D. H. Lawrence
and the Experience of Italy

D. H. Lawrence and the Experience of Italy

Jeffrey Meyers

University of Pennsylvania Press
Philadelphia • 1982

Library of Congress Cataloging in Publication Data

Meyers Jeffrey.
    D. H. Lawrence and the experience of Italy.

    Includes bibliographical references and indexes.
    1. Lawrence, D. H. (David Herbert), 1885–1930—
Homes and haunts—Italy. 2. Authors, English—20th
century—Biography.   3. Italy in literature.   4. Italy—
Description and travel—1901–1944. I. Title.
PR6023.A93Z679 1982   823′.912 [B]   82–60261
ISBN 0–8122–7861–5

Printed in the United States of America

For David and Lee Porter,
remembering Sicily

Contents

	Acknowledgments	viii
	Plates	ix
	Chronology	xv
	Maps of Italy and Sardinia	xvi
1	Lawrence in Italy	1
2	The Aesthetics of Travel	12
3	Maurice Magnus	29
4	Translations of Verga	50
5	*Look! We Have Come Through!* and *Birds, Beasts and Flowers*	72
6	*The Lost Girl*	94
7	Fascism and the Novels of Power	105
8	The Paintings	137
9	The Resurrection Theme	149
	Notes	171
	Index	185

Acknowledgments

The author and publisher would like to thank Viking Penguin Inc. of New York and Laurence Pollinger Ltd. for permission to reprint poems from *The Complete Poems of D. H. Lawrence,* collected and edited by Vivian de Sola Pinto and F. Warren Roberts. Copyright © 1964, 1971 by Angelo Ravagli and C. M. Weekley, Executors of the Estate of Frieda Lawrence Ravagli; Lord Astor, Saki Karavas and the Humanities Research Center, University of Texas for permission to reproduce paintings in their collections by D. H. Lawrence; and the University of Colorado Committee on Scholarly Publications for a grant.

Plates

1. D. H. Lawrence, *Italian Landscape,* 1928 (Lord Astor Collection).
2. D. H. Lawrence, *Boccaccio Story,* 1926 (Humanities Research Center, University of Texas).
3. D. H. Lawrence, *Fauns and Nymphs,* 1928 (Saki Karavas Collection, Taos, New Mexico).
4. D. H. Lawrence, *Flight Back into Paradise,* 1927 (Saki Karavas Collection, Taos, New Mexico).
5. D. H. Lawrence, *Resurrection,* 1927 (Humanities Research Center, University of Texas).

D. H. Lawrence, *Italian Landscape,* 1928.

D. H. Lawrence, *Boccaccio Story,* 1926.

D. H. Lawrence, *Fauns and Nymphs,* 1928.

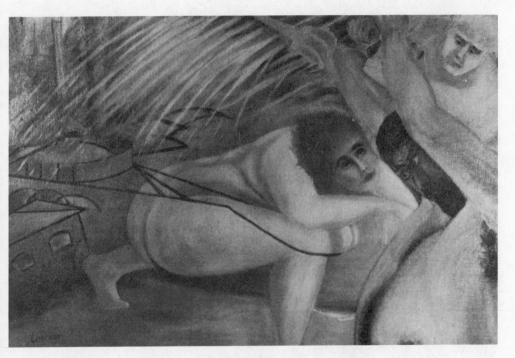

D. H. Lawrence, *Flight Back into Paradise*, 1927.

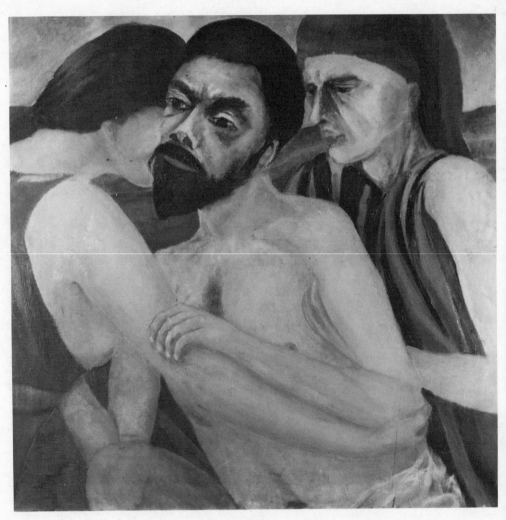

D. H. Lawrence, *Resurrection*, 1927.

Chronology

September 1912–March 1913	Villa Igéa, Gargnano, Lago di Garda
April 1913	San Gaudenzio, near Gargnano
October 1913–June 1914	Villa Gambrosier, Fiascherino, near Lerici
November 1919	Pensione Balestri, Florence
December 1919	Picinisco, in the Abruzzi
January–February 1920	Palazzo Ferraro, Capri
February 1920	visits Montecassino
March–July 1920	Fontana Vecchia, Taormina
September 1920	Villa Canovaia, San Gervasio, Florence
October 1920–April 1921	Fontana Vecchia, Taormina
January 1921	visits Sardinia
September 1921–February 1922	Fontana Vecchia, Taormina
November 1925–April 1926	Villa Bernarda, Spotorno
May–July 1926	Villa Mirenda, Scandicci
October 1926–July 1927	Villa Mirenda, Scandicci
April 1927	visits Etruscan towns
October 1927–January 1928	Villa Mirenda, Scandicci
March–June 1928	Villa Mirenda, Scandicci
June 1929	Pensione Giuliani, Forte dei Marmi
July 1929	Lungarno Corsini and Hotel Porta Rossa, Florence

Lawrence's Italy

Lawrence's trip to Sardinia, January 1921

1

Lawrence in Italy

Italy has given me back I know not
what of myself, but a very, very
great deal. She has found for me
so much that was lost.

Sea and Sardinia

I

THE IMPORTANCE OF LAWRENCE'S RELATION to Italy was suggested
by Edward Nehls, who wrote that a fruitful approach would be
"to combine the fragments of his life in Italy, and to study the
resultant literary output in an effort to see his evolution as both
man and artist."[1] *D. H. Lawrence and the Experience of Italy*
traces this development, concentrates on his less-known works
which have not been subjected to intense critical scrutiny—the
letters, travel books, essay on Maurice Magnus, translations,
poetry, novels of power, paintings, late works on the resurrection theme—and shows the unity of his artistic achievement
during the last decade of his life. Lawrence's art is discussed
in relation to his experience in Italy, though that rich, protean
country has a different function and meaning in each of his
works. In his letters Italy represents freedom and inspiration,
in the travel books a search for an ideal community, in the
Magnus essay a dramatic background, in the translations of
Verga a source of primitive passion, in the poetry a test of love
and expression of non-human life, in *The Lost Girl* a way to
self-discovery, in the novels of power the conflict between
chaos and authority, in the paintings a pagan landscape, in the
resurrection works a way to rebirth.

After 1912, Lawrence spent one third of his life in Italy. He never lived permanently in England after 1919, and during the 1920s Italy was his principal home. That country transformed him from Bert to Lorenzo, from young prig to bold exile, and had a profound effect on his life and work. The climate, landscape, culture and people provided comfort, nourishment and stimulation. Italy was a secure refuge after the scandalous flight with Frieda and the persecution of the war years. After his journey to America, it became an attractive alternative to New Mexico. Lawrence's vision of England was sharpened by the experience of another civilization, for Italy provided new imaginative material and inspired him to transform it into art. His informed and sympathetic response to Italy enabled him to see English beliefs and conventions in a new light, and to make a valuable critique of his own culture. The impact of Italy—perhaps the strongest unifying force in Lawrence's work during the last decade of his life—combined with his native genius to create the quintessential passion of his art.

"A poet who goes from country to country," says Philip Larkin, permanently immobile in Hull, "might find that his sense of cultural identity becomes blurred and weakened."[2] Lawrence was aware of the intellectual limitations of living among peasants in an isolated and exotic locale. And Middleton Murry mentions "the old, terrible mistrust which comes over Lawrence when he lives among unspiritual, pre-mental people, after whom he hankers—the same fearful mistrust that uttered itself in *Sea and Sardinia,* and in Pancrazio's grim warning to Alvina in *The Lost Girl:* 'These people are bad.' In *The Plumed Serpent* Lawrence cannot conceal his mistrust and his terror."[3] He confessed that he disliked the Mexican Indians and could not penetrate their barrier of alien blood. And he set the last chapter of *Mornings in Mexico* (1927) in Italy, as if to place savage America in the classical perspective of the Mediterranean norm. But Lawrence was both a regional novelist and a good European; his sense of cultural identity was certainly strengthened, not weakened, by continuous travels and prolonged residence in foreign countries. As Robert Louis Stevenson said in Samoa in 1894: "It is all the better for a man's work, if he wants it to be good and not merely popular, to be removed from these London influences. Human nature is always the same, and you can see and understand it better when you are standing outside the crowd."[4]

Why was Lawrence attracted to Italy and why did he

choose to live there when he first left England—with a fortune of £11—in 1912? Italy provided a vital contrast to what Lawrence called the hopelessness, "the oldness and grubbiness and despair" of mechanized and materialistic England, with "its enervation and misty miserable modernness." When a group of middle-class English poets turned up in Fiascherino, they "seemed so shadowy and funny, after the crude, strong, rather passionate men at the wedding." Lawrence expressed his intense relief on leaving moribund England in his incantatory description of Alvina's escape from Folkestone: "For there behind, behind all the sunshine, was England. England, beyond the water, rising with ash-grey, corpse-grey cliffs, and streaks of snow on the downs above. England, like a long ash-grey coffin slowly submerging. She watched it, fascinated and terrified. It seemed to repudiate the sunshine, to remain unilluminated, long and ash-grey and dead, with streaks of snow like cerements. That was England!"[5]

Lawrence had grown up in the gloomy industrial Midlands and taught school in the dreary suburbs of London. He wanted to go south for the winter, to enjoy the sunshine and drowsy uneasiness of spring, which roused the earth and made the flesh restless, and which also strengthened his body and prolonged his life. He had always responded to the natural beauty of the countryside around the mining villages; and in Italy was stimulated by the colors of Lake Garda, the scent of roses, oleanders and grapes, and the snow on the hovering mountains.

In the days before the War, when the pound was strong, Italy was a good deal cheaper than England. Though Lawrence had a minute and precarious income, he could always afford what he wanted to buy. Compared to the peasants, he was "a howling gentleman and swell," who could pay for a language teacher, a comfortable flat, plentiful food and wine, and still have enough left over for his travels.

Unlike many writers, who were primarily concerned with Italian culture—and with acquiring villas, furniture, antiques—Lawrence was seriously interested in folk art and the common people. He admired the generous, handsome, sensual peasants who walked proudly, adored their children and led healthy, leisurely lives. The Italians gave Lawrence a standard of masculine behavior that made his fellow Englishmen seem repressed and even impotent. The warm, extroverted people worshiped the mother, were devoted to the family and maintained clear sexual divisions between men and women—a notable contrast to the cocksure women and henpecked men in the "more advanced" society of England. The fierce opposition between men and women, which he observed in Italy and in the fiction of Giovanni Verga, reinforced his belief that sexual relationships were an endless struggle of clashing wills in which man either maintains a precarious dominance or is overcome by humiliating defeat. This conviction led to Lawrence's fear of merging with a woman in sexual union, and was expressed in *Look! We Have Come Through!* and *Aaron's Rod.*

The peasants still led a traditional, almost ritualistic life, symbolized by the Good Friday procession in Fiascherino: "A white, ghostly winding procession, with dark-dressed villagers crowding behind. It was gone in a minute. And it made a fearful impression on me. It is the *mystery* that does it—it is Death itself, robbed of its horrors, and only Fear and Wonder going humbly behind."[6] Exile in a Catholic country enabled Lawrence to distance himself from the Protestant tradition and formulate his critique of Christian mythology. The mysterious aspect of the procession, beneath the Christian ceremony, suggested to Lawrence the pagan and even barbaric quality that still existed in Italy. He was aroused by the pagan art of the Etruscans, which gave him a sense of historical and aesthetic continuity. This primitive element confirmed his belief that traditional life was superior to the industrialization of the modern age, and put him back in touch with essential traits that had been lost in contemporary society. The lack of physical vitality, the emptiness in the lives of civilized people, was his definition of modern tragedy. The peasants provided a way for him to mediate between mechanized humans and the nonhuman world of animals and flowers. They expressed the regenerative power of nature, the rebirth into a new state of being, and the hope of a physical resurrection.

Jessie Chambers records that even in his college years Lawrence "was vehemently of Schopenhauer's opinion that a white skin is not natural to man. . . . 'For me a brown skin is the only beautiful one.' "[7] He admired the ageless virtues of the peasants: simplicity, fidelity, courage, power to endure; and believed they fortified and inspired him: "I find, here in Italy, for example, that I live in a certain silent contact with the peasants who work the land of this villa. I am not intimate with them . . . and they are not working for me; I am not their *padrone.*

Yet it is they, really, who form my *ambiente,* and it is from them that the human flow comes to me. . . . I want them to be there, about the place, their lives going on along with mine, and in relation to mine. I don't idealize them. . . . I don't expect them to make any millennium here on earth, neither now nor in the future. But I want to live near them, because their life still flows."[8]

Lawrence's silent contact with the peasants led directly to his doctrine of vitalism, for Italy—more than any other place— seemed to realize his hope, expressed in *Apocalypse,* for a more intense existence: "For man the vast marvel is to be alive. For man, as for flower and beast and bird, the supreme triumph is to be most vividly, most perfectly alive. Whatever the unborn and the dead may know, they cannot know the beauty, the marvel of being alive in the flesh. . . . We ought to dance with rapture that we should be alive and in the flesh, and part of the living, incarnate cosmos."[9]

It is generally believed that Lawrence's endless discussions with his wife about Jessie Chambers and Frieda's revelation of Freud's ideas, especially the Oedipus complex, led Lawrence to become more critical of his mother and more sympathetic to his father in *Sons and Lovers.* While this is true, the Italian experience, which reinforced his belief that men and women are natural enemies, also led Lawrence to a more positive attitude toward his father, whom he identified with the instinctive life of the peasants, and to a rejection of his mother's genteel culture, which he associated with the repression he had fled in England. In "Nottingham and the Mining Countryside" Lawrence (who grew a beard in 1914 in imitation of his father) makes an implicit connection between the miners and peasants: "The people lived almost entirely by instinct, men of my father's age. . . . The physical, instinctive, and intuitional contact between men [was] very highly developed, a contact almost as close as touch, very real and very powerful. This physical awareness and intimate *togetherness* was at its strongest down pit."[10] As Keith Alldritt observes: "The effect of Italy upon Lawrence is one of the important causes of the striking development in his fiction between *Sons and Lovers* and *The Rainbow.* "[11]

All these things—the contrast to England, the sunshine, the natural beauty, the cheap food and wine, the sympathetic people, the traditional life, and especially the pagan, primitive element—revitalized Lawrence and inspired his astonishing creative achievement. Like Thomas Mann, he felt "the need for completion and deliverance through the completely other, the south, the brightness, clarity and lightness, the gift of the beautiful."[12] Lawrence's discovery of Italy was also a discovery of himself.

II

Lawrence's letters from Italy—the greatest in English since Keats and Byron—are marked by intuition, energy, intellectual audacity and imaginative intensity. They evoke the spirit of the place, convey his lively response to new experience and make the Italian landscape leap to life. They immediately establish a personal contact with each correspondent, and express the extremes of enthusiasm and disappointment. They are always human, always alive, and reveal his innermost sensitive self. When he first came to Gargnano and was trying to learn the language, he started a conversation with an olive gatherer: "Summoning up all my Italian, I say to him, 'It's a late harvest.' *'Come?'* he says. I repeat, 'A late harvest, Signore'; he grins. 'It's very early.' I feel like saying to him: 'Don't be a pig, I've done my best.' "[13]

Lawrence lived in Gargnano, "a rather tumble-downish place" on Lake Garda in northeast Italy, from September 1912 to April 1913. "You can only get there by steamer," he wrote, "because of the steep rocky mountainy hills at the back—no railway. You would come via Brescia, I should think. There are vineyards and olive woods and lemon gardens on the hill at the back. There is a lovely little square, where the Italians gossip and the fishermen pull up their boats, just near. Everything is too nice for words—not a bit touristy—quite simply Italian common village."[14]

At the Villa Igéa in Gargnano, Lawrence, for the first time in his life, lived with a woman and had a home of his own. He and Frieda self-consciously saw themselves as Vronsky and Anna Karenina. They were well aware of the dangers and difficulties of living together in a foreign country and establishing a deeper love, but the isolation of Italy only heightened their relationship and brought them closer together.[15]

Lawrence's emotional life and literary career were closely

connected, for his art was stimulated by passion. Italy intensified his extremist ideas about sex and society, and sharpened
the contrast between his beliefs and those of conventional English writers like Galsworthy, Bennett and Wells. In January
1913, four months after arriving in Italy, he recorded the impact of the new experience in his credo of blood knowledge:
"My great religion is a belief in the blood, the flesh, as being
wiser than the intellect. We can go wrong in our minds. But
what our blood feels and believes and says, is always true.
. . . That is why I like to live in Italy. The people are so unconscious. They only feel and want: they don't know."[16] Italy
seemed to support Lawrence's need to assert the rights of the
body. He had just escaped from a restrictive psychological conflict between his love for his mother and for Jessie Chambers,
which prevented him from experiencing sexual fulfillment,
and from a rigid class system, which he defied by eloping with
Frieda. He was in love with Frieda and had to stress the importance of sexual feeling in order to live with his guilt about her
husband and children. At this stage of his artistic career he had
to put his intellect in abeyance—or seem to do so—in order to
develop emotionally after the inhibiting relationship with his
mother. Italy, therefore, provided exactly what he had hoped
to find. He believed the hot-blooded Latins who trusted their
own feelings lived a more sensual and spontaneous mode of existence than the intellectual English. But in *The Lost Girl,*
"Sun" and *Lady Chatterley's Lover* he sometimes carries this
doctrine of mindlessness to absurd extremes; and in *The
Plumed Serpent,* he connects Cipriano's participation in blood-
sacrifice with sexual potency and praises him as a "column of
blood, with a voice in it"—a kind of eloquent penis.

When Lawrence left for northern Europe in April 1913, he
noted the depth of his attachment to the place and the freedom
he had enjoyed: "It broke my heart to leave Italy. . . . One must
love Italy, if one has lived there. It is so non-moral. It leaves the
soul so free. Over these countries, Germany and England, like
the grey skies, lies the gloom of the dark moral judgment and
condemnation and reservation of the people. Italy does not
judge. I shall want to go back there."[17] Since Lawrence's life
and works were condemned in England from 1912 until his
death, and long afterwards, he felt more comfortable in a country that allowed him, as a foreigner, to lead an instinctive life,
based on fidelity to his own emotions, without fear of moral

judgment, censure or persecution; and that helped to integrate his old life in England with his new marriage to Frieda. Lawrence's seven months in Gargnano was the most intensely creative period of his entire career. During that time he finished *Sons and Lovers;* wrote the series of personal poems, *Look! We Have Come Through!;* completed two plays, *The Fight for Barbara* and *The Daughter-in-Law;* and began *Twilight in Italy, The Rainbow* and *The Lost Girl.*

Lawrence returned to Italy in the fall of 1913 and settled in Fiascherino, near La Spezia on the Ligurian coast. He was conscious of his place in the Byron-Shelley tradition of rebellious expatriate poets and lived an hour's walk from San Terenzo, where Shelley had drowned. Once again, he found an inexpensive and isolated village, with a spectacular view, far from the cities where foreigners usually resided, which inspired his work on *The Rainbow* and *Twilight in Italy:* "There is a little tiny bay half shut in by rocks, and smothered by olive woods that slope down swiftly. Then there is one pink, flat, fisherman's house. Then there is the *villino* of Ettore Gambrosier, a four-roomed pink cottage among vine gardens, just over the water and under the olive woods. There, D.V., is my next home. . . . You run out of the gate into the sea, which washes among the rocks at the mouth of the bay. The garden is all vines and fig trees, and great woods on the hills all round."[18]

Lawrence was confined to England during the War, but escaped to Italy as soon as he could. In December 1919 he pitched up (like Alvina in *The Lost Girl*) at Picinisco in the wild Abruzzi. As usual, the approach to the village was difficult: "Rome being vile, we came on here. It is a bit staggeringly primitive. You cross a great stony river bed, then an icy river on a plank, then climb unfootable paths, while the ass struggles behind with your luggage. The house contains a rather cave-like kitchen downstairs—the other rooms are a wine-press and a wine-storing place and corn bin: upstairs are three bedrooms, and a semi-barn for maize cobs: beds and bare floor."[19]

But Picinisco was too remote, icy and mountainous—even for Lawrence. After ten torturous days he moved to the milder climate of Capri and took a small flat above Morgano's restaurant, looking across the bay to Naples. Though Lawrence had friends on the island—Compton Mackenzie, Brett Young and Mary Cannan—it was not at all his sort of place. He felt the English crowd were the uttermost limit for spiteful scandal. In February 1920 he left that "stewpot of semi-literary cats" for Taormina, at the foot of volcanic Mount Etna, where he lived for eighteen months during 1920–22.

Lawrence liked Sicily even more than Gargnano and Fiascherino. In Fontana Vecchia he enjoyed the sensation of being "on-the-brink," able to hop out of Europe and to the ends of the earth at any moment: "We have quite a lovely villa on the green slope high above the sea, looking east over the blueness, with the hills and the snowy, shallow crest of Calabria on the left across the sea, where the straits [of Messina] begin to close in.— The ancient fountain still runs, in a sort of little cave-place down the garden."[20] In Sicily Lawrence finished *The Lost Girl,* and wrote *Birds, Beasts and Flowers, Aaron's Rod, Sea and Sardinia* and the essay on Maurice Magnus.

Within a few months Lawrence, whose motto was "When in doubt—move," was seized by his habitual dissatisfaction and restlessness. The prewar idyll was irrevocably lost. Things had become expensive and now cost about the same as in England. The inefficiency was often exasperating. And he began to mistrust and dislike the people: "The Italians are really rather lowbred swine nowadays: so different from what they were. . . . The Taorminisi natives are as mean and creeping as ever—I really begin to feel that one must have done with Italy." The south seemed so torpid and lifeless (though it "cured one of caring") and began to go rancid in his mouth: "I have been hating Taormina—but one hates everywhere in fits and starts." As riots and strikes increased and the Fascists prepared for their coup of October 1922, Lawrence felt he had to leave: "Such a muddle ever increasing. I am tired of it. There are not many *forestieri* [foreigners] here, all afraid of strikes and railway smashes."[21] Lawrence's view of Italy was intensely subjective, and his interpretation was both influenced and intensified by his personal relation to the country.

In February 1922, summoned to New Mexico by Mabel Luhan, Lawrence left Italy by way of Ceylon, Australia and the South Seas. But Italy would not release him from its emotional hold, and he soon longed to return: "We saw our Etna like a white queen or a white witch there standing in the sky so magic-lovely. She said to me, 'You come back here,' but I only said, 'No,' but I wept inside with grief, grief of separation." He carried as talisman a gaily painted panel of a Sicilian cart; and seven months later wrote from Taos: "My heart still turns most readily to Italy. . . . My spirit always wants to go south."[22]

After visiting Mexico, Lawrence returned to Italy, via England and Germany, in November 1925. His publisher Martin Secker recommended Spotorno, between Genoa and the French frontier, as a quiet place that did not attract many foreigners. Though Lawrence was not especially drawn to the Riviera, it was convenient for the visits of friends and Frieda's children. The sun glistened on the Mediterranean and Italy felt familiar, "like the ghost of one's self." They rented Villa Bernarda from Lieutenant Angelo Ravagli, who married Frieda after Lawrence's death: "We are sitting quietly here, in this not very exciting village. But the house is on the hill above the roofs, just under the castle, and the sea goes in and out its bays, and glitters very bright. There is something forever cheerful and happy about the Mediterranean: I feel at home beside it. We've got a big garden of vines and almond trees, and an old peasant Giovanni."[23] Lawrence worked a bit, walked in the hills when it was not too cold, sat out on the terrace in the daytime and huddled round the kitchen stove at night.

Lawrence moved to the isolated village of Scandicci, seven miles outside Florence, in May 1926, and lived there until June 1928—his longest residence in Italy. (You can still find the Villa Mirenda by following his directions from Florence.) His friends were not surprised to hear: "We have made a little move—taken the top of this heavy old Tuscan villa for a year. . . . It's very rough and no comforts, but nice: stands on a bluff looking over the Val d'Arno. . . . It's very pretty country— Tuscan—farms on little green hills, and pine woods fringing the ridges." A month later, when he had settled in to paint, visit the Etruscan tombs and write *Lady Chatterley's Lover,* he described the tranquility of his existence: "I'm sitting on the little balcony upstairs—you can so easily imagine this old square whitish villa on a little hill all of its own, with the peasant houses and cypresses behind, and the vines and olives and corn on all the slopes. It's very picturesque, and many a paintable bit. Away in front lies the Arno valley and mountains beyond. Behind are pine woods. The rooms inside are big and rather bare—with red brick floors: spacious, rather nice, and very still. Life doesn't cost much here."[24]

Lawrence suffered a violent hemorrhage in June 1927 and was seriously ill for two months. But he would never admit the gravity of his illness and blamed the Italian climate for exhausting him and bleeding him emotionally: "One needs a tonic, after Italy." In the fall, the old restlessness came over him again. He was rather bored and irritated by the excitable people and languid country that seemed to rub against his grain, and thought Italy had "gone sort of dead for me." Like Mann's Tonio Kröger, he sometimes felt "The whole *bellezza* business makes me nervous. All those frightfully animated people down there with their black animal-like eyes. I don't like them."[25] He pondered the prospects of Ireland, Spain and America, which was "tough and anarchic and soulless, but not as mercenary as Italy."

During the next year Lawrence wandered through Vevey and Gsteig, Baden Baden, Port Cros and Bandol, and Majorca, but none of these places could satisfy—or cure—him. He spent his last month in Italy during June–July 1929. He found Forte dei Marmi, on the coast south of La Spezia, "beastly, as a place: flat, dead sea, jelly fishy, and millions of villas." During the last two weeks he lived with his friend and publisher Pino Orioli on the Lungarno Corsini in Florence. As he lay dying in the south of France in September 1929, the exhausted Ulysses wrote: "I want to take a nice house in Italy now, and settle down a bit."[26]

2

The Aesthetics of Travel

It is my destiny, this wandering. . . .
I must go on till I find something
that gives me peace.

D. H. Lawrence,
Letters of May–June 1922

I

LAWRENCE'S GREATEST CONTRIBUTION to the travel-writing tradition was to shift the center of interest from the external world to the self. His desire to discover the landscape and culture of Italy was a means of exploring his own inner nature, and the revelation of his feelings and thoughts is the most interesting aspect of his travel books. For he defines himself in relation to the country and shows the response of an extraordinary personality to the stimulating experience of Italy. His books are both an escape from industrial England and a search for a climate and culture that will reveal a new mode of consciousness. For Lawrence, travel was "a stream of reflections, where images intertwine with dark thoughts and obscure emotion, and the whole life flows on turbulent and deep and transitory. It is reflection, thinking back on travel and on life, and in the mirror sense, throwing back snatches of image."[1]

The classical travel books on Italy—from Dickens, Ruskin and Butler to Gissing, James and Douglas—evoked antiquarian, aesthetic and cultural associations. They told prospective travellers what to see and provided an imaginative substitute for those who could not journey to the exquisite peninsula. Lawrence, by contrast, was much more subjective and wanted "to write some sketches of these Etruscan places, not scientifically, but only as they are now and the impression they make."[2]

Though some travellers tried to provide more subjective accounts, they lacked Lawrence's inspired response to exotic places. Mark Twain thought all foreigners were funny; Rudyard Kipling was omniscient, condescending, even hostile; H. M. Tomlinson verbose, platitudinous, and banal; Rupert Brooke rather commonplace and flat. Though none of these men influenced Lawrence, their works allowed him to test himself against writers who were more interested in the people and landscape than in the history and art.

Two travel books that Lawrence greatly admired were Melville's *Typee* (1846) and *Omoo* (1847), which were based on his voyages to the Marquesas and Tahiti in the early 1840s and initiated the Rousseauistic myth of primitive man in a South Seas paradise. Both Lawrence and Toby in *Typee* "go rambling over the world as if pursued by some mysterious fate they cannot possibly elude."[3] Both writers contrast pagan and Christian societies, and describe the destructive effect of civilization on traditional culture.

Lawrence's observations on Melville in *Studies in Classic American Literature* apply with equal force to himself: "Never was a man so passionately filled with the sense of vastness and mystery of life which is non-human. He was mad to look over our horizons. Anywhere, anywhere out of *our* world. To get away.... Human life won't do. He turns back to the elements." Though Melville was drawn to the Golden Age of the past and portrayed the paradise he was searching for in *Typee,* Lawrence insists there is an impassable gulf in time and consciousness between civilized and primitive man: "Melville couldn't go back: and Gauguin couldn't really go back: and I know now that I could never go back. Back towards the past, savage life."[4] Yet Lawrence did "go back" while in Italy and deliberately retreated from the hateful modern life of the peninsula. He moved from Lake Garda to the more traditional life in Sicily and then to the primitive island of Sardinia. All these places eventually disappointed him; so he finally went further back to the remote past of the Etruscans, who no longer existed, and like a god, resurrected and transformed them into his ideal society.

Like Lawrence, Stevenson was drawn to the South Seas by Melville's travel books. Both Stevenson and Gauguin lived on Pacific islands during the 1890s and, by the end of the century, had firmly established the legend of an exotic paradise. But when Lawrence (stimulated by Frederick O'Brien's *White Shadows on the South Seas,* 1919) passed through Raratonga and Tahiti, en route from Sydney to Taos in 1922, the islands could no longer sustain the myth. Lawrence found the tropics rather rancid and the people "ugly, false, spoiled and diseased": "Papeete is a poor sort of place, mostly Chinese, natives in European clothes, and fat. . . . I never want to *stay* in the tropics. There is a sort of sickliness about them, smell of cocoa-nut oil and sort of palm-tree, reptile nausea. . . . These are supposed to be the earthly paradises: these South Sea Isles. You can have 'em."[5]

The savage pilgrimage of Stevenson anticipates, in a number of significant ways, the character, life and travels of Lawrence. Both Stevenson and Lawrence were archetypal expatriate writers whose cultural identities and artistic insights were strengthened by residence in foreign lands. Both rejected their family background but retained a strong sense of their native place. Both had adulterous affairs with and then married older, foreign, impractical women who had children from their previous marriages. Both remained childless themselves. Both were spontaneous, warm-hearted, enthusiastic, generous men who inspired the adoration of possessive friends, despite their volatile temperaments and furious rages during sickness. Both wanted to live the life they wrote about, willingly endured the "incidental beastliness of travel," and sought a simple and even Spartan existence. Both were oppressed by civilization and hoped to create an ideal community. Both were brought up in puritanical households but believed, as Stevenson told his cousin Bob, that man should "honour sex more religiously. THE DAMNED THING of our education is that Christianity does not recognise and hallow sex."[6]

Both Stevenson and Lawrence were adept at peripatetic composition, continued to write despite constant travel and debilitating illness, and produced a great number of novels, poems and essays in less than twenty years. Both had been invalids since infancy, suffered severe bronchial infections, combined fragility and endurance, and had extraordinary vitality. Both had tuberculosis, lived most of their adult lives abroad, tried and disliked the Alpine cure among the sick and dying, wandered restlessly in Italy, France, the South Seas and America to repair their tissue and regain their nerve. Stevenson's comments on his illness apply with equal force to Lawrence, and place them both in the tradition of tubercular writers whose intensity was closely connected to their stimulating but devastating disease—Schiller, Novalis, Keats, Elizabeth Barrett Browning, Emily Brontë, Thoreau, Chekhov, Crane, Beardsley, Flecker, Kafka, Mansfield and Orwell: "I have never been well enough really to enjoy life, except for a day or two at a time, and I fear my character has suffered, and I know that troubles have grown upon me. . . . For nearly ten years my health had been declining; and for some while before I set forth upon my voyage, I believed I was come to the afterpiece of life, and had only the nurse and undertaker to expect. . . . Every bit of brisk living, and above all when it is healthful, is just so much gained upon the wholesale filcher, death."[7] Both sailed close to the "tradewinds of death" and perished in mid-career at the age of forty-four. After their deaths, their families and many friends wrote controversial books about them and shifted the emphasis from the works to the man.

There are also striking similarities between Stevenson in Silverado and Lorenzo in Taos. Both became interested in America through Whitman and American literature, and were drawn to the continent by an older, divorced woman (Fanny Osbourne and Mabel Luhan). Both established a private and isolated life in a remote, rustic, mountain cabin, near canyons and pine woods, eagles, lions and bears. Both lived with their wives and a painter as guest and companion, repaired and improved a dilapidated house, drew water, cut wood, practiced carpentry, fetched milk from a neighboring ranch, gave lessons in their household, bathed in medicinal springs. Both admired the Indians, defined their identity and revalued civilization in relation to a primitive society. Stevenson captured the essence of their tranquil mood in the last chapter of *The Silverado Squatters* (1883): "The household duties, though they were many, and some of them laborious, dwindled into mere islets of business in a sea of sunny daytime; and it appears to me, looking back, as though the far greater part of our life at Silverado had been passed, propped upon an elbow, or seated on a plank, listening to the silence that there is among the hills."[8]

Though Stevenson, whose style was more constrained and self-conscious, did not write the same kind of travel books as Lawrence, who saw the natural world with his imagination rather than with his eye, they shared a similar aesthetic of travel: a preference for a rough and relaxed rather than a comfortable and formal journey, popular rather than high culture, colloquial rather than mandarin style. Both *An Inland Voyage* (1878) and *Sea and Sardinia* end with a description of a marionette theater and return to their starting point in a final chapter called "Back to the World" and "Back."

Unlike most men, whose lives are narrow and restricted, Stevenson and Lawrence had an infinite number of possibilities (especially in the days when the Empire and the pound were strong) and wanted to explore many of them before they finally decided where to live. Both wished to go to geographical as well as emotional extremes of temperature, height and distance. They were always excited by change and movement, by the exhilaration of departure and recourse to flight, by the opportunity to avoid people and mail, to clear out and be free. In *Travels with a Donkey* (1879) Stevenson wrote: "I travel not to go anywhere, but to go. I travel for travel's sake. The great affair is to move."[9] Lawrence opened *Sea and Sardinia* by exclaiming: "Comes over one an absolute necessity to move."

For both men travel was a method of inner exploration and a source of immediate inspiration. It intensified their sense of being British at the same time that it removed them from Britain and allowed them to see it more clearly. Both searched for a wild landscape and people that would reflect their own mood. "The frame of mind was the great exploit of our voyage," Stevenson observed. "It was the farthest piece of travel accomplished."[10] Both felt the excitement more than balanced the discomfort of travel, that hardship intensified experience and made it more real. Stevenson declared: "Discomfort, when it is honestly uncomfortable and makes no nauseous pretensions to the contrary, is a vastly humorous business. . . . Six weeks in one unpleasant country-side had done more, it seemed, to quicken and educate my sensibilities than many years in places that jumped more nearly with my inclination."[11]

Both men craved direct contact with an untouched landscape that still retained its savagery. They were attracted to people who rejected the modern form of civilization and cared nothing about possessions, and to primitive life that harmonized the elements and avoided the machine. They were extremely sensitive to atmosphere, preferred the natural to the man-made world: Stevenson travelled by donkey and canoe,

Lawrence walked into Italy in 1912 and wrote under a tree with his back against the living trunk.

The initials of Richard Lovat Somers, wanderer in the antipodes and autobiographical hero of *Kangaroo,* are doubtless a subtle acknowledgement of Stevenson's pervasive influence. For in 1923, the year that novel was published, Lawrence expressed a desire to travel exactly as Stevenson had done: "I think I shall go to California, and either pack with a donkey in the mountains, or get some sailing ship to the islands."[12]

II

The meaning of Lawrence's travel books becomes clearer when seen not only in the context of a literary tradition but also in relation to his own aesthetics of travel. In *Aaron's Rod* the hero asks Lilly: " 'What's the good of going to Malta? Shall *you* be any different in yourself, in another place? You'll be the same there as you are here. . . . What's the use of going somewhere else? You won't change yourself.' 'I may in the end,' said Lilly."[13] Lawrence was both changed and stimulated by travel, inspired by places where his imagination could have free play. As Mark Schorer observes: "To discover a place where the vital connections could be maintained intact was the motive of Lawrence's life as it increasingly becomes the motive of his heroes. . . . All the time that Lawrence was moving, he was also writing, and the settings of his works follow upon the march of his feet. . . . There is probably no other writer in literary history whose works responded so immediately to his geographical environment as Lawrence, and certainly there is no other modern writer to whose imagination 'place' made such a direct and intense appeal, and in whose works, as a consequence, place usurps such a central role."[14]

Lawrence planned to write a novel about each continent but died before he could capture Africa and Asia. In 1913, before he was confined by the War, he wrote from Italy: "I'm not going to settle down. I shall be in England sometime in spring. Then I shall come abroad again for the winter. There's nothing like keeping on the move." When the War severely restricted his movements, he dreamed of escaping to the farthest corners of the earth: "I wish I were going to Thibet—or Kamschatka—or Tahiti—to the ultima, ultima, ultima Thule. I feel sometimes I shall go mad, because there is nowhere to go, no 'new world.' One of these days, unless I watch myself, I shall be departing in some rash fashion, to some foolish place."[15]

After the War, Lawrence's travels were marked by restlessness and indecision. In January 1922, when he had finally decided to travel from the East Coast to Taos, he suddenly changed plans, visited the Brewsters in Ceylon and approached the New World from the west: "Perhaps it is necessary for me to try these places, perhaps it is my destiny to know the world."[16] The great trouble was that he always longed to be in another place: he yearned for Europe in America and wished he were in America as soon as he returned to Europe.

In the mid-1920s, when more money and better health allowed him to roam the earth, Lawrence contemplated visits to Greenland, Russia, China and India. When he was unhappy in Mexico, he thought: "perhaps I've no business trying to bury myself in out-of-the-way places." But as soon as he was back in Europe, the Mediterranean inspired him to wander like Ulysses. From Italy he planned trips to Ragusa, Dalmatia, Crete, Cyprus, Constantinople, Damascus, Jerusalem, Jaffa, Egypt, Tunisia and Morocco. He inevitably realized: "As one gets older, one's choice in life gets limited—one is not free to choose any more." But three months before his death, he was thankful "to escape anything like a permanency" and told Maria Huxley: "I sort of wish I could go to the moon."[17] Lawrence continued to move about after death, for in 1933 his body was disinterred from the cemetery in Vence and cremated. His ashes were taken by Frieda to New Mexico, lost and recovered at the railroad station in Fort Lamy, and nearly stolen by Mabel Luhan before he was finally cemented into place near the chapel at the ranch above Taos.

Lawrence had three main reasons for travelling, as Mark Schorer briefly mentions: he moved because of poor health; he was looking for a place where he might establish his ideal community, Rananim; and he travelled to discover a place "that was in every way better than any other place he had known."[18] Travel, for Lawrence, was at times simply a struggle for existence, a pilgrimage from country to country in search of warm climate and good health. Both Taormina and Taos had extreme summer and winter climates which forced him to leave for part of the year. He always felt he had to abandon places, like Oaxaca and Scandicci, where he had been gravely ill, and often blamed the place for his sickness. "I hate this country like poison, sure it would kill me,"[19] he wrote from Florence in the summer of 1929; then wandered through Majorca, Germany and France during the last year of his life.

The origin of Rananim went back to Lawrence's youth in Nottingham, when he exclaimed to the dubious Jessie Chambers (his mother's greatest rival): "I should like to have a big house—you know there are some lovely old houses in the Park with gardens and terraces. Wouldn't it be fine if we could live in one of those houses, mother and all the people we like together?"[20] During the War he told Ottoline Morrell (as well as Murry, Mansfield, Brett and Carswell): "I want you to form the nucleus of a new community which shall start a new life amongst us." And after the War, in New Mexico, he refused to abandon his obsessive quest. As Knud Merrild reports: "The one thing that Lawrence never got tired of speaking of was the 'new life' that he wanted to start or create. . . . He wanted to find a place away from civilization where he felt that the possibility of its growth would be fairly secure. It was an old idea of his, but he had not yet found a suitable place for it, although he had circled half the globe in its pursuit. Now he thought the possibility might be in old Mexico."[21]

The quest for Rananim was closely connected to his search for a perfect place where he could live with Frieda, if not with his followers. (How many friends, buried in the gloom of England, must have been attracted by his enticing descriptions of the beautiful places he had found—from Lerici to Vence—and frustrated by their leaden inability to follow his course through Europe and around the world.) Lawrence would agree with Christopher Isherwood that "The ideal travel book should be perhaps a little like a crime story in which you're in search of something and then either find it or find that it doesn't exist in the end."[22] But Lawrence was forced to admit, despite his enthusiastic despatches: "Travel seems to me a splendid lesson in disillusion—chiefly that." In his review of H. M. Tomlinson's *Gifts of Fortune,* Lawrence confirmed that though the pattern of his travels and travel books moved from enchantment to disillusion, the quest itself was valid: "We travel, perhaps, with a secret and absurd hope of setting foot on the Hesperides, of running our boat up a little creek and landing in the Garden of Eden. This hope is always defeated. There is no Garden of Eden, and the Hesperides never were. Yet, in our very search for them, we touch the coasts of illusion, and come into contact with other worlds."[23]

Lawrence found it easy to fantasize about Sicilians and Sardinians but quite another matter to live and travel with them. He hated Sardinia and sadly wrote, after his "dash" from Palermo to Cagliari: "It was an exciting little trip—but one couldn't live there—one would be weary—dreary. I was very disappointed."[24] But most critics, aware that the worst trips make the best reading and perhaps misled by the fact that Lawrence's initial expectations, charged with curiosity and energy, postponed (but did not prevent) the inevitable disappointment, credit Lawrence's travel books with an array of positive qualities. Richard Aldington, who established the misleading critical tone, first calls *Sea and Sardinia* "that magical little book" and then states: "All the time Lawrence is giving out life, giving you the sensation of his unique perception of a world which to him was marvellously alive and variously interesting."[25] Anthony Burgess follows Aldington and describes this work as "perhaps the most charming of all the books Lawrence ever wrote." Clive James maintains it "is a remarkable piece of lyrical visualization." And Harry Moore agrees that it is "a masterpiece of lyric and sharply observational prose, of bright colours that fill the reading eye."[26] They all manage to ignore the dark, despairing mood of his travel books.

III

Twilight in Italy (1916) is neither an account of a journey nor a description of Lawrence's life on Lake Garda, but rather a portrayal of a series of symbolic figures who illustrate his didactic and often digressive argument. The book is essentially about the opposition of the Christian and the sensual life, the conflict between the mechanical and the natural mode of existence. Lawrence expresses this tension in a sequence of clashing opposites: life–death, blood–law, phallic–spiritual, immediacy of experience–hope of salvation, lemon gardens–mechanical door, the old peasant Paolo who returned to San Gaudenzio–the young worker Giovanni who intends to go back to America, the unconscious, self-absorbed spinner–the neutral, regimented monks. *Twilight* describes how these unresolved conflicts affect the emotional lives of men and women, and has close affinities with *The Rainbow* and *Women in Love,* which were mainly written between Lawrence's sojourn on Lake Garda in 1912–1913 and the revised composition of his travel book in 1915.

Both *Twilight* and *The Rainbow* describe intoxicating harvest and dancing scenes, and a woman who obliterates her husband with her child. *Twilight* begins and ends, as *Women in Love* concludes, in the austere and deathly Alps. Both portray the effect of war on the emotional life of civilians and the inherent hostility of men and women; both explore the possibility of male love, and the conflict between sexual consummation and a contented, self-contained existence, like that of the wool-spinner and the vine-grafter.

Lawrence believes the greatest, most deeply-rooted enemy of the intuitive and sensual life is Christianity; and he opens *Twilight* in Catholic Austria with a chapter on "The Crucifix Across the Mountains," a Nietzschean account of the twilight of the idols. Though Lawrence does not believe that death, the complete disillusionment, gives the answer to the soul's anxiety, he is fascinated by the almost obscene crucifixes, pious monuments to physical death, which are genuine expressions of a people's soul. When he sees a rough-hewn broken figure under a wooden hood, he "dared not touch the fallen body of the Christ, that lay on its back in so grotesque a posture at the foot of the post. I wondered who would come and take the broken thing away, and for what purpose."

The monks, who live in the pallor between night and day, express the neutrality of the twilight that provides the thematic title of the book: "The flesh neutralising the spirit, the spirit neutralising the flesh, the law of the average asserted, this was the monks as they paced backward and forward." In contrast to the sterile, solitary and mechanical monks, Lawrence believes in the possibility of unity and consummation and attempts to achieve this ideal in his own marriage: "Night and day are one, light and dark are one, both the same . . . in the moment of ecstasy, light fused in darkness and darkness fused in light. . . . Where is the transcendent knowledge in our hearts, uniting sun and darkness, day and night, spirit and senses? Why do we not know that the two in consummation are one; that each is only part; partial and alone for ever; but that the two in consummation are perfect, beyond the range of loneliness or solitude?"

But none of the Italians have been able to achieve Lawrence's ideal. Nearly all the evidence presented in the book, and the whole disastrous tendency of modern Italy—with its materialism, money, emigration, machinery, factories, nationalism and war—opposes this fruitful and harmonious consummation of man and woman. Even Hamlet, whom Lawrence sees in the theater, becomes "the modern Italian, suspicious, isolated, self-nauseated, labouring in a sense of physical corruption," and personifies the true frenzy of unresolved polarities. The brief, doomed twilight, eclipsed by the powerful forces of the modern world, is destined to die into darkness: "This great mechanised society, being selfless, is pitiless. It works on mechanically and destroys us, it is our master and our God." It disintegrates the old way of life and precipitates the deracinated peasants into unfamiliar chaos.

The anarchistic Italians in exile, who work in a raw Swiss factory and inhabit drab stone tenements, explain the reasons for the imminent extinction of the spinner, lemon gardens and traditional way of life: "They loved Italy passionately; but they would not go back." They opposed government policy, refused to serve as soldiers in the colonial war against Turkey that led to the annexation of Libya, and were forced into permanent exile.

Anthony Burgess believes that *Twilight in Italy* is "an inept title, as Lawrence's biographer Richard Aldington says, for so sunlit a book." And Paul Fussell agrees that it "effuses something of Lawrence's ecstasy and security . . . it is unforgettable for its lyric richness."[27] But *Twilight* is a much darker book than these critics suggest. It is a lament for a lost life; and its lyricism is radically undermined by its portrayal of "the hideous rawness of the world of men, the horrible, desolating harshness of the advance of the industrial world upon the world of nature. . . . It is as if the whole social form were breaking down, and the human element swarmed within the disintegration, like maggots in cheese." Lawrence, who foresaw that Italy would become like industrialized England, fought unavailingly against this dehumanization. He described the exploitation of miners in *Sons and Lovers, Women in Love* and *Lady Chatterley's Lover,* which opens with the same angry despair that concludes *Twilight in Italy:* "Ours is essentially a tragic age, so we refuse to take it tragically. The cataclysm has happened, we are among the ruins."

IV

Only the powerful compulsion to travel, to go anywhere, expressed in the brilliant opening sentence of *Sea and Sardinia* (1921)—"Comes over one an absolute necessity to move"—enabled Lawrence to endure the tedious vicissitudes of Sardinia for ten wintry days in January 1921. Unlike most of his predecessors in the travel tradition, who romanticize and glorify their experience, Lawrence is engagingly frank about the torments of his trip and his own self-created discomfort. Economic necessity determined his mode of travel. He could not afford luxury—or even comfort—and had to accept crude transportation and lodging. As soon as he had devoured the good English bacon and tea that he brought from Taormina, his food became horrible.

Lawrence's motives for travelling to Sardinia are both complex and irrational. He takes Ulysses as his model and wants "to be free of all the hemmed-in life—the horror of human tension, the absolute insanity of machine persistence." He feels a change of place will lead to a change of mind and wants—through a kind of metamorphosis—to trade a Sicilian for a Sardinian soul. He has a prewar nostalgia for a lost past, and is attracted to a remote place—free of cultural associations—which he can penetrate (like Marlow in *Heart of Darkness*) in a "fascinating act of self-discovery—back, back down the old ways of time." Sardinia, which "has no history, no date, no race, no offering," lies outside the circuit of civilization. There the strange, sinister and diverse spirit of the place still prevails against the grey, mechanical oneness that extinguishes individuality.

Lawrence also wants to escape from the intensely irritating Sicilians, whom he now lumps with the Italians. In *Sea and Sardinia* they are portrayed as shamelessly intimate, physically all over one another, infatuated with ill-mannered children, vain, mercenary, prying, ignorant, insolent, indiscreet, callous, restless, slovenly and extortionate. The Sardinians provide a welcome contrast: "There was a certain pleasant, natural robustness of spirit, and something of a feudal free-and-easiness"—without constraint or presumption. The solitary self-contained men do not idealize their women, and are courteous, hospitable and unselfconscious.

Though Lawrence is pleased with the people, he is misinformed about the conditions on the island and disappointed when the coarse reality fails to match his fascinating expectations. In Sicily, Messina is dismal and horrible; Palermo windy and desolate. The ship is late, the cabin smelly, the food disgusting. Trapani, which looks so lovely from a distance, is filthy and crude. Cagliari is "rather bare, rather stark, rather cold and yellow," with a hideous cathedral that "oozed out baroque and sausagey." The sea-plain is malarial; Mandas freezing cold and with nothing to do: "one goes to bed when it's dark, like a chicken." The waiter in Sorgono, a dreary hole, is disgustingly dirty and outrages Lawrence by his maculate shirt-breast. The proud inhabitants gather in groups to relieve themselves in the shit-filled streets.

By the time Lawrence gets to Nuoro, where, of course, there is nothing to see, he begins to make a virtue of necessity: "sights are an irritating bore. Thank heaven there isn't a bit of Perugino or anything Pisan in the place: that I know of. Happy is the town that has nothing to show. What a lot of stunts and affectations it saves!" But it is also an affectation for Lawrence to pretend (after the manner of Norman Douglas) that he is a complete philistine. As Lawrence continues northward, he finds Orosei a dilapidated, god-forsaken hell; Siniscola "just a narrow, crude, stony place, hot in the sun, cold in the shade." Even Civitavecchia, on the Italian mainland, is scrubby and desolate.

Sea and Sardinia, then, is an essay in the psychology of travel, in which the traveller is a victim. His suffering validates his experience and adds a heroic element to the pestiferous journey. No wonder Lawrence portrays himself as critical, impatient, irascible; and Frieda, the queen-bee dislodged from her hive and accompanied by an ineffectual drone, as foolish, irrational, irritable, officious and aggressive. They travel *déclassé,* are furious when the Italians rejoice when conveying bad news, are besieged by tourist touts and parasites. They are often cold, hungry and acutely uncomfortable; but are also accused of mercenary exploitation and transformed into an ugly stereotype: "You are a State usury system, a coal fiend and an exchange thief. Every Englishman has disappeared into this triple abstraction."

Though Paul Fussell maintains "The *Sea* of the title has largely an alliterative office,"[28] the book begins and ends with voyages to Sardinia and to Sicily. The carefully wrought, cyclical structure links Lawrence with Sicily rather than Sardinia. He frequently departs before dawn; and chained convicts, the constellation of Orion and the *Città di Trieste* appear at the start and finish of the book to emphasize the futility of the journey. The marionette theater in Palermo, which is meant to represent the qualities Lawrence admires in the island people, seems strangely detached from the realities of Sardinia, and provides a forced rather than a natural conclusion: "Truly I loved them all in the theatre: the generous, hot southern blood, so subtle and spontaneous, that asks for blood contact, not mental communion or spirit sympathy." For these qualities are what Lawrence sought, not what he found. The great merit of *Sea and Sardinia* is the honesty with which he recorded his profound disenchantment.

V

Etruscan Places (1932), based on a week's travel with Earl Brewster in April 1927, is a synthesis of history and direct experience. It combines description and interpretation with social criticism and political commentary, and concerns both the past and present of Italy. The central paradox of the book, reinforced by four allusions to the ephemeral moments captured in Keats's "Grecian Urn," is that the Etruscans, though destroyed by the Romans, are still more vital than their conquerors: "the carved figure of the dead rears up as if alive, from the lid of the tomb. . . . The underworld of the Etruscans becomes more real than the above day of the afternoon."

Though Lawrence relies heavily on Etruscan scholars like Dennis, Ducati and Weege, he instinctively opposes their traditional interpretation of the people. He also condemns their efforts to tear Etruscan art from its customary setting ("Museums anyhow are wrong") in the "rough nothingness of the hillside," where the guide kneels to light his lamp and the travellers quite naturally dive down into the little one-room tombs, "just like rabbits popping down a hole."

The vague and mysterious quality of the Etruscans, who "half emerge from the dim background of time," allows and even encourages Lawrence to construct an imaginative but entirely convincing picture of their vanished life, to re-create them in his own image. He laments: "We have lost the art of living"; and believes the Etruscans, who express all the qualities he admires, can by their still-vivid example restore their precious gifts to modern man.

Paul Fussell, a critic who is always worth arguing with, provides a neatly simplified and schematic summary of Lawrence's travel books, and states that they seem to sketch the stages of his life: *"Twilight in Italy,* with its fervors about 'reconciliation,' is about youth; *Sea and Sardinia,* devoted to social comedy, is about young adulthood . . . *Etruscan Places,* about dying happily."[29] But *Twilight,* dominated by opposition rather than reconciliation, is not about youth any more than the bitterly despairing *Sea and Sardinia* is about young adulthood. Nor is *Etruscan Places* about dying happily. It is, like all the major works of Lawrence's last, moribund years, about the theme of resurrection, about the hope of rebirth and life after death.

Lawrence announces, on the opening page, that he is instinctively attracted to the Etruscans, who "get into his imagination" and will not go out. He makes specific connections between the ancient Etruscans and the modern Italian peasants. According to Lawrence, Etruscan places have a stillness and repose. The Etruscans were connected to a primitive and prehistoric Mediterranean world, were in touch with the gods, and (like the peasants in *Twilight*) had a phallic consciousness as opposed to the present-day mental and spiritual consciousness. They possessed a delicacy, sensitivity, carelessness and fullness of life; they had an originality, spontaneity, gaiety and ease that saw everything—including death—as a pleasant continuance of life, with luxurious jewels, wine, flutes and dance. Their religion, which preceded gods and goddesses, was expressed in terms of ritual, gesture and symbol; the ship of death represented "the mystery of the journey out of life." Everything they made was ephemeral, conveyed a sense of touch and the everlasting wonder of things, and provided immediate pleasure without the tedious burden of imposing works of art (which Lawrence was pleased to avoid in Nuoro). Their confederacy of loosely linked, independent city-states expressed the Italian political instinct and resembled modern Italy before unification in 1861—and afterward. "To the Etruscan," Lawrence exclaims in a beautiful passage that proclaims his doctrine of vitalism, "all was alive; the whole universe lived; and the business of man was himself to live amid it all. He had to draw life into himself, out of the wandering huge vitalities of the world. The cosmos was alive, like a vast creature. The whole thing breathed and stirred. . . . The active religious idea was that man, by vivid attention and subtlety and exerting all his strength, could draw more life into himself, more life, more and more glistening vitality, till he became shining like the morning, blazing like a god."

The antithesis of the Etruscans are the brutal, imperial Romans. They dominated and destroyed their weak though charming neighbors, who held out against overwhelming mechanical force for more than one hundred years. The historical justification for the destruction of Etruria was that the people were vicious. Lawrence stoutly defends them against the charge of cruelty and refutes the traditional "picture of a gloomy, hellish, serpent-writhing, vicious Etruscan people who were quite rightly stamped out by the noble Romans."

Lawrence associates the ancient Romans with the modern Fascists, just as he equates the Etruscans with the peasants. He thus gives a satiric twist to the nationalistic propaganda of the contemporary conquerors, who revived the Roman salute, spoke of the Mediterranean as *mare nostrum* and were inspired by imperial ambitions to invade Africa. But Lawrence notes, with considerable perspicacity, that Fascist (like Roman) power is doomed because the party members do not trust themselves and cannot trust their leaders: the Nietzschean "will-to-power is a secondary thing in an Italian, reflected onto him from the Germanic races that have almost engulfed him. . . . Brute force and overbearing may take a terrific effect. But in the end, that which lives lives by delicate sensitiveness." Though the will to power may be foreign to the Italians, the Fascists still ruled as the Romans once did.

Etruscan Places, like *Sea and Sardinia,* ends with a symbolic scene that expresses the dominant themes of the book. The impulsive composer who suddenly kills his nagging wife recalls the passionate shepherd of the opening pages, who represents the Etruscans and whose "face is a faun-face, not deadened by morals." And the two prisoners who escape after sculpting bread into life-like effigies that deceive the flashing light of the warder and cost the Fascist governor his job, subtly recall the Etruscans who sail out of the world with their ephemeral household effects on the ship of death, revealed by the guide's sudden light in the underground tombs.

Lawrence's letters, novels and travel books imposed the image of Italy on the modern imagination as Conrad did for Africa, Forster India and Hemingway Spain. Lawrence did not follow a specific literary tradition, he created one; and his profound influence can clearly be seen in the travel writers who followed his innovative example. The works of Huxley, Auden, Isherwood, Graham Greene, Henry Miller and Lawrence Durrell all reflect Lawrence's themes: his escape from a mechanical to a natural life, his quest for inspiration, his idealistic search for a personal connection with ordinary people, his vital response to landscape and culture, his imaginative rather than realistic view of the world, his self-exploration and self-revelation. These travel writers also reflect his honest portrayal of discomfort, disillusionment and despair.

3

Maurice Magnus

I

LAWRENCE WAS ESPECIALLY PROUD of his long and little-known Introduction to Maurice Magnus' *Memoirs of the Foreign Legion* (published in 1924 and reprinted in *Phoenix II,* 1968) and declared it was "the best single piece of writing, as *writing,* that he had ever done."[1] The Introduction is geographically structured by Lawrence's restless movements around Italy as the scene shifts six times from Florence (November) to Capri and Montecassino (February), Taormina (April), Syracuse and Malta (May). Each place evokes a distinctive mood; all are linked by a recurrent pattern of emotional encounters and financial demands, by Lawrence's search for a postwar haven and Magnus' desperate quest for money. Throughout the Introduction Lawrence oscillates between the solace of the Italian landscape and the torments of Magnus, for Italy, much more than a background to Lawrence's story, is a place where rootless postwar exiles, like Magnus, can operate. The lush countryside (which also appears in Renaissance paintings) provides a natural contrast to the horrors of war and the tragic fate of Magnus—who was a victim of the war.

Lawrence describes the actual circumstances of his relationship with Magnus "as truthfully as a man can tell a thing,"[2] but he also intensifies essential traits and uses novelistic elements (plot, structure, setting, symbol and theme) to create one of his greatest literary portraits. Because Lawrence was deeply engaged with Magnus, he describes his own involvement as part of this portrait; the truth about Magnus must be true to himself and include the truth about himself. The creative act thus becomes a moral act, and the analysis of Magnus' character reveals some obscure aspects of Lawrence's own personality. The artistic integrity of the Introduction is based on Lawrence's honesty about his fascination with Magnus' homosexuality. Once this is fully understood, the meaning of Lawrence's controversy with Magnus' defender, Norman Douglas, becomes much clearer.[3]

The story opens dramatically just after Lawrence has escaped from censorship, persecution and the "Nightmare" experience of the war (described in *Kangaroo*) which brought him to the verge of a physical and emotional breakdown: "On a dark, wet, wintry evening in November, 1919, I arrived in Florence, having just got back to Italy for the first time since 1914."

Lawrence asked Norman Douglas, who had been assistant editor on Ford's *English Review* and had "never left him in the lurch," to find him a room in a cheap hotel. He met Douglas at the Pensione Balestri in the Piazza Mentana, where he was paying ten lire per day. The grandiose but courtly Douglas "was decidedly shabby and a gentleman, with his wicked red face and tufted eyebrows." Douglas never opened the windows of his dreadful room and the queer smell was something new to Lawrence: "But I didn't care. One had got away from the war." When they had eaten dinner, Douglas made the waiter measure the remaining half-liter of wine and deduct it from the bill.

Lawrence's sketch complements his satiric portrait of Douglas, who appears as James Argyle in *Aaron's Rod* (1922). Argyle admits "I'm a shady bird, in all senses of the word" and asks "what is life but a search for a friend?" Though handsome in his day, "now his face was all red and softened and inflamed, his eyes had gone small and wicked under his bushy grey brows." He is extremely cynical about men's claim to heterosexuality and women's to purity. While in his cups he insists that "Impotence set up the praise of chastity.... They can't do it, and so they make a virtue of not doing it." Aaron's attitude toward Argyle foreshadows Lawrence's view of Magnus: "He had never met a man like Argyle before—and he could not help being charmed";[4] Argyle's hedonistic ideas anticipate Douglas' homosexual friendship with Magnus.

Lawrence is clearly intrigued by the paradoxical Maurice Magnus, whom he meets through Norman Douglas. Magnus resembles a common actor-manager down on his luck and is "just the sort of man he had never met": "He looked a man of about forty, spruce and youngish in his deportment, very pink-faced, and very clean, very natty, very alert . . . little smart man of the shabby world. . . . His voice was precise and a little mincing, and it had an odd high squeak." Lawrence portrays Magnus' fussy and finicky character through his possessions as well as his person, for he acts like a little pontiff, surrounded by essences, pomades and powders in cut-glass silver-topped bottles. Like Mr. Jones in Conrad's *Victory,* he wears a blue silk dressing gown, has affected manners and speech, insists on his status as a gentleman and is a rabid woman-hater.

Lawrence can never quite make up his mind about the elusive Magnus, a Catholic convert who had been Isadora Duncan's manager, had edited the *Roman Review* which began and ended in 1914, had translated Gordon Craig's *Art of the Theater* into German and Barbier's opera *Tales of Hoffmann* into English. He is common yet queer and sensitive as a woman, a bounder yet delicate and tender, pompous and superior yet so intelligent.

The characterization of Magnus as the theatrical manager Mr. May in *The Lost Girl* (1920) illuminates Lawrence's attitude toward him. Like Magnus, Mr. May is an American Catholic who attended a German school and wears expensive clothes: smart overcoat, velour hat, blue silk underwear. He is afraid of being stranded without cash, but stays at the best hotel; is married, but hates women and prefers mental to physical friendship. He appears as a tempter "whose pink, fat face and light-blue eyes had a loud look" and convinces Mr. Houghton to start a cinema that eventually ruins him. He is "blatant, but fastidiously so," a "disconsolate bird pecking the crumbs of Alvina's sympathy."[5] Yet Alvina (the emotional touchstone of the novel) likes him and they become almost inseparable. Harry Moore's statement: "Here he showed the worst of Magnus: the pushing, worldly man of theatrical back-alleys, oozing guile and seething with bitchiness,"[6] misses the subtlety of Lawrence's portrait and his attraction to this smart but shady personage.

In the Introduction, Lawrence suggests that Magnus is in love with Douglas, whom he indulges and spoils in every way. Like John Wilkes with Dr. Johnson, Magnus offers Douglas the choicest pieces of food before he helps himself and is patient, fastidious, deferential. He dashes around town, arranges Douglas' affairs, runs his errands, settles his bills. Douglas appears to accept this as his due and despises his friend as "a little busybody and an inferior"—though he does buy him a Volterra marble bowl as a birthday present.

Lawrence is careful to detach himself from this ménage, and to define his own way of life and moral values in opposition to this repulsive yet somehow attractive homosexual. Magnus is neat and smartly dressed. Lawrence, who has a horror of strange barbershops, wears an old overcoat and ragged beard (Magnus asks him what he uses to dye his hair). Magnus travels first class, favors luxurious hotels, makes constant demands on the servants and dines in expensive restaurants. Lawrence goes third class, stays in cheap rooms, dislikes chambermaids, often eats bread and cheese in his room. Magnus feels the mind endures when the physical beauty of the peasant has passed away. Lawrence chooses the mindlessness of the peasant and his strong blood-presence. Magnus thinks only mental friendships last forever. Lawrence believes, "If there is no profound blood-sympathy, I know the mental friendship is trash."

Magnus exclaims that the very time to spend money is when you have none. He foreshadows his own sad end by asking: "If you're going to live in fear of the world, what's the good of living at all? Might as well die." Lawrence is extremely careful with money and feels Magnus despises him for hoarding it. But he mistrusts the world and would never let himself be penniless. Magnus ultimately adopts the bourgeois rather than the bohemian viewpoint and chooses to die rather than face the world without money. Magnus is a reckless hedonist who wants to escape from the real world into the monasticism of the Middle Ages. Lawrence is a cautious puritan who knows that he is, unhappily, rooted in the present. Magnus, who has a childlike dependence on the authority of the Church, sees the monastery as a refuge. Lawrence, who is intensely individualistic, views it as a temptation.

Lawrence leaves Florence in December and after a few

cold weeks in the primitive Abruzzi mountains, moves to Capri
and reminds Magnus of his invitation to visit him at Montecassino. This Benedictine monastery, the oldest in western Europe,
educated St. Thomas Aquinas and was destroyed by bombs in
1944. Magnus' curiously indirect response makes Lawrence
feel he needs money. Since Lawrence has just recieved an unexpected £20 from Amy Lowell in America, he sends £5 to Magnus—both to avenge Magnus' scorn for his own frugality and
to satisfy his muted appeal for help. Magnus, grateful that Lawrence has intuitively "saved his life," asks him to come to the
monastery. Lawrence enjoys the excitement of the boat ride
from Capri across the bay to the mainland: "I always loved
hanging over the side and watching the people come out in
boats from the little places of the shore, that rose steep and
beautiful. I love the movement of these watery Neapolitan
people, and the naive trustful way they clamber in and out of
the boats, and their softness, and their dark eyes."

When Lawrence arrives alone at the fortress-palace, Magnus seductively looks into his eyes "with that wistful, watchful
tenderness rather like a woman who isn't quite sure of her
lover." Lawrence then assumes a passive role and is treated by
Magnus with the same affection he had previously lavished on
Douglas. He lends Lawrence five francs to pay the driver. Because of the cold in the mountains, he incongruously envelops
Lawrence (his secret sharer) in his luxurious "coat made of
thick, smooth black cloth, and lined with . . . silky black seal-
skin." To seal their intimacy, Magnus shows him a photograph
of a lovely lady and asks for Lawrence's opinion. Irritated by
Magnus' anticipation of praise, Lawrence replies that he finds
her rather cheap and trivial. He is embarrassed when Magnus
dramatically states: "That's my mother." Magnus then con-
fesses that he has just given Lawrence his last five francs and
attempts to wheedle more money out of his guest. But Lawrence is reluctant to give what Magnus seems to expect. As he
leaves he offers 20 lire to Magnus, who refuses this paltry sum.
Lawrence also reads the manuscript of the *Memoirs of the Foreign Legion,* but finds it rather mediocre: "vague and diffuse
where it shouldn't have been—lacking in sharp detail and definite event." He suggests specific improvements and Magnus
agrees to revise. When Lawrence sees the final version, he admires it and sends the manuscript to his American publisher,
Thomas Seltzer, who rejects it.

The monastery stands alone above "the gulf where the world's valley was, and all the mountains that stand in Italy on the plains as if God had just put them down ready made." It represents not only a refuge from the world, but also a violation of Lawrence's soul, a temptation to succumb to "the poignant grip of the past, the grandiose, violent past of the Middle Ages, when [Lawrence imagines] blood was strong and unquenched and life was flamboyant with splendours and horrible miseries." He is finally able to resist what attracts Magnus when he realizes that the Bramante courtyard is empty of life and the gay, red-legged gentry who decorate Italian paintings are dead forever. Such troubled thoughts do not disturb the enthusiasm of Magnus, a worldly, sybaritic, swindling, would-be monk who has offended the Benedictine brothers by his pompous manner and is actually hiding from the police.

When Lawrence moves from Capri to Sicily, he experiences on the ship to Palermo the same sensation of well-being he had felt on the boat to Naples. He is inspired by the heights of Taormina, as he had been by Montecassino, and senses the possibility of a personal renaissance: "Whatever had died for me [in the War], Sicily had not then died; dawn-lovely Sicily, and the Ionian sea. We came back, and the world was lovely: our own house above the almond trees, and the sea in the cove below."

But once again the serpent, in the form of Magnus, creeps obsessively into Lawrence's Eden. Magnus had paid his hotel bill in Anzio with a worthless check; and as the police climbed up to the monastery to search for him, the monk Don Bernardo gave him some money and urged him to escape down the back of the hill. He had spent an agonizing time hiding in the toilet of the train until he reached Naples, assumed Lawrence would be responsible for his welfare and comes straight to him for help. He evades the effects of his extravagance by continuing to live beyond his means at the luxurious San Domenico hotel (a former monastery, where the opening scene of Antonioni's *L'Avventura* was filmed).

Magnus praises Lawrence's house and wants to reestablish their intimacy—and Lawrence's responsibility—by moving in with him. When Lawrence refuses, Magnus accepts 100 francs to pay his hotel bill and exclaims, in his most pathetic manner: " 'I shouldn't have come to Taormina at all, save for you. Don't be so unkind to me—don't speak so coldly to me.'—He put his hand on my arm, and looked up at me with tears swimming in his eyes." Lawrence, who established his friendship with Magnus when Frieda was absent, now tries to use his domestic life with Frieda as a barrier between himself and Magnus. Magnus returns when Lawrence is out to plead with Frieda in her native language, for he is the Kaiser's illegitimate grandson and she is the daughter of a German baron. He appeals for sympathy, breaks down her reserve and forces her to give in to his demands. When Lawrence returns home, he finds Frieda "shivering with revulsion and excitement, and even a sense of power"—a perfect reflection of his own ambivalent response.

In *Not I, But the Wind,* Frieda rather disingenuously denies her own emotional involvement ("To me it was no problem"), but admits that Magnus had a profound emotional effect on Lawrence: "He came almost taking for granted that we would be responsible for him, that it was our duty to keep him. . . . I felt he made a fool of Lawrence. . . . But Lawrence felt deeply disturbed by Magnus and did feel a responsibility for him."[7]

Lawrence also manages to resist Magnus' outrageous request that he make a forty-hour train journey to recover Magnus' possessions from the monastery. Lawrence does not know exactly what mischief he has been up to, but does not trust him for a second. When the simpering Magnus claims that Lawrence has betrayed him, Lawrence feels repelled by his charity-demanding insolence. As usual, the landscape reflects his current mood and turns ugly when he is tormented by Magnus: "Never had the Ionian sea looked so sickening to me."

To save money, Magnus compromises his principles and rents a room in a local house. When he fails to pay his bill, the Italian landlord (who makes Lawrence intensely aware of his own absurd relationship with Magnus) complains to Lawrence about Magnus' behavior. Lawrence sorts matters out by advancing Magnus seven guineas in return for a supposedly misplaced check that was sent to Magnus as payment for an article. Magnus then promises to leave Taormina for Malta, where he has friends and his prospects seem more promising. At this point in the narrative, the exasperated Lawrence abandons his tolerant attitude and condemns Magnus' behavior: "He was one of these modern parasites who just assume their right to live and live well, leaving the payment to anybody [i.e., Lawrence] who can, will, or must pay. The end is inevitably swindling."

Having freed himself—he thinks—from Magnus' clutches, Lawrence accepts an invitation from Mary Cannan to visit Malta as her guest. For the third time he experiences a kind of (temporary) euphoria as he surveys the port of Syracuse and succumbs to the healing powers of the landscape: "beyond, the long sinuous sky-line of the long flat-topped table-land hills which run along the southern coast, [are] so different from the peaky, pointed, bunched effect of many-tipped Sicily in the north" of the island. But Magnus, still "sweating blood," spots Lawrence in the street and extracts, as a final request, another hundred lire to settle the bill of his expensive hotel in Syracuse.

When Lawrence (travelling second class) boards the ship for Valetta and breathes free for the first time since leaving the monastery, he spots Magnus smoking a cigar and chatting with the captain on the first-class deck—his ticket paid for, of course, with Lawrence's money. As they sail into Malta, Magnus, still pompous and patronizing, echoes his benefactor's sentiments and states: "I love approaching these islands in the early morning."

In Valetta, Lawrence inevitably runs into Magnus, who introduces him to two Maltese friends of the monk Don Bernardo, and they all go for a motor-car drive together. Magnus loves the island, which had been a strategic center in the fight against Moslem power in the eastern Mediterranean and was then controlled by the British. Lawrence, by contrast, finds the place dreadful and dislikes its "fearful and stony bay, arid, treeless, desert, a bit of stony desert by the sea, with unhappy villas and a sordid, scrap-iron front . . . a bone-dry, bone-bare, hideous landscape." He leaves Malta secure in the knowledge that he has finally rid himself of his incubus and that Magnus is "safely shut up in that beastly island."

The tragic climax occurs six months later, in November 1920, exactly a year after he first met Magnus. Lawrence writes that one of Magnus' Maltese friends, Walter Salomone, withdrew his financial guarantee (necessary for residence in the island) after he learned that another Maltese, Michael Borg, had loaned Magnus £55 and that Salomone might be responsible for this debt. The Italian police finally caught up with Magnus and were about to arrest and extradite him for defrauding a hotel in Rome. Magnus, who seriously contemplated suicide, had prepared for this possibility by hiding poison in his room. While the police were waiting outside for him to change his clothes, he killed himself by swallowing prussic acid—and damning himself in the eyes of the Church. In his will Magnus left all his literary property to Douglas and characteristically demanded: "I want to be buried first class, my wife will pay." (She refused at first but later refunded the money for the expensive funeral.) Magnus, like Lawrence, died at the age of forty-four.

At the end of the Introduction there is a distinct change in tone as Lawrence shifts from psychological narrative to moral judgment. Only after Magnus' death does he realize "what it must have meant to be the hunted, desperate man." Just as Italy had looked lovely to Lawrence when he was free and ugly when pursued by Magnus, so it must have seemed pleasant to Magnus when he was sustained by Lawrence and hideous when hunted by the police. Lawrence's final judgment of Magnus is harsh but convincing: "The worst thing I have against him, is that he abused the confidence, the kindness and the generosity of unsuspecting people like Mazzaiba [i.e., Borg]"—as well as Don Bernardo; the hotel-keepers in Rome, Anzio and Taormina; Frieda; and Lawrence himself; but not, significantly, Douglas. Magnus, "a little loving vampire," had the power to arouse affection and used that power to get money from people who were attracted to him.

But Lawrence's judgment of himself is even more severe. He has the moral courage to oppose the humanist tradition and dare to suggest that human life is not sacred. He admits that he could have saved Magnus' life by giving him half his money and allowing him to escape to Egypt (where he could get beyond the reach of the Italian police and earn money as a journalist) but deliberately "chose not to save his life." But he did not know that Magnus would kill himself; he merely refused to support Magnus and forced him to face the consequences of his own actions. Lawrence reveals that even with the knowledge of Magnus' suicide: "I would not help to keep him alive, not if I had to choose again."

Douglas claimed to be Magnus' friend and said he was corresponding with him just before his suicide, but he knew Magnus far too well to give him anything: "You won't get me to lend you money; I never do."[8] Douglas had given Magnus the impression that Lawrence was well off, though he could barely support himself as a writer. Lawrence, who had been robbed of £10 in Rome en route to Capri, was extremely poor when he arrived in Florence. After nine years of writing books like *Sons and Lovers* and *The Rainbow,* he had only £21, or perhaps £24 if Frieda returned from Germany with £3 left over. During a period of six months, when the rate of exchange was 45 lire (or francs) to the pound, Lawrence gave Magnus, who was merely an acquaintance, a total of £20—nearly as much as he had started with. He sent £5 from Capri to Montecassino, gave Magnus £2.25 (100 francs) at first and then about £5.50 to pay the hotel bill in Taormina (Magnus had been at the San Domenico for several days at 50 lire per day and Lawrence gave him 100 lire extra), and finally presented him with £7.35 as an advance against a check for an article that was mistakenly returned to *Land and Water.* (It is not clear if this check actually existed— the landlord told Lawrence that a letter had come for Magnus but said he did not know what it contained—or if Lawrence ever received it, for the magazine folded in 1920.) Lawrence was hostile to Magnus, but he was also extraordinarily generous to him.

Having judged Magnus' character and justified his own actions, Lawrence turns to the ostensible subject of the Introduction, the *Memoirs of the Foreign Legion,* which casts new light on Magnus' background and behavior. Magnus claims that he joined the Legion in 1915 for patriotic reasons, but Douglas says he enlisted because of domestic tragedy (perhaps his mother's death or his broken marriage). Magnus spent two months in Algeria and was then sent back to France. Before seeing combat, he deserted and "hopped it" across the border to neutral Italy, after the fashion of Douglas. His book, originally called *Dregs,* was written in 1917 and contained homosexual passages that were expurgated from the published version. The *Memoirs,* which has the sharp details and definite events that Lawrence urged Magnus to include, is a vivid account of life among the brutal outcasts of society that emphasizes Magnus' social and moral superiority. Though some of his old snobbery and taste for luxury surfaces when he abandons his soldier's uniform and plans his escape, there is no hint in the book of the pampered, spoiled sponger portrayed by Lawrence. It seems surprising, when one compares the two disparate portraits, that Magnus survived the extreme hardships of the Legion only to kill himself over a hotel bill. Douglas calls Magnus' suicide "an almost inexplicable phenomenon" and Nancy Cunard agrees that "the whole tangle around the death of Magnus is such that it will probably remain a puzzle forever."⁹ The most convincing explanation is implicit in the dominant theme of the Introduction, for Lawrence, with great insight, suggests that Magnus was a victim of the war, which exhausted his resilience and sapped his will to live.

Lawrence is amused by Magnus' misplaced indignation in the *Memoirs,* wonders what Magnus did "in the way of vice," is surprised to find he is a pure Prussian, and suspects that he may even have been a cast-off German spy. In order to explain the inconsistency between the tough legionnaire and the helpless parasite, Lawrence points out that Magnus' trick of exploiting affection works all through his book. But he more generously concedes: "He had his points, the courage of his own terrors, quick-wittedness, sensitiveness to certain things in his surroundings. I prefer him, scamp as he is, to the ordinary respectable person."

Lawrence also praises Magnus for his resourceful escape from the Legion and for his determination not to be trapped by the military machine: "Magnus carried the human consciousness through circumstances which would have been too much for me. I would have died rather than be so humiliated, I could never have borne it."¹⁰ Though Magnus survived the Legion, he did not, when trapped by a similar authority, survive the Italian police. Lawrence, who said that he mistrusts the world and would "never let myself be penniless while I live," implies that in the same circumstances he would rather die, like Magnus, than live in fear of the world. He respects Magnus for dying when he was cornered, suggests that his suicide was morally right and maintains that he was also right to let Magnus kill himself. He ascribes Magnus' weakness to the fact that he was the adored only son of a woman who imagined she had royal blood. When his beloved mother died, he turned to the Catholic Church for consolation. He suffered from the "cruel illusion of importance *manqué,*" which protected him from reality, enabled him to escape the Legion and allowed him to exploit his friends.

Lawrence then returns to his opening theme—the disastrous effects of the War—and ends with a peroration against modern militarism which was opposed, successfully and even heroically, by both Lawrence and Magnus. In a prophetic strain, he urges his readers to "Take the foul rotten spirit of mankind, full of the running sores of the war, to our bosom, and cleanse it there." The collapse of civilization during the War and the postwar chaos in Europe led Lawrence to search for a new mode of life and a renewal of his senses and spirit in a setting that would stimulate his creative work. Magnus—a poor, rootless exile—deeply disturbed Lawrence by suggesting parallels to Lawrence's own life and giving in to two temptations: homosexuality, which evades the conflict between man and woman; and the Church, which evades the problems of the modern world by retreating into a medieval sense of order.

The disturbing portrait of Magnus that emerges from the Introduction bears a close resemblance to the character of Frederick Rolfe, the self-styled Baron Corvo. It also shows Magnus as a would-be artist, like Huysmans' Des Esseintes or Mann's Detlev Spinell, in the Decadent tradition of the 1890s—a tradition that Lawrence disliked but also found intriguing. Both Corvo and Magnus were overt homosexuals, masochists, pornographers, aesthetes, snobs, parasites, petty criminals, shady con-men operating (to the embarrassment of their respectable friends) in Italy. (Both men died there in middle age.) Both were escapists and escape-artists who suffered from delusions of grandeur and a persecution complex. Both were bogus aristocrats, Catholic converts and spoiled priests, who sought refuge in the Church and had ecclesiastical fantasies. Both endured, as Graham Greene wrote of Corvo, "the long purgatories in foreign *pensions,* the counted coppers, the keeping up of appearances."[11] Lawrence's review of *Hadrian the Seventh* in 1925 clearly shows his fascination with Corvo and the revealing parallels with Magnus, whom he refers to as a tempter in both the Introduction and *The Lost Girl:*

> He seems to have been a serpent of serpents in the bosom of all the nineties. That in itself endears him to one. The way everyone dropped him with a shudder is almost fascinating. . . . [He] is sexually chaste, because of his almost morbid repugnance for women. . . . Fine, subtle, sensitive, and almost egomaniac, he can accept nothing but the momentary thrill of aesthetic appreciation. . . . His medievalism makes him a truly comical royalist. . . . It is all amazing, that a man with so much insight and fineness, on the one hand, should be so helpless and just purely ridiculous, when it comes to actualities.[12]

Douglas Goldring observed that "Poor Magnus was almost everything that Lawrence disliked and disapproved of. He was a decayed 'gentleman', incapable of earning his living, always in debt, always borrowing money, and homo-sexual into the bargain."[13] While there is some truth in this statement, it is essentially misleading. For Lawrence was also fascinated by decayed gentlemen (Norman Douglas, Reggie Turner, Harry Crosby) and aristocrats (Lady Ottoline Morrell, Lady Cynthia Asquith, the Hon. Dorothy Brett). Though he stresses the differences between himself and Magnus throughout the Introduction, he closes the gap between them at the end to emphasize certain similarities and concludes on a sympathetic note. Both men experience the same exhilarating response to landscape, both were hurt by the war but stood up to militaristic brutality, both mistrusted the world and (would have) preferred to die rather than be humiliated. In the end, Lawrence praises Magnus' book and admires "the courageous isolated little devil" for facing risks and accepting the consequences.

It is significant that Lawrence, not Magnus, revived their friendship by writing to ask if he could visit Montecassino. Yet Lawrence was uneasy in the monastery, left after only two days (though he had planned to stay a week), and spent the rest of the year attempting to elude Magnus. Magnus, who gained some sort of hold on Lawrence, establishes a comical pattern, pursues Lawrence throughout Sicily and Malta, and obsessively reappears whenever Lawrence thinks he has escaped. Lawrence is stubborn but passive: helpless, uncomfortable, susceptible to Magnus' wheedling ways, unable to refuse his exacting demands. He tries to use Frieda to fortify himself against temptation, but she also succumbs. He cannot quite free himself because Magnus appeals to him on a subconscious level, and Lawrence can never resolve the conflict between overt rejection and covert acceptance.

Lawrence destroyed his homosexual treatise "Goats and Compasses" in 1917, depicted homosexual scenes in *The White Peacock, Women in Love, Aaron's Rod* and *The Plumed Serpent,* and was also attracted to William Henry Hocking and John Middleton Murry.[14] He declared: "I believe in what [Whitman] calls 'manly love', the real implicit reliance of one man on another: as sacred a unison as marriage: only it must be deeper, more ultimate."[15] Homosexuality, the implicit reliance that Magnus established, was the source of his strange power over Lawrence. Magnus, who behaved as if he had honored Lawrence by coming to Taormina and as if Lawrence had betrayed him there, appealed for protection to the masculine side of Lawrence's nature and for sympathy to the feminine side (which Lawrence recognized in himself). Lawrence, who associated man-for-man love with death, felt he was right to let Magnus die so that he could also kill his own fearful homosexuality: "I would let him go over into death. He shall and should die, so should all his sort." This admission is strikingly similar to his discussion of Whitman's homosexuality and explains why Lawrence believed "his sort" was morbid and deserved to die: "Woman is inadequate for the last merging. So the next step is the merging of man-for-man love. And this is on the brink of death. It slides over into death."[16] The paradox of Whitman's solution is that the merging of men goes beyond women—but into a dead end, into morbid masturbation and sterility. Lawrence's Introduction is not only a memoir, memorial, critique, confession and apologia, but also an exorcism.

II

The death of Magnus did not end his controversial connection to Lawrence, whom he continued to plague from beyond the grave. Douglas responded to the Introduction in a long pamphlet, *D. H. Lawrence and Maurice Magnus: A Plea For Better Manners.* It was privately published by Douglas in Florence in December 1924 (in an edition of 500 copies) and twice reprinted during 1925. Douglas, who adopts a charming, chatty, familiar, roguish and worldly persona that confirms Lawrence's portraits, softens his criticism by calling the Introduction a wrongheaded "masterpiece of unconscious misrepresentation." As Magnus' sometime collaborator and literary executor, he claims that he should have been consulted about the publication of the *Memoirs* and has a right to half the profits. Lawrence, who appropriated the manuscript, "has now recouped himself many times over by the sale of these Memoirs." Douglas maintains that Lawrence hated being pestered for money by bounders (which was correct) and that "those borrowed pounds are the key to this whole feline Introduction" (also correct, but in a different sense than Douglas intended, for Lawrence wrote the Introduction to get the *Memoirs* published and repay Magnus' debts). Douglas is most acute when he observes that Lawrence's pity for Mazzaiba (Borg) is really vicarious pity for himself.

Douglas also objects to his appearance in *Aaron's Rod* as a high-handed old swaggerer, unsteady on his legs. He argues that Lawrence was unfair to Magnus and distorted Douglas' attitude to his old friend. He admits that he gave Lawrence permission "to put me in as you please," but objects to the wine-weighing scene which makes him look mean. He defends himself by claiming that wine is "sold by weight, and that the man who does not act as I did is held to be weak in the head." But, as Richard Aldington explains, it is customary to take back a liter or more of wine, though one is expected to leave less than this amount as a tip for the waiter.

Douglas relates that his first, characteristic, encounter with Magnus took place in Capri in 1909 when the childlike and forlorn stranger approached him in the street and in an ingratiating, offhand manner extracted 37 francs. Douglas confirms that he inspired deep and lasting affection in the "finicky, fussy and fastidious" Magnus, who seemed to delight in anticipating his slightest wish. But he insists that he did *not* despise his friend. Magnus had a terrific zest for work and a strange reluctance to give pain (to Douglas, but certainly not to Lawrence.) He was brave, amusing and likeable, far more civilized and multi-facted than Lawrence suggests, and had a greater capacity for giving than for borrowing. (Lawrence agrees that Magnus was generous when he had money, but he never had any when Lawrence knew him.) Douglas excuses Magnus' lack of literary success by explaining that it was difficult to sell his work in the postwar period, though the same constraint applied to both Lawrence and himself. Like Lawrence, Douglas attributes Magnus' habit of reckless expenditure to the fact that his mother, the illegitimate daughter of Kaiser Wilhelm I, had lived with him until her death in 1912 and had never been able to deny him anything.

He mentions that the police followed Magnus from the bilked hotels in Rome and Anzio to Montecassino and Malta. He wonders (but offers no explanation) how Magnus, "a rare alloy of cunning and grit," could face the unspeakable horrors among the "sharpers and sodomites" of the Foreign Legion only to poison himself because he owed a little money to hotels and might have to serve a month or two in prison. Douglas does not seem to share Lawrence's good opinion of the *Memoirs,* which he says was written in a bare and undistinguished style. He is sorry that Magnus was forced to expurgate many allusions "to certain ultra-masculine peculiarities of legionary life." (Douglas also regretted that Charles Doughty was not more explicit about homosexual habits in *Arabia Deserta,* though he did not describe these acts in his own North African travel book, *Fountains in the Sand.*)[17]

He concludes his criticism of Lawrence by angrily declaring that the novelist's touch "is hitting below the belt, and a damnably vulgar proceeding"—a snobbish swipe at Lawrence's working-class origins. This point leads to a digressive plea for better literary manners, in which he temporarily abandons his urbane and tolerant persona and condemns the unscrupulous writer (i.e., Lawrence) as a *"cloaca maxima* for the discharge of objectionable personalities." But Douglas, who satirizes his former friends in *South Wind* and other novels, is in no position to criticize Lawrence for doing the same thing. Even his most serious criticism of Lawrence is not as grave as Lawrence's own admission that he could have saved Magnus' life and chose not to do so.

Douglas' pamphlet was provoked partly by Lawrence's penetrating if inhumane dissection of Magnus' unfortunate character in the Introduction, which was meant to present his posthumous work to the public, and by his fictional satire in *Aaron's Rod* of Douglas' gentlemanly upper-class pretence. But Douglas—who maintained a respectable front, had a predilection for little boys, was often in trouble with the Italian police and had to "hop it" over the frontier—was really infuriated and frightened by Lawrence's potentially dangerous and damaging suggestions about his homosexual relationship with Magnus.

Mark Holloway notes that in their controversy "the advantage was with Douglas throughout. Lawrence's views were so unorthodox, his behaviour was so eccentric and cantankerous, his morals [unlike Douglas'] were so suspect to the ignorant—above all, he was so open, so honest, so vulnerable—that everything he did and said was liable to be turned to sensational account by the press."[18] Graham Greene calls Douglas' pamphlet "one of the finest passages of invective written in our time."[19] But Douglas, like his rival, revealed more of his own weakness than he perhaps intended and allowed

Lawrence, despite his considerable disadvantage, to get the better of the argument.

Lawrence, who had moved to New Mexico in 1922, was willing to tolerate Douglas' carelessly printed Italian pamphlet. But when Douglas included this polemic in *Experiments* (1925), Lawrence was roused to defend himself publicly. He first worked out the strategy of his counterattack in two letters to his agent, Curtis Brown, in April 1925, soon after the pamphlet appeared. He states that he acted more generously toward Magnus than Douglas did, received *carte blanche* from Douglas to deal with the *Memoirs* as he wished, wrote the Introduction only to repay Borg, refused offers to publish it separately (though this entailed financial sacrifice), deserved 50 percent of the royalties since he wrote nearly half the book himself and was entirely responsible for the publication of the *Memoirs.* He also denies the importance of Douglas' supposed collaboration:

> I hear Norman Douglas attacks me on behalf of Magnus. Rather disgusting, when one knows what N. D. is: and how he treated M., wouldn't give him a sou: and when I have a letter from Douglas telling me to do what I liked and say what I liked about that MS: and when one knows how bitter Magnus was about Douglas, at the end. And when one knows how much worse the *whole* facts were, than those I give. . . .
>
> I bothered about that MS. only for the sake of those two Maltese. From 1921 to 1924 I tried to get the thing published. The New York publisher [Seltzer] wanted to publish my introduction, alone, as an essay, without the *Legion* MS. I refused, and waited.
>
> Having written half the book, surely half the proceeds are due to me. As for Douglas' co-writing—it's a literary turn. Besides, Magnus re-wrote the *whole* thing, after I talked with him at Monte Cassino. I really wanted to get that fellow money, and Douglas wouldn't give him a cent. . . .
>
> He only thinks I am hard on M. M. But in *life,* Douglas was much harder on him—very much.[20]

Lawrence elaborated these arguments in an extremely strong and effective letter that appeared in the *New Statesman* on February 20, 1926, soon after a review of *Experiments.* Lawrence's most devastating weapon, which decisively won the argument, was a letter from Douglas that gave Lawrence permission to act as he wished and hinted at his own immorality:

> By all means do what you like with the MS. As to M. himself, I may do some kind of memoir on him later on—independent of *Foreign Legions.* Put me in your introduction, if you like.
>   *Pocket all the cash yourself.* [Borg] seems to be such a fool that he doesn't deserve any.
>   I'm out of it and, *for once in my life,* with a clean conscience.[21]

In the *New Statesman* letter Lawrence also states that after Magnus' death Borg, who never met Douglas and knew of him mainly through Magnus, said he "would never put anything into the hands of Douglas." (Douglas admits that he applied for, but failed to obtain, Magnus' papers.) Borg then urged Lawrence to publish the *Memoirs* so he could recover his money. Though Lawrence states that the "MS. was detained by Magnus' creditors, at his death, and handed by them to me,"[22] Holloway is probably correct in stating that all Magnus' possessions were held by the American consul as security for his debts and that Lawrence actually got the manuscript from Grant Richards, who was considering the book for publication. In any case, Borg received half the royalties and the £55 were repaid in full.

Despite the acrimonious quarrel, Lawrence and Douglas were reconciled by Pino Orioli in his bookstore on the Lungarno during the winter of 1926–27. Though Douglas disliked certain aspects of Lawrence's character, he admired his gifts. According to Aldington, when Douglas met Lawrence in the shop he courteously offered his snuffbox and said: " 'Have a pinch of snuff, dearie.' Lawrence took it. 'Isn't it curious'—sniff—'only Norman and my father'—sniff—'ever gave me snuff?' "[23] This symbolic gesture renewed their friendship, if not their old intimacy. A painting by Collingwood Gee (reproduced in Moore's biography) shows Lawrence reading *Lady Chatterley's Lover* (1928) to Douglas, Orioli and Reggie Turner.

Though Lawrence seemed to have the last word, the notorious and still volatile quarrel was continued after his death by the contentious Richard Aldington, disparaging friend and biographer of Lawrence and Douglas. In his autobiography *Life for Life's Sake* (1941), his book on Lawrence *Portrait of a Genius, But* (1950) and his memoir of Pino Orioli and Norman Douglas *Pinorman* (1954), Aldington sides with Lawrence and makes some serious charges against Douglas. In the first book Aldington states that Lawrence's portrait of Argyle—not his dissection of Magnus—was the real reason for Douglas' pamphlet; that Douglas, who was Magnus' friend and had more money than Lawrence, did not lend Magnus the funds that could have prevented his suicide; and that Douglas "accepted a gift of a hundred pounds to write the pamphlet, from a rich woman who had a grudge against Lawrence."[24]

Douglas' letter of March 11, 1942 about *Life for Life's Sake,* quoted in Nancy Cunard's effusive and adoring *Grand Man: Memories of Norman Douglas* (1954), anticipates his more formal and direct response to Aldington's accusations that appeared in *Late Harvest* (1946). Douglas insists "I am far too tough to care tuppence what anyone thinks" and reaffirms that his motive was to defend Magnus. He attempts to evade the second charge by quoting Aldington's statement about Douglas' "loyalty and generosity to old friends." He does not deny the charge of bribery (though he had denied it in the letter to Nancy Cunard quoted in *Grand Man*), but merely challenges Aldington to explain the origin of the "legend" and to name the lady. And he supports his statement that Lawrence was not a gentleman because "nothing was sacred; all was grist to his literary mill,"[25] by saying that though Compton Mackenzie had gone out of his way to help Lawrence in Capri, Lawrence satirized him in "The Man Who Loved Islands."

Aldington once again stokes up the old fires of controversy in *Pinorman* and does further damage to Douglas' unconvincing refutation of his charges. He notes that Douglas' annoyance about *Aaron's Rod* was vividly shown in his pamphlet. Holloway provides more proof of this when he quotes Douglas' malicious comment: "Lawrence is all wrong about my room; *table* obviously untidy: as to my keeping windows shut, I can afford to do so; I haven't got a syphilitico-tuberculous throat like he has."[26] Aldington's statement about Douglas' generosity clearly did not apply to his treatment of Magnus; Douglas had never disappointed Lawrence, but he did leave Magnus "in the lurch." Most damagingly, Aldington cites Pino Orioli, Douglas' closest friend, as the source of the story about the £100 bribe.

This not only reveals Douglas' mercenary motives, but also destroys the basis of his attack on Lawrence for appropriating the royalties due to Douglas. For Douglas, who sold out three printings of the pamphlet and also received £100 from the vengeful lady, earned much more money from Magnus than Lawrence ever did. Since Aldington accepted Douglas' challenge, named his source and repeated the potentially libelous accusation in 1954, after Douglas had denied it in Cunard's book of 1946, the story was probably true.

Aldington's conclusion—"warfare between two such free spirits and great writers as Norman Douglas and D. H. Lawrence was a misfortune for both literature and themselves. The Magnus pamphlet was by far the cleverest and most damaging attack made on Lawrence, and did him more harm than he realised"[27]—is not convincing, for the Magnus controversy inspired two brilliant memoirs and sparked a lively literary battle that still reverberates today. Lawrence is more direct and honest than Douglas, who never questions his presentation of the facts (except about the amount of money that Magnus spent in Malta) or accuses him of lying. And Lawrence's portrait of Magnus is more vivid and convincing, if less humane and sympathetic. Douglas' finest insight comes on his final page when he observes that "in exposing the frailties of Maurice Magnus he has contrived, like a true Boswell, to expose his own." But this is the strength, not the weakness, of the Introduction, a profound and richly rendered character study of Magnus as well as an honest and even lacerating self-revelation. Lawrence, whom Douglas justly called an "inspired provincial with marked puritan leanings,"[28] wrote: "I believe tremendously in friendship between man and man, a pledging of men to each other inviolably. But I have not ever met or formed such a friendship."[29] His fascination and repulsion with the homosexual Magnus, who is now remembered only through his association with the two greater writers, illuminate the puritanical repression and moral scruples that prevented Lawrence from achieving his long-sought male friendship.

Lawrence and Frieda, who led a rather isolated existence in Italy, usually lived and travelled alone. But Lawrence's relations with Magnus brought him into distasteful contact with the world of homosexual expatriates (described in *Aaron's Rod*), interfered with his work and intensified his need for isolation. His study of Giovanni Verga provided a salutary contrast to his agonizing involvement with Magnus. He was able to compare Verga's fiction about Sicilian peasant life with his personal observations and to reflect on the social and sexual conflicts so important to his own work.

4

Translations of Verga

I

LAWRENCE'S FIRST REACTION TO VERGA, whom he read in December 1916, was bemused condescension: "We have read the 'Cavalleria Rusticana': a veritable blood-pudding of *passion!* It is not at all good, only, in some odd way, comical, as the portentous tragic Italian is always comical." Lawrence felt he could speak with authority about the idiosyncrasies of the Italian character. In the disastrous context of the War, the jealousy in Verga's most famous story seemed a trivial provocation for murder; the excessive emotion appeared, to Lawrence's northern temperament, operatic rather than tragic.

After the War Lawrence moved to Sicily and returned to the fiction of Verga, the preeminent novelist of that region. As Lawrence reread Verga, he became more absorbed in his work: "He exercises quite a fascination on me, and makes me feel quite sick at the end. But perhaps that is only if one knows Sicily.—Do you know if he is translated into English?— *I Malavoglia* or *Mastro-don Gesualdo*—or *Novelle Rusticane,* or the other short stories."[1] He was immediately fascinated by Verga's language, which tried to express the workings of unsophisticated minds and, as Thomas Bergin has observed, "to arrange good Tuscan words in Sicilian word order and to make the reader aware of the rhythm of dialect under the Italian sentence."[2] Unlike the ornamental style of his early work, the ordinary speech and limited vocabulary of his Sicilian stories were concentrated and sparse. Lawrence's "sickness" was caused by Verga's emphasis on the squalid, brutal and depressing aspects of peasant life. But Lawrence's fascination with Verga's brutal details shows that he was determined to penetrate below the surface and discover the truth about primitive existence.

As Lawrence's understanding of Verga deepened, he moved from disgust to admiration and felt challenged by the prospect of translating him. Though Lawrence later translated A. F. Grazzini's sixteenth-century tale, *The Story of Dr. Manente* and wrote an introduction to the Sardinian novelist Grazia Deledda, he called Verga "The only Italian who does interest me." "He is *extraordinarily* good," Lawrence told Edward Garnett, "—peasant—quite modern—Homeric—and it would need someone who could absolutely handle English in the dialect, to translate him. He would be most awfully difficult to translate. That is what tempts me. . . . If I don't, I doubt if anyone else will—adequately, at least."[3] He saw that Verga captured the essence of peasant life with the realistic techniques of the modern European novel, believed there was a similarity between the Sicilian and Midlands dialects, and felt a kind of instinctive affinity with Verga that made him the ideal translator of his work. Lawrence admired, in *Mastro-don Gesualdo,* the passion that reached beyond convention and law, and told Thomas Seltzer, who published Lawrence's translation in 1923: the novel "interests me very much, as being one of the genuine emotional extremes of European literature."[4]

The first draft and final version of Lawrence's Introduction to *Mastro-don Gesualdo* interpret Verga's works and help to explain his attraction to them. Lawrence observes that modern Italian literature has had very little influence on the European mind. Though Verga is a great novelist and master of the short story, with his own weird, distinct quality, he is considered too depressing and is ignored. Lawrence makes an important distinction between Verga's mannered and sentimental early novels of love in the fashionable society of Florence and Milan and his portrayals of peasant life in Sicily in the 1880s. Though *I Malavoglia (The House by the Medlar Tree)* presents a striking picture of poverty in Sicily, there is too much wallowing in the tragic fate of the humble poor. Lawrence prefers *Mastro-don Gesualdo.*

Lawrence calls Verga a Flaubertian realist who portrays characters toiling against the odds of circumstance and doomed to misery. Gesualdo Motta makes a great deal of money, but his wealth cannot protect him from cancer and bitterness. Despite Verga's lack of faith in heroes, Lawrence thinks Gesualdo is attractive and truly heroic: he has extraordinary force, sagacity and humanity; is bold, daring and manly. Lawrence notes the tender as well as the tragic side of Gesualdo: "We see him so patient with his family, with the phthisical Bianca, with his daughter, so humane, and yet so desperately enduring. In affairs he has an unerring instinct, and he is a superb fighter. . . . Yet he blindly brings most of his sufferings on himself, by doing the wrong things to himself."[5]

Lawrence emphasizes Gesualdo's heroism by relating the modern Sicilians to the classical Greeks, who had colonized the island before the age of Theocritus. He asserts that Gesualdo has the old Greek impulse toward splendor and self-enhancement, and might really be a Greek in a modern setting: "He has the energy, the quickness, the vividness of the Greek, the same vivid passion for wealth, the same ambition, the same lack of scruples, the same queer openness." He also stresses Verga's archaic quality by stating that his novel is nearer to the true medieval than anything else in modern literature: "The island is incredibly poor and incredibly backward. There are practically no roads. . . . The land is held by the great landowners, the peasants are almost serfs. It is as wild, as poor, and in the ducal houses of Palermo even as splendid and ostentatious as Russia."[6] These remarks illuminate the novel, whose very title—"Artisan-Gentleman Gesualdo"—suggests Gesualdo's futile and tragic attempt to unite the peasant with the aristocratic class.

Lawrence concludes his Introduction on a personal note by returning to his fascination for Verga, who evokes the deepest nostalgia he has ever felt, and by noting the powerful distinction between the depressing peasant life and the exhilarating landscape: "Sicily, the beautiful, that which goes deepest into the blood. It is so clear, so beautiful, so like the physical beauty of the Greek. Yet the lives of the people all seem so squalid, so pottering, so despicable: like a crawling of beetles. And then, the moment you get outside the grey and squalid walls of the village, how wonderful in the sun, with the land lying apart."[7]

Lawrence had made precisely the same distinction two years earlier in *Sea and Sardinia* (1921), which begins in Taormina and Messina and concludes in Palermo. Lawrence praises Mount Etna, the Ionian Sea, the changing jewel of Calabria, and the clouds and stars at night; and contrasts the landscape with "These maddening, exasperating, impossible Sicilians, who never knew what truth was and have long lost all notion of what a human being is." They absolutely refuse to uphold their classical and medieval heritage, throw open their slummy doors and hurl their garbage into the street. Though the wild mountain scenery clashes with the broken houses and concrete shanties that remind Lawrence of a vast mining settlement, he still admires the dishonest and dirty Sicilians for their "generous, hot southern blood, so subtle and spontaneous."[8]

II

Lawrence identified with certain aspects of Verga's life—"As a man, Verga never courted popularity, any more than his work courts popularity. He kept apart from all publicity, proud in his privacy"[9]—and was personally drawn to *Mastro-don Gesualdo* (1888), for the novel suggested his parents' life as well as his own. It portrays the marriage of a superior woman and working-class man, and the delicate child who rejects its earthy father. Lawrence's own novels, which portray a series of rebellious men and women breaking free from the restrictions of English life, oppose Verga's determinism and present an interesting reversal of his themes. In *Sons and Lovers,* Paul Morel is eventually reconciled with his father through his vicarious relationship with Baxter Dawes (the husband of his actual, as opposed to his symbolic, lover). And in *Lady Chatterley's Lover*—the culmination of a long series of Nausicaa-Polypheme liaisons that began with *The White Peacock*—the superior woman is revitalized rather than repulsed by her lower-class lover.

Mastro-don Gesualdo, as Lawrence noted, is in the French realistic tradition. The clearest model for the story of an obsessively devoted father who sacrifices all his material wealth for a daughter—who has married an aristocrat, is ashamed of the father and visits him only for mercenary reasons—is Balzac's *Père Goriot* (1834). Except for Gesualdo and his daughter Isabella, who uses his wealth to make an aristocratic marriage, the major characters in the novel—his wife Bianca, her cousin and lover Baron Nini Rubiera, Isabella's husband the Duke of Leyra and Gesualdo's mistress Diodata—marry for money, not for love. Though Verga prides himself on his objective realism and straightforward style, his book is limited as well as strengthened by these qualities, and does not achieve the symbolic meaning and poetic power of novels like *Women in Love.* Verga's art is best revealed in the structural complexity of the novel, in which the tragic errors of the first generation are ironically repeated by the second.

In both generations the women (Bianca and Isabella) are seduced by their cousins (Rubiera and Corrado). Both women are forced to give up their impoverished lovers, who have ruined their reputations, and to marry—in the same church—men they dislike. Just as Gesualdo willingly marries Bianca, who is carrying Rubiera's child,[10] to improve his social status, so Nanno willingly marries Diodata, who is carrying Gesualdo's child, to improve his material status. Bianca's aunt, the Baroness, refuses to attend her niece's wedding; Gesualdo's father refuses to attend his granddaughter's baptism. Isabella, who wallows like Emma Bovary in romantic fantasies, rejects her putative father and uses her mother's maiden name (Trao) at her convent school; Gesualdo's two sons by Diodata reject their real father and use Nanno's family name in the village. The collapse of the bridge constructed by Gesualdo, which is meant to connect him, through his new wealth, to the upper class, reflects his *hubris* and foreshadows his doom. Only Diodata sympathizes with Gesualdo when everyone else gloats over his defeat.

Verga's novel suffers from a Russian proliferation of undeveloped characters and a consequent lack of focus. But Gesualdo is an impressive, if unsympathetic hero; and his relationships with the devoted Diodata, the distant Bianca and the icy Isabella bring out the vulnerable side of his rough character. Despite his self-destructive materialism, he has a fierce pride, an admirable energy and independence, and an idealistic, if deluded, desire for happiness.

Gesualdo's marriage, destined to bring frustration and bitterness, is foreshadowed by two brief but poignant scenes. First,
Bianca, in a shabby dress, hangs out her own worn washing as
Gesualdo chews his simple meal and Diodata looks up at the
lovely lady, "saying nothing, her heart swelling." And second,
as the priest is persuading Bianca to save her honor and family
fortune by marrying Gesualdo, there "appeared a skinny, thin
woman with her ragged shift lifted from her thin legs by her
stomach that was big with child, dirty and unkempt, as if she
had done nothing else all her life but carry that belly in front
of her"[11]—to warn Bianca of her shameful fate if she refuses
the proffered husband.

The moving scene just after Gesualdo's wedding, when he
anticipates the pleasure—and Bianca the repulsion—of their
first embrace, is one of the masterful moments of the novel:

> An unusual tenderness swelled his heart, as he helped
> her to comb her hair. Actually his big hands helping a
> Trao, and feeling themselves become light as feathers
> [as Lawrence translated *leggere leggere,* anticipating
> the "wings" of the next sentence] among her fine hair!
> His eyes kindled on the lace that veiled her white, deli-
> cate shoulders, on the short, puffed sleeves that almost
> gave her wings. The golden down that bloomed on the
> last nodes of her spine pleased him, as did the scars left
> by the inexpert vaccination on her slim, white arms,
> and the little hands that had worked like his own, and
> that trembled now under his eyes, and her bent neck
> that flushed and paled, all those humble signs of priva-
> tion that brought her near to him.[12]

In order to soften this unnatural contact of the crude with the
refined, Gesualdo exalts Bianca into an angel and becomes a
mute adorer at her shrine. The signs of privation, which he
looks on with tenderness, explain why she was forced to marry
him. She is unable to confess that she is carrying another man's
child; and Gesualdo senses the bitterness of his marriage before he tastes the joys.

The pattern of naive hope and cruel disappointment is reflected in the structure of the novel and in the climactic
events that emphasize the themes of love and money, marriage and death, and conclude each of the four sections. The
first part ends with the marriage of Gesualdo; the second with

the illness of the Baroness, which prevents her from taking the property away from her son, Rubiera. The conclusions of parts three and four repeat those of one and two: the former ends as Isabella agrees to marry the impoverished Duke of Leyra (sacrificing love, like her mother, and trading wealth for prestige, like her father); the latter with the disease and death of Gesualdo.

The same disillusionment recurs when Gesualdo holds the newborn Isabella after her baptism, and when he reflects on his wife's illness and inability to give him a son:

> Nothing, nothing had that marriage brought him, neither dowry, nor male child, nor the help of the relations, nor even that which Diodata gave him formerly, a moment of happiness, an hour of pleasantness, such as a glass of wine brings to a poor man who has worked all day! Not even that!—A wife who wasted away between your hands, who made your caresses go cold, with that face and those eyes and that being frightened, as if you were going to make her fall into mortal sin, every time; as if the priest hadn't made the sign of the cross over you both, in the beginning, when she had said yes. It wasn't Bianca's fault. It was the blood of her race which refused. You can't graft peaches on an olive tree. She, poor thing, inclined her head, and even went so far as to offer herself, all blushing, so as to obey the commandment of God; as if she was paid to do it.[13]

This moment of insight recalls the sacrifices made and pleasures lost, the failure of their sexual life, the resistance of her racial blood to his unnatural grafting, and the painful confusion of religion, sex and money.

The marriage intensifies rather than alleviates Gesualdo's estrangement—which began when he first acquired wealth—not only from Bianca but also from his father, his friends and his relations. This becomes clear to Gesualdo when his servants abandon him (for fear of cholera infection), and he has to put his father into the coffin with his own hands.

Just as Gesualdo's father was ashamed of his coarse manners, so Gesualdo—who wants to die in the country but is brought to Isabella's ducal mansion in Palermo—feels awkward and uncomfortable amidst the luxuries which he has paid for but never used. (He finally escapes to his own room and takes his meals there alone.) There is a touch of irony—which would have appealed to both Hardy and Lawrence—when Gesualdo examines the architectural details of the palace from a builder's point of view and calculates the cost of the luxury in terms of agricultural labor: "How many good strokes of the hoe, how much labourers' sweat would it not have paid for! Farms, whole villages it might have built—land sown, as far as you could see."

The death of the hero, a set-piece in nineteenth-century fiction, is magnificently done. The aristocratic Bianca dies of tuberculosis—the most "refined" disease of the period—while the cruder Gesualdo is killed by cancer. As the disease continues to gnaw at his guts and the shadows encircle him, Gesualdo finally realizes the basic theme of Ecclesiastes and of the novel: *Vanitas vanitatum*—money brings only bitterness. Isabella withdraws from him, the Duke molests the chambermaids, the household servants become more insolent, and the blood and money themes converge. Gesualdo speaks of his rightful heirs, Diodata's sons (one of whom bears the name of Gesualdo's father), and begs Isabella to defend the remnants of his wasted property against the reckless extravagance of the Duke. The class conflict is reinforced, and in his dying moments "he felt himself become a Motta again, as [Isabella] was a Trao, suspicious, hostile, another flesh."

The novel portrays the rise and fall of Gesualdo against the background of the Sicilian countryside, where the hot sun can set a man's heart on fire or drive him to tear his hair, bite his arms and spit into the sky:

Growling still, he went off at the ambling pace of his mule, under the burning sun; a sun which split the stones now, and made the stubble crackle [or burst: *scoppiettare*] as if it was catching fire. At the gully between the two mountains he seemed to enter into a furnace; and the village on top of the heights, hanging [or climbing: *arrampicato*] above the precipices, scattered between enormous rocks, mined with caverns which made it seem suspended in the air, blackish, rusted, appeared abandoned, without a shadow, with all the windows wide open in the heat, like so many black holes, the crosses of the church-towers in the sun-dark [*caliginoso*] air.[14]

As his story "Sun" reveals, Lawrence was attracted to this harsh landscape and to the emotional extremes that it produced: the sense of honor, the hot blood, the sudden violence.

In *Mastro-don Gesualdo* the major scenes of birth, baptism, courtship, marriage, illness and death mark the stages of the life cycle. Verga's great scenes must have reminded Lawrence of his own rendering of the birth of Ursula, the courtship of Will and Anna, Tom Brangwen's speech at their wedding feast and Tom's death in the flood in *The Rainbow.*

The political theme of the novel is expressed through two revolutions which emphasize the pattern of expectation and disappointment. In both 1821 and 1848 the revolutions spread from Palermo to the remote village near the east coast of the island. In both risings Gesualdo, a hard-working man of the people whose career refutes the revolutionary slogans of equality, whose riches seem unnatural to the mob and who is resented more bitterly than the long-standing aristocratic exploiters, is threatened by the crowd, warned by neighbors and hidden by Nanno (Diodata's husband) in return for money. Verga maintains a fatalistic attitude toward the revolutions, which are destined to erupt and fizzle out as the mob works off grudges, accepts its punishment and returns to its oppressive existence. The rigid class structure both provokes violent hatred and prevents the possibility of social change. Gesualdo may alter his social position, but his blood will always remain the same.

Verga presents Sicilian peasant life as a series of overwhelming disasters, but scorns the revolution because there is no one competent to replace the corrupt people who hold power. He remains intensely conservative—a typical product of his landowning class. In *The Plumed Serpent* (1926) Lawrence also presents a society of peasants oppressed by landlords; and like Verga, he identifies with the landowning class (Ramón) and conservative generals (Cipriano). Both Verga and Lawrence fear the mob and share authoritarian beliefs.

Politically, and in other significant ways, *Mastro-don Gesualdo* influenced the greatest Italian novel of the twentieth century: Tomasi di Lampedusa's *The Leopard* (1957). In both novels the landscape of Sicily is a dominant influence, and there is a significant shift in tone and values when the characters move from the town to the country. Both novels portray a moribund aristocracy, sliding toward extinction in their crumbling Palermitan palaces. In both works the authors express disdain for the revolutionary mob; and both describe the infiltration of the aristocracy by an energetic lower-class usurper (Gesualdo and Sedàra) who attempts to "graft peaches on an olive tree."[15]

III

The *Little Novels of Sicily (Novelle rusticane,* 1883) are much more limited in theme and expression than the later novel *Mastro-don Gesualdo.* But Lawrence was drawn by Verga's emotional portrayal of the peasants' struggle to survive and to preserve their instinctual life. Lawrence also admired these qualities in the Sardinian novels of Grazia Deledda, who wrote in the tradition of Verga's *verismo* and portrayed the same pulsating life as Verga's Sicily: "An island of rigid conventions, the rigid conventions of barbarism, and at the same time the fierce violence of the instinctive passions. A savage tradition of chastity, with a savage lust of the flesh. A barbaric overlordship of the gentry, with a fierce indomitableness of the servile classes. A lack of public opinion, a lack of belonging to any other part of the world, a lack of mental awakening, which makes inland Sardinia almost as savage as Benin, and makes Sardinian singing as wonderful and almost as wild as any on earth. It is the human instinct still uncontaminated."[16]

Five of Verga's twelve stories—"So Much for the King," "Don Licciu Papa," "The Orphans," "History of the Saint Joseph's Ass" and "The Gentry"—are variations on a single theme: the equal and interchangeable value of humans and animals when men are degraded by poverty to the level of beasts. The rich own the poor in the same way as the poor own their mules, and force them to behave in a bestial way.

In "So Much for the King" a devoted but impoverished litter driver, who once carried the Queen of Naples, has his mules seized and his son taken away to serve in the army. The lack of a human bond between the bearer and his burden leads to merciless exploitation when his loyalty to the Queen is repaid by rapacity. In "Don Licciu Papa" the fate of the shepherd Arcangelo, who wants to die in the house of his birth, is symbolized by the squealing pig, tied to the bedpost like a tortured soul in purgatory. The story exposes the cruelty of the law that allows the rich to exploit the poor, to steal the houses and daughters of helpless people. In "The Orphans" the peasant mourns for his dead wife in the same way that he mourns for his dead donkey, whose hide, at least, can be sold for money. In this base and brutish society, there is no place for human emotions. In "The History of the Saint Joseph's Ass," which describes the degeneration of a donkey as he is exploited by poorer and poorer masters, the metaphor becomes reality. The animal, who symbolizes the condition of man, turns men into beasts. "The Gentry" reveals that the rich are also vulnerable and can be forced to share the misfortunes of the poor. The main difference between the suffering peasants and gentry is that the common people cannot restrain themselves and are punished for their violence in the galleys.

The other stories in this collection explain the environmental, religious and political reasons for these barbarous conditions. In "Malaria" the disease becomes a palpable threat that rises out of the claustrophobic landscape: "And you feel you could touch it with your hand—as if it smoked up from the fat earth, there, everywhere, round about [*torno torno*] the mountains that shut it in, from Agnone to Mount Etna capped with snow—stagnating in the plain like the sultry heat of June."[17] The peasant loses his job on a farm, must work on the railway, and envies the speeding passengers, who are destined for a more salubrious climate and seem impervious to the malaria that will surely take his life.

"The Mystery Play" and "His Reverence," like *Mastro-don Gesualdo,* are intensely anti-clerical. They may have reinforced Lawrence's own feelings and contributed to the attack on Christianity in *The Plumed Serpent.* In the former the rapacity of the priest and hardship of the people are dramatized in the village play. The latter exposes the religious hypocrisy of a swindling former friar, who is a social climber and commits each of the seven deadly sins.

"Liberty," a reactionary story that foreshadows the political ideas of *Mastro-don Gesualdo,* describes the blood bath during the revolution of 1860—"The crowd was heard howling along the twisting of the passages, advancing like a river in flood"—which leads to a sudden change of mood when the mob becomes tired of slaughter. The stern retribution of the authorities, the swift imprisonment and executions, quickly dispel the peasants' naive infatuation with liberty. Verga's condemnation of the status quo and rejection of the possibility of political amelioration reinforce his Hardyesque theme of hopeless characters doomed by fate.

The two most substantial stories, "Black Bread" and "Property," express the dominant ideas of the book. In the former, the only story with developed characters and a moving theme, "bread is scarce, and children come quick," married couples "help one another like two oxen yoked to the same plough," and watch in stony silence as "the field goes yellow under their eyes, like a sick man departing to the other world." The story reveals that peasants must sacrifice pride, love, honor and virginity for economic survival. Lucia, impoverished by her father's death and exploited by Santo and Red-head, her brother and sister-in-law, is courted by the unattractive frog-catcher, Tome, who then rejects her for a lame but wealthy widow. (The widow had previously been rejected by Santo, who now regrets his mistake.) Lucia becomes the servant of Don Venerando, who bribes her with jewelry and a dowry, and forces her into his bed. Lucia, obviously pregnant at her mother's funeral, is condemned by Santo for disgracing the family and grieves that she was unable to pay for a doctor with her newly earned money. Red-head ironically remarks that Brasi, the kitchen slave in Venerando's house, who "would have both his eyes pulled out for ten guineas," will certainly marry Lucia. Lucia's parallel courtships with Tome, Venerando and Brasi, and the marriages of Santo (who is impoverished), Tome (who is humiliated) and Brasi (who is betrayed), portray desperate lives in hopeless compromise.

"Property" is a fable of obsessive acquisition, of a peasant who gains possession of his master's land but, like Gesualdo, is devoured by manic materialism. The opening description of the swampy Lake of Lentini, "stretched out there like a piece of dead sea," the burnt-up stubble-fields of the Plain of Catania, the deserted pasture-lands, the long dusty road, the heat-heavy sky and the sad-sounding bells of the immense campagna, is an ironic parody of Manzoni's classic description, on the opening page of *I Promessi Sposi* (1827), of the beautiful scenery surrounding Lake Como. It also suggests the seeds of destruction that lie in the landscape. Though Mazzaro emerged from the depths of back-breaking poverty, inexorably annexed the Baron's olive groves, vineyards, pastures, farm and mansion, and seemed to own even the setting sun and whirling cicadas, he retains the psychology of the poor, ends in bitterness and laments that he must abandon his wealth when he dies. The moral of the story is the same as in Tolstoy's parable, "How Much Land Does a Man Need?"

IV

Cavalleria Rusticana (1880) initiated the great decade of Verga's literary career. Lawrence's Preface notes that the stories were a regenerative return to his roots amidst the soil and peasants of Catania. Verga worshipped "every manifestation of pure, spontaneous, passionate life, life kindled to vividness"; his characters are sensitive and honorable men, despite their brutality and violence.

Lawrence's attitude toward Verga's vengeful husbands was extremely personal. According to Frieda, he was rendered impotent by his wasting disease toward the end of 1926 and countenanced her infidelity in October 1928 with Angelo Ravagli. In his 1928 Preface, Lawrence observes that the passions of Verga's characters are too extreme and uncontrolled: "How stupid of Alfio, of Jeli, of Brothpot, to have to go killing a man and getting themselves shut up in prison for life, merely because the man had committed adultery with their wives. . . . Nowadays we have learnt more sense, and we let her go her way." But the unusually tolerant Anglo-Saxon forgets that even the mild Ernest Weekley went into a jealous rage about Frieda. He overlooks the fact that the wife of the Sicilian peasant is his most important possession: the only adult person he can absolutely dominate and control. If he loses his wife, he loses everything, and is inexorably driven to murder. Though Lawrence admires the passion of Verga's Sicilians, he is forced to admit that in the ironically titled story, "Rustic Chivalry" is simply murder.

Yet Lawrence, who recovered from his early "sickness" over Verga, believed that Verga's characters ultimately transcend their limitations. "Jeli the Herdsman" and "Rosso Malpelo" are "among the finest stories ever written" because their tragic heroes represent a vital response to the destructive rationalism that dominated the consciousness of northern Europe. For Lawrence, the greatest tragedy "is the ugly trespass of the sophisticated greedy ones upon the naive life of the true human being: the death of the naive, pure being."[18] Lawrence's comments on Verga suggest that he puffed the stories he had translated and interpreted them in the light of his own life and art. Lawrence was much more concerned than Verga about the fate of instinctual man, and the revival of blood-consciousness ("a belief in the blood, the flesh, as being wiser than the intellect") became a dominant idea in both *The Plumed Serpent* and *Lady Chatterley's Lover.*

The themes of Verga's stories, as we have seen in the *Little Novels of Sicily,* can be essentially reduced to the indifference of nature, the tyranny of the rich, the oppressive existence of the poor, domestic love and jealousy. Three of the tales— "Cavalleria Rusticana," "Jeli the Herdsman" and "Brothpot"— portray a *delitto d'onore* in which the husband kills his wife's lover with a knife, with scissors and with an iron bar. In "La Lupa" the wife's mother, who is almost demonically possessed, seduces her son-in-law, who can free himself only by killing her with an axe.

"Gramigna's Lover" and "Rosso Malpelo," which are more ambitious stories, describe, in a strangely moving way, hopeless devotion and resignation to destiny. Peppa, an attractive girl destined for a fortunate marriage, suddenly feels a burning love for Gramigna, a brigand pursued by the police, whom she has heard about but never seen. She finds him pale with fasting and parched with fever, and announces: "I've come to stay with you."[19] She is wounded by a soldier's bullet while bringing water for Gramigna, and the blood under her clothes symbolizes her sacrificial defloration. When he is finally captured, she turns into a wild beast. Carrying his child at her breast, she follows him to the city and settles outside the prison where he was once shut up. Though he has been sent to the galleys, she remains there because she has nowhere else to go—a tragic example of "respectful tenderness, a sort of brute admiration of brute force." Peppa's instinctive ritual of love is reminiscent of stories like "The Fox" and "The Horse-Dealer's Daughter" (both 1922).

Lawrence was attracted to "Rosso Malpelo" because it describes the life of a miner who quarries stone beneath the surface of the earth. The red-headed, Judas-cursed, animal-like, underground man knows the sand is treacherous, for his father was buried alive in the mine. But he is also destined to be crushed to death or lost in the depths. He is lured toward his fate when his father's body is discovered and he inherits his shoes, trousers and tools. His doom is foreshadowed by the death of the miners' donkey and of his pathetic tubercular friend, Frog. He believes it is better to die than to suffer, deliberately accepts an extremely dangerous job and disappears in the darkness of the mine. There is nothing attractive about Rosso Malpelo but his ability to endure hardship and his stoic resignation to fate. But his story had a strong appeal to Lawrence, whose mother had prevented him from following his father into the mines.

V

Lawrence did half his translation of *Mastro-don Gesualdo* in Taormina, worked on it while sailing from Naples to Colombo on the *Osterley*—between finishing *Aaron's Rod* and beginning *Kangaroo*—and completed it in Kandy in March 1922. He started work on the *Little Novels of Sicily* soon afterward and continued the translation on the *Orsova* en route from Ceylon to Australia. Achsah Brewster provided a detailed picture of her friend translating Verga in Ceylon: "Lawrence sat curled up with a schoolboy's copy-book in his hand, writing away. He was translating Giovanni Verga's short stories from the Sicilian [i.e., Italian]. Across the pages of his copy-book his hand moved rhythmically, steadily, unhesitatingly, leaving a trail of exquisite, small writing as legible as print. No blots, no scratchings marred its beauty. When the book was finished, he wrapped and tied it up, sending it off to the publisher."[20]

Though Lawrence could speak and read Italian fluently, there is strong evidence that his knowledge of Italian grammar and vocabulary was imperfect, that he translated (as he wrote) very quickly and that his versions of Verga are filled with hundreds of minor errors. But there is little agreement about the quality of his translations. It is essential, therefore, to give some precise sense of how Lawrence translated Verga and to judge the quality of his performance.

Lawrence remains close to the original text, adds almost nothing of his own and does not use Italian words to give a foreign flavor to his English. Most of the striking, unusual or colloquial phrases in Lawrence are the same in Verga:

rannicchiò il capo . . . al pari di una testuggine—drew his head inside . . . like a tortoise

portarsi la pancia a spasso nel paese—taking his belly for a walk round the village

Apriti, terra, e inghiottimi—Open, earth, and swallow me

lasciarsi aprir le vene . . . a bersi il sangue suo—let his veins be opened . . . to drink his blood

crampi allo stomaco . . . come tanti cani arrabbiati dentro—cramps in his stomach . . . like mad dogs inside him.

Lawrence sometimes gives a more colloquial equivalent rather than a literal translation:

tutti pezzi grossi—big guns

una porcheria—mucked-up business

maneggi [plots] *sottomano*—underhand dodges.

Writing of the Baron Ninì Rubiera, Lawrence makes an English pun that is impossible in Italian:

quello sciocco [fool]—that ninny.

At times, Lawrence effectively intensifies the original:

denti . . . acchiappare [to catch] *un marito a volo*—teeth . . . to *snatch* a husband on the wing

Sarina dei miei stivali—Sarina *lick*-my-boots

mi costa un occhio—it costs me the eyes *out of my head.*

Lawrence also brings in his own characteristic phrase to fortify an English word that is stronger in Italian:

> *e lo feriva sin lí nell'amore della sua creatura* [the one
> created by him]—and it wounded him even there,
> in the *quick* of his love for his child.

This has an ironic force since Isabella is not actually Gesualdo's child, though he loves her as if she were his own blood.

Though Lawrence's translations have recently come under
critical attack, they were extremely well received when they
first appeared in the 1920s. The *Boston Evening Transcript* review of *Mastro-don Gesualdo* stated: "Mr. Lawrence has suc-
ceeded in reproducing marvellously the poignant irony and
elliptical style so characteristic of Verga's later work." The reviewers of the stories were equally enthusiastic. The *Dial,* a
distinguished journal, agreed that "Mr. Lawrence's translation
is good fortune for the reader no less than for the author";[21] and
Edwin Muir, the translator of Kafka, also commended his
work: "Mr. Lawrence's selection of Verga's short stories, rap-
idly and vigorously translated, is admirable." The authoritative
reviews in the *Times Literary Supplement* were both favorable: "Mr. Lawrence has done his work very well, better even
than in *Mastro-don Gesualdo.* A careful comparison of his
translation with the original has revealed to us extremely few
places where an improvement could even have been suggested.
... The problem of the translator was to be neither too polished
nor too uncouth, and Mr. Lawrence, with the insight of a very
gifted writer, has solved it." Three years later *TLS* added: "His
translation of *Mastro-don Gesualdo* is a brilliant version of the
book. . . . The translation [of *Cavalleria Rusticana*] is as good
as it could be—spirited, supple and true to the original."[22] Carlo
Linati, an Italian critic with an expert knowledge of English,
agreed with the reviewers and in 1933 wrote that Lawrence's
translations "are accomplished with an exact knowledge of our
language and of its colloquial accents, with true artistic taste."[23]

The perversely negative appraisal of Lawrence's translations by Giovanni Cecchetti was clearly motivated by personal
bias, for he felt obliged to demolish Lawrence's work in order
to clear the path for his own translations of Verga's stories and
novel. Cecchetti notes that Lawrence never studied Italian sys-
tematically, learned it by speaking to Italians and had an imperfect command of the language. In 1957 he dismissed
Lawrence's work as "nothing but a hasty and often inaccurate
transcription of the Italian, word for word, comma for comma.

. . . As a result, his translations do not belong in the realm of art, but rather in that of commerce." Cecchetti, whose comfortable academic salary allowed him to reside in the world of art while hacks like Lawrence grubbed about in commerce, revised his Pecksniffian opinion of Lawrence's translation in the 1958 Introduction to his own translation of *La Lupa (The She-Wolf)*, where he gave Lawrence higher marks for the same work: "Lawrence's translations are by far the best known. Although they have some good passages, on the whole they are rather unsatisfactory. Lawrence did not know Italian sufficiently well, nor did he have enough time to do justice to the original. As a result, his Verga is full of oddities. He misunderstood or misread many Italian words."[24]

Armin Arnold, writing in 1968, rashly concedes that "Cecchetti's translations are immaculate," but convincingly argues that Lawrence's translations are superior: "Cecchetti did, philologically, a painstaking job, but his language is pedestrian and uninspired. Lawrence's translations, on the other hand, have all the fire, poetry, and vitality of his other writings."[25] Andrew Wilkin, whose notes to the 1973 Penguin edition of the *Little Novels of Sicily* are largely devoted to pointing out Lawrence's philological errors, also demonstrates that Cecchetti himself has misunderstood and mistranslated many Italian words and phrases.[26] But he takes a somewhat more favorable view than Cecchetti of Lawrence's performance. Wilkin begins with an acknowledged repetition of Cecchetti—"Lawrence let himself be guided largely by personal instinct and artistic taste"[27]—which mistakenly suggests that these were Lawrence's weaknesses instead of his strengths. He concludes that "Lawrence's reliance in many cases on the dictionary (his knowledge of Italian was limited) does not detract greatly from the value of the translations, which often capture the tone and atmosphere of the original."[28]

Despite Lawrence's frequent errors, which do not make much difference to the English-language reader, the judgments expressed by Muir, Linati and Arnold seem much more convincing than the pedantic, self-serving and condescending carping of Cecchetti and Wilkin. I would agree with the former and with the balanced evaluation of Mary Corsani, who in 1965 concludes: "In *Mastro-don Gesualdo,* one notes, especially in the first part, that Lawrence lacks knowledge of Italian grammar and vocabulary, and makes gross errors of interpretation.

But in mastering the language and penetrating its spirit, he translates with extreme fidelity to the original."[29]

Two passages from "Rosso Malpelo" show that Lawrence's translations—which clearly influenced Cecchetti's—are more forceful and vivid than the correct versions by the Italian professor:

Outside the pit the sky was swarming with stars, and down there the lantern smoked and swung like a comet; and the great red pillar, disembowelled by the strokes of the pick, twisted and bent forward as if it had belly-ache.	Outside the quarry, stars were swarming in the sky, and down below, the lantern smoked and turned like a spinning-wheel. The big red pillar, gutted by the strokes of the hoe, twisted and bent itself into an arch, as if it had a stomach-ache.

Lawrence's version, which is four words shorter, sharpens the contrast between the sky and the mine by a more active rhythm (sky was swarming), metaphorical expression (swung like a comet), effective diction (disembowelled) and colloquial language (belly-ache).

Only when they drew near with the light they saw him, his face distorted, his eyes glassy, his mouth foaming, so that they were afraid; his finger-nails were torn, and hung bloody and ragged from his hands.	And when they came close with a lamp they saw such a distorted face, such ugly glassy eyes and foam at the mouth, that would frighten anybody; his nails were torn and were hanging from his bleeding hands.

Lawrence's description of Rosso, who has just been buried in a mountain of sand, emphasizes the ghastly way Rosso appears to the other miners, avoids the rhetorical parallel (of such-such) and uses the direct "they" instead of the vague "anybody." Lawrence's "hung bloody and ragged" is more immediate than the two awkward present participles "hanging from his bleeding." These characteristic passages reveal that Lawrence intensifies while Cecchetti dilutes Verga.

After *Mastro-don Gesualdo,* his last major work, Verga virtually stopped writing and went into eclipse. During the last thirty years of his life he was mainly known as the author of "Cavalleria Rusticana," which he rewrote as a one-act tragedy that in 1890 inspired the famous opera by Mascagni. Verga was not fully recognized in Italy until the publication of Luigi Rosso's book in 1919. Lawrence's translations—not, as Wilkin would have it, a "passotempo," but a labor of love for a greatly admired kindred spirit—were primarily responsible for establishing Verga's international reputation.

VI

Lawrence's fascination with Sicily gave him the opportunity to confirm, in another race, his credo of blood-consciousness and to develop the implications of this idea in his own art. His awareness of the people and the place was intensified by reading Verga. As he translated and reevaluated the novels and stories, he subjectively interpreted Verga's social and political ideas in order to bring them in line with his own views and to diminish the differences between himself and the Sicilian. For in Lawrence's novels, the characters achieve a sexual freedom that is impossible in Verga's deterministic fiction. And Lawrence, an outsider who tended to see peasant life as an anthropological spectacle, presents a more idealized view of the common people than did Verga, who wrote realistically from within the community.

Yet their similarities were more significant than their differences. The main reason for Lawrence's attraction to Verga was undoubtedly the raw power and emotional extremes of the characters, driven by brute force and blind fate. Though Verga himself maintained an impersonal coolness toward his characters and even expressed scorn for the mob, their "life kindled to vividness" matched both the primitive quality that Lawrence admired in American novelists like Cooper and Melville, and the personal emotions that he poured into his own work. The lives of Verga's peasants, like Lawrence's miners, are dominated by toil and poverty but redeemed by spontaneous warmth.

There are also many other, less obvious, reasons that drew Lawrence to the Sicilian novelist. In works like "Jeli the Herdsman" (where "Jeli seemed to feel within his own body the dull noise which the shot . . . made within the living flesh of the animal") and Lawrence's Sicilian poem "Snake," there is a vital connection between animals and men. In Verga this expresses man's degradation and bestiality; in Lawrence, the mysterious forces of life. Lawrence was also deeply moved by Verga's evocation of the "spirit of place," which depressed many readers but aroused his nostalgia for the Sicilian scene.

In Verga, in Hardy (his close contemporary) and in Lawrence's *The Rainbow,* the characters have a strong family sense, a bond with the rural community, an organic relation to the eternal round of the seasons and a connection to the landscape which seems to exist as an independent force: "The whole day-life of the people passes in the open, in the splendour of the sun and the landscape, and the delicious, elemental aloneness of the old world. This is a great *unconscious* compensation."[30] Through Verga, Lawrence could link himself with what he found most valuable in both the Italian and the English traditions.

Lawrence, who used Midlands dialect in almost all his novels to suggest a more natural and realistic form of lower-class speech (Mellors speaks dialect to Connie Chatterley in order to establish their intimacy), was fascinated by the directness of Verga's taut prose, and by the challenge of finding the convincing English equivalent for Verga's unusual rhythm and diction. Both writers felt their language had its roots in the vernacular and transmuted the speech of their childhood into sophisticated art.

Lawrence personally identified with aspects of Verga's character. As he wrote in the self-reflective Preface to *Cavalleria Rusticana:* "His nature was proud and unmixable. At the same time, he had the southern passionate yearning for tenderness and generosity. . . . He was a handsome man, by instinct haughty and reserved: because, partly, he was passionate and emotional, and did not choose to give himself away." Lawrence shared Verga's anti-clericalism and political conservatism, his belief that the masses were corrupt and the aristocracy defunct. He also sympathized with Verga's disdain for the ugly reality of practical politics: "Verga seems to have taken little interest in politics. He had no doubt the southern idea of himself as a gentleman and an aristocrat, beyond politics."

Lawrence rightly believed that Verga was the greatest contemporary Italian writer and that his works were the most powerful portrayal of Sicilian life. He admired Verga's fiction for its documentary value, and wrote: "As a picture of Sicily in the middle of the last century, it is marvellous. But it is a picture done from the inside. . . . The thing is a heavy, earth-adhering organic whole. There is nothing showy."[31] Lawrence also felt that Verga was a seriously underrated writer who deserved wider recognition; and his translations enhanced Verga's reputation in English-speaking countries. Lawrence's identification with Verga was his way of associating himself with Italian, as opposed to the more fashionable French and Russian literature. Lawrence saw Gesualdo in the Homeric tradition, in contrast to the pitiful, commonplace characters of Flaubert, and the obsessively subjective creations of Dostoyevsky and Chekhov. For in Russian novels, "The merest scrub of a pickpocket is so phenomenally aware of his own soul, that we are made to bow down before the imaginary coruscations that go on inside him. That is almost the whole of Russian literature: the phenomenal coruscations of the souls of quite commonplace people."[32]

Most important of all, Lawrence saw aspects of his own work portrayed in Verga's. He surely identified "Rosso Malpelo" with the miners in "Odour of Chrysanthemums" and *Sons and Lovers;* the peasants, like Gesualdo, with Ciccio in *The Lost Girl,* with the gamekeepers Annable and Mellors who also love superior women in *The White Peacock* and *Lady Chatterley's Lover,* and with the Indians who oppose the destructive rationalism of the modern age in "The Princess" and "The Woman Who Rode Away"; the significant moments in the human life cycle and the sense that past generations still live in the present characters with *The Rainbow;* the intuitive rituals of love with "The Fox" and "The Horse-Dealer's Daughter"; the contrast between the squalor of the town and the magic of the countryside with *Twilight in Italy* and *Sea and Sardinia;* and the conservative political attitudes with the antirevolutionary ideas in *Aaron's Rod, Kangaroo* and especially *The Plumed Serpent.* Inspired by imaginative insight, Lawrence's translations of Verga were both re-creations of a sympathetic spirit and variations of the major themes and values of his own art.

5

Look! We Have Come Through! and Birds, Beasts and Flowers

I

LAWRENCE'S SEQUENCE OF LOVE POEMS, *Look! We Have Come Through!*, was mainly written in 1912 during his first months with Frieda in Germany and Italy. In Europe, where the two lovers could approach each other on new territory, Lawrence was inspired to write about his passion. The poems are "an essential story, or history, or confession," as Lawrence wrote in the Foreword, "revealing the intrinsic experience of a man during the crisis of manhood, when he marries and comes into himself."[1] The title invites the reader to be both voyeur and participant in the most intimate of all Lawrence's writings, to share in the emotional convulsions and joyful consummation as he comes into a new awareness of himself—achieves self-knowledge and self-fulfillment—*through* his marriage to Frieda and life in Italy.

These love poems express what Lawrence called "pure passionate experience," a kind of emotion recollected in emotion that attempts to simulate and convey "the quality of life itself." In his essay "Poetry of the Present," his Introduction to the American edition of *New Poems* (1918) which "should have come as a preface to *Look!*," Lawrence exclaims: "Free verse is, or should be, direct utterance from the instant, whole man . . . the insurgent naked throb of the instant moment. . . . Free

72

verse has its own *nature,* it is neither star nor pearl, but instantaneous like plasm."[2] Though Lawrence's essay suggests the dominant mood of the poems, they vary considerably in tone and feeling, and express much more than "passionate experience." The imagery is both mythical and biblical; and the style changes from the traditional forms of the early poems written under the influence of the Georgians to the loose, long-lined doctrinal assertions in the mode of Walt Whitman. The poems were composed between 1911 and 1916, and are extremely uneven in quality. The best ones—"Bei Hennef," "First Morning," "On the Balcony," "Gloire de Dijon," "Meeting Among the Mountains," "Doe at Evening" (which leads straight into *Birds, Beasts and Flowers*)—are lyrical, pictorial, intuitive, sensual and dramatic poems that often celebrate the landscape and the woman's body. The worst—"New Heaven and Earth," "Manifesto," "People," "Frost Flowers"—are self-pitying, repetitive, satirical, assertive, homiletic and didactic.

The "Argument" makes clear that the poems are a direct expression of Lawrence's own character, an intensely personal case history, "a biography of an emotional and inner life." Amy Lowell called the volume "a greater novel than *Sons and Lovers,"* for the themes are expressed through the characters and the story, which describes Lawrence's life after the break with Jessie Chambers: "After much struggling and loss in love and in the world of men, the protagonist throws in his lot with a woman who is already married. Together they go into another country, she perforce leaving her children behind. The conflict of love and hate goes on between the man and the woman, and between these two and the world around them, till it reaches some sort of conclusion, they transcend into some condition of blessedness."[3] Though Lawrence specifies Frieda's abandoned children (rather than inconstancy, jealousy and betrayal) as the major cause of their love-hate conflict, he is deliberately vague about the achievement and definition of their "condition of blessedness." But the poems show that the pain of his past struggles and loss in love—the death of his mother; his rejection of a teaching career; uncertainty about the future; affairs with Jessie Chambers, Alice Dax, Louie Burrows and Helen Corke—all prepared him to respond fully to Frieda.

"It is a great thing for me to marry you, not a quick, passionate coming together," Lawrence wrote Frieda in May 1912. "I know in my heart, 'here's my marriage.' " And during that year he explained to an Eastwood friend why he rejected Jessie and chose Frieda: "She is the one possible woman for me, for I must have opposition—something to fight or I shall go under." Frieda also seemed to thrive on the violent but open and honest quarrels that so frequently shocked their friends, and affirmed in her autobiography, *Not I, But the Wind:* "It was a long fight for Lawrence and me to get at some truth between us; it was a hard life with him, but a wonderful one. . . . We fought our battles outright to the bitter end. Then there was peace, such peace."[4]

The battles raged because Lawrence, though attracted to Frieda, felt threatened by dominating and possessive women. From his experience with them he learned to see love as a struggle of wills in which man either dominates women or suffers defeat. Frieda perceptively observes: "His courage in facing the dark recesses of his own soul impressed me always, scared me sometimes. In his heart of hearts I think he always dreaded women, felt that they were in the end more powerful than men." Lawrence resented his dependence on Frieda, was awed by her sexual experience and sexual demands, was fiercely jealous of the longing for her three children (they had no children of their own) and hated her willful refusal to submit to him. Frieda's divided loyalty to her lover and her children was similar to Anna Karenina's anguished conflict between Vronsky and her son, Seriozha; and like Vronsky, Lawrence could not sympathize with or understand his mistress' attachment to her children. He demanded absolute devotion and rather callously said: "You don't care a damn about those brats really, and they don't care about you."[5]

In December 1912 Lawrence confided to an Eastwood friend: "We've had a hard time, Frieda and I. It is not so easy for a woman to leave a man and children like that. And it's not so easy for a man and a woman to live together in a foreign country for six months, and dig out a love deeper and deeper."[6] *Look! We Have Come Through!* reveals their scarifying but successful attempt to dig out a deeper love. The poems go beyond the merely personal, describe the real difficulties in achieving fulfillment in love, and illuminate the connection of Lawrence's emotional and creative maturity.

When Frieda asked him, "What do I give you, that you didn't get from others?" he answered: "You make me sure of myself, whole"—complete as a man and an artist. Lawrence freely admitted: "It is hopeless for me to try to do anything, without I have a woman at the back of me. . . . A woman that I love sort of keeps me in direct communication with the unknown."[7] Lawrence's love for Frieda stimulated his creative life, for she inspired most of his heroines, helped him to imagine fictional scenes, was sympathetic yet critical about his books and believed in his genius.

Critics of Lawrence's poetry, misled by his emphasis on "inconclusiveness and immediacy" in his essay "Poetry of the Present," have neither sought nor found a discernible structure or unity in *Look! We Have Come Through!* Amy Lowell, who admired the book, concedes that it is "a rather disconnected series of poems." Conrad Aiken speaks of the poems as a "sequential, though somewhat disjointed, autobiography." And Tom Marshall follows this critical line by stating: "Lawrence attempted to make a book of poems that would have the effect of an important long poem. . . . But, unfortunately Lawrence's performance does not equal his conception."[8] But the arrangement of the poems in this volume is both careful and complex. Chronologically, the poems move from his mother's death in December 1910, through his months in Germany (May–August 1912) and Italy (September 1912–April 1913), to his return to England, the outbreak of the War (another threat to love), his third anniversary with Frieda and his move to Zennor in March 1916. Several poems—like "Frohnleichnam,"[9] "Giorno dei Morti," "All Souls" and "New Year's Eve"—are connected to specific days in 1912. Geographically, the poems progress from Eastwood, Croydon and Bournemouth to the Rhineland, Bavaria, the Tyrol and Lake Garda, and then back to Kent, Sussex and Cornwall. The cosmic setting (moon, sun, stars, sea) reflects the striving for transcendence. Lawrence feels pain in England, doubt in Germany and joy in Italy, where he achieves sexual fulfillment and "comes through" at Eastertide ("I feel new and eager / To start again") in "Spring Morning"—the last of the Italian cycle, written in San Gaudenzio, in the mountains above Gargnano, in April 1913.

Thematically, the poems follow a cycle from death to rebirth—in a reversal of its prototype, *Modern Love* (1862). Meredith describes the extinction, Lawrence the growth of love; Meredith the breaking, Lawrence the forging of the bond of marriage. Both Meredith and Lawrence deal with the pain and suffering of modern love; but Meredith ends with suicide, Lawrence with rebirth. Many of Lawrence's poems are also linked by affinity or contrast: "Elegy" and "Everlasting Flowers," "Nonentity" and "Quite Forsaken," "Don Juan" and "Priapus," "First Morning" and "Bad Beginning," "Mutilation" and "Wedlock," "Doe at Evening" and "Rabbit Snared," "Song of the Man Who Is Not Loved" and "Song of the Man Who Is Loved," "Sinners" and "Paradise Re-Entered."

The poems are unified by the two dominant themes: the natural conflict between men and women, and the striving for transcendence and consummation. Lawrence found the perfect expression of this sexual conflict in Italy, where "there is no comradeship between men and women, none whatsoever, but rather a condition of battle, reserve, hostility. . . . There is no synthetic love between men and women, there is only passion, and passion is fundamental hatred, the act of love is a fight." Lawrence developed this idea in "The Reality of Peace" (1916), where he asserted: "It is not of love that we are fulfilled, but of love in such intimate equipoise with hate that the transcendence takes place."[10] For Lawrence, then, the physical union of man and woman, which symbolizes spiritual consummation and expresses the crucial mystery of human life, evolves directly from this love-hate polarity.

The meaning of the poems lies in the progress of Lawrence's love and the development of his life, and is revealed in swift, radical alternations of dark and light, despair and hope, isolation and union. The sequence opens with "Moonrise," a celebration of the female deity who gives three assurances of bliss:

> That beauty is a thing beyond the grave,
> That perfect, bright experience never falls
> To nothingness,

and that full consummation will not "tarnish or pass away." But we know from the scenes in *The Rainbow* where Ursula dances before the moon and in *Women in Love* where the wounded Birkin throws stones into the moon-filled pond, that such consummation is not easily achieved. Though the moon promises that beauty and experience will lead to consummation, Lawrence believes that women hinder this ideal by an individualism and exclusiveness that express their fundamental hostility to men. He writes in *Fantasia of the Unconscious* (1921): "The moon, the planet of women, sways us back from our day-self, sways us back from our real social unison, sways us back, like a retreating tide, in a friction of criticism and separation and social disintegration. That is woman's inevitable mode, let her words be what they will. Her goal is the deep, sensual individualism or secrecy and night-exclusiveness, hostile, with guarded doors."[11] But this intensely subjective statement conveys Lawrence's essential loneliness and expresses his own hostility to a woman who would not "yield her goal" to his and might choose to be alone or with her children rather than with him.

The "Elegy" for his mother begins with an invocation of the male sun and describes her death as a willful act: "you closed your eyes forever against me." Her death leaves Lawrence with an "empty existence," and he reaches out to her—to woman—for his salvation. The next five poems reflect his desolate condition. "Ballad of a Wilful Woman" (the Virgin Mary), a transitional poem and the first to be written in Germany, portrays his love for a married woman as a religious experience which brews "hope from despair." A sharp change of mood occurs in "Bei Hennef" with the entrance of Frieda near "The little river twittering in the twilight." She soothes anxieties and pain, brings "almost bliss . . . perfectly complete"—though not yet free from an element of suffering.

Frieda's wedding night with Ernest Weekley had been a disaster. When she undressed, climbed upon a cupboard and waited to be carried down, he was shocked at her behavior. "She had expected unspeakable bliss," Frieda wrote of that night, "and now she felt a degraded wretch."[12] And in the bravely honest "First Morning," Lawrence admits his own sexual repression and the failure of their first night together:

> In the darkness
>> with the pale dawn seething at the window
>> through the black frame
>> I could not be free,
>> not free myself from the past, those others—
>> and our love was a confusion,
>> there was a horror,
>> you recoiled away from me.

This pain is prolonged—"I wish it would be completely dark everywhere"—in "And Oh—That the Man I Am Might Cease To Be," whose title comes from Tennyson's "Maud" and echoes Keats's sonnet "When I Have Fears That I Might Cease To Be." The reason for this pain is explained in "She Looks Back" where Frieda, as Lot's salty wife, looks guiltily back to the Sodom of England: "Back to those children you had left behind." As Frieda recalls: "Again we would be thrown out of our paradisial state. Letters would come. The harm we had done; my grief for my children would return red hot"[13]—and destroy all the happiness they had achieved. But affirmation returns in "On the Balcony" and "Frohnleichnam" (June 12, 1912), where he sees the body of Frieda "Glistening with all the moment and all your beauty."

Conflict returns in "In the Dark" as Frieda pleads: "There is something in you destroys me." They separate in the crucial "Mutilation," and Lawrence aches "Where she is cut off from me." He realizes "She has not chosen me finally, she suspends her choice"; fears she will return to England and pathetically prays to the dark Celtic gods: "Leave her no choice, make her lapse me-ward." "Humiliation" results when he recognizes he is lost without Frieda: "she is *necessary!* / *Necessary,* and I have no choice!" In "A Young Wife" he also admits (as in a popular song): "The pain of loving you / Is almost more than I can bear."

The lyrical core of the book—when he first achieves consummation—is signalled by "Green," the color of Frieda's eyes, reflected in the dawn sky and the moon, and continues in the series of five poems on roses. In the splendid "Gloire de Dijon," the antithesis of "First Morning," "Reality streams through the body of Frieda, through everything she touches, every place she steps, valued absolutely":[14]

> She drips herself with water, and her shoulders
> Glisten as silver, they crumple up
> Like wet and falling roses, and I listen
> For the sluicing of their rain-dishevelled petals.
> In the window full of sunlight
> Concentrates her golden shadow
> Fold on fold, until it glows as
> Mellow as the glory roses.

In "Youth Mowing," one of the few poems that looks beyond their concentrated passion, Lawrence balances Frieda's longing for her children, seeks an alternative to his frustrating humiliation with a woman and attempts to achieve what he calls " 'manly love,' the real implicit reliance of one man on another: as sacred a unison as marriage: only it must be deeper, more ultimate than emotion and personality, cool separateness and yet the ultimate reliance."[15] He claims the handsome youth mowing down by the Isar and boldly announces in dialect—as if he were a woman, impregnated by a man:

> Lad, thou hast gotten a child in me,
> Laddie, a man thou'lt ha'e to be.

In "Quite Forsaken" and the pitiful "Forsaken and Forlorn," he is once again alone, annihilated by the darkness. Frieda attacks his self-pity in "Fireflies in the Corn" and criticizes the unmanly Lawrence for:

> Limping and following rather at my side
> Moaning for me to love him!

Just as Lawrence made an intuitive identification with the youth mowing, who carried "His head as proud as a deer," so he makes another strange connection with "A Doe at Evening":

> Has she not fled on the same wind with me?
> Does not my fear cover her fear?

—in which "cover" means both mate and conceal. "Song of a Man Who Is Not Loved" conveys the isolation that made him respond to the deer.[16]

The last three German poems—"Sinners," "Misery" and "Meeting Among the Mountains"—express Lawrence's guilt about the people in England whom he and Frieda have hurt. In the last poem, which takes place among the "Christs in Tirol" described in the opening chapter of *Twilight in Italy,* Lawrence associates the accusing eyes of the bullock-driver— "The brown eyes black with misery and hate"—with his guilty memory of Ernest Weekley, the man he betrayed. While Lawrence stands with a chill of anguish beneath the carved crucifix, "trying to say / The joy I bought was not too highly priced," the pale dead Christ breathes "the frozen memory" of his crime.

"Everlasting Flowers," the immortelles one places on a grave, recalls the "Elegy" for his mother. It is the first of nineteen poems in the Italian cycle—a new beginning of a new life. As he watches the mountain peaks, the sails on Lake Garda, the light olive-leaves and the oxen-wagon, his thoughts turn back to her and prevent him from enjoying the loveliness of Italy:

> I know you here in the darkness,
>   How you sit in the throne of my eyes
> At peace, and look out of the windows
>   In glad surprise.

"Sunday Afternoon in Italy" portrays the natural enmity of man and woman. "In Winter Dawn," which brings the new year, he renounces their hurtful and hateful love. Despite the joy of Italy, their difficulties recur in "A Bad Beginning" when her throat, bruised with his kisses, reveals his cruelty. The lake steamer, drumming in from across the Austrian border, stands for the outside world; and he asks her to choose him instead. In "Why Does She Weep," he promises Frieda, who is homesick, fearful, "disturbed by the stress / of our loving," that they must and will begin to love each other properly. The procession in "Giorno dei Morti" (All Saints Day) and the chanting in "All Souls" (November 1 and 2, 1912) once again recall the sorrow of his mother's death and his emotional bondage to her. She is the affective equivalent of Frieda's children, and he must try to exorcise her.

"Lady Wife" recalls "She Looks Back" and the terrible conflict Frieda feels as mother and wife. Their love-hate polarity is described in "Both Sides of the Medal," which suggests the resolution that is later found in "Manifesto":

> But we will learn to submit
> each of us to the balanced, eternal orbit
> wherein we circle on our fate
> in strange conjunction.

Frieda is still unable to make up her mind about Lawrence in the transitional "Loggerheads"; and he pretends to be "quite indifferent / To your dubious state." But they achieve a secure reconciliation in the next five end-of-the-year poems in which Frieda, "the naked sacrifice," is born again, like Eve from the body of Adam. "Rabbit Snared in the Night" develops the idea of a naked sacrifice; and like "Doe in the Evening," uses an animal to symbolize his own emotions. The snared rabbit, like the rabbit in "Love on the Farm" and Bismarck in *Women in Love,* sexually arouses the lover, who is "implicated with you / in your strange lust." The rabbit's passion inspires the last three Italian poems in which the "Beautiful, candid lovers, / Burnt out of our earthly covers," are resurrected and reenter paradise on a spring morning. Christ's last words on the cross in the Gospel of St. John, "It is finished" *(consummatum est),* express the end of their earthly torment and the beginning of their consummation. The "gorgeous world" of Italy has inspired them to come through.

The retrospective poems in the last, English phase of the cycle celebrate their triumph and express the doctrine that has enabled them to reach fulfillment. In "Wedlock" Lawrence acknowledges Frieda's inspiration—"Where I touch you, I flame into being"—and claims they are vitally connected, yet "awfully distinct." The five quatrains of "History" recapitulate their emotional progress through Germany and Italy until:

> Your life, and mine, my love
> Passing on and on, the hate
> Fusing closer and closer with love
> Till at length they mate.

The imagery of the joyful "Song of the Man Who Is Loved," which was deleted from the original volume when the publishers objected to the strange sensuality, comes from the Song of Solomon 1:13: "A bundle of myrrh is my well-beloved unto me, he shall lie all night betwixt my breasts." Lawrence has discovered a tower of strength and haven of peace in the sweet softness of Frieda's body:

> So I hope I shall spend eternity
> With my face down buried between her breasts;
> And my still heart full of security,
> And my still hands full of her breasts.

There is also an embarrassing element of infantile regression in Lawrence's search for passionless maternal security between the breasts, and in his attempt to resolve the conflict between his roles as son and lover (analogous to Frieda's mother-mistress conflict) that was expressed in "Elegy," "Everlasting Flowers," and "All Souls" and led to the disastrous wedding night described in "First Morning." It was probably this "Song" (and the poems about swinging breasts and neck bites) that provoked Bertrand Russell's witty remark: "They may have come through, but I don't see why I should look," and Huxley's dry comment: "Reading these poems was like opening the wrong bedroom door."[17] Though Russell and Huxley, both highly intellectual and fastidious, were repelled by Lawrence's frank treatment of sex and marriage, his confessional tone and courageous self-exposure led to a radical change in taste and taught contemporary readers to admire the raw psychological anguish in the poetry of Lowell, Sexton, Plath and Berryman's *Love Sonnets.*

It is ironic that Lawrence was criticized for using the imagery that he condemned in Meredith, for in *Women in Love* the besotted Ursula "made great professions, to herself, of her willingness to warm his foot-soles between her breasts, after the fashion of the nauseous Meredith poem."[18] In Sonnet 23 of *Modern Love,* the husband is forced to share the same room as his adulterous wife after a Christmas party in the country, and prefers to sleep on the floor rather than in her bed. He prays to the demons who have tormented him to sustain him against temptation, yet still hopes for a reconciliation:

> I know not how, but, shuddering as I slept,
> I dream'd a banish'd Angel to me crept:
> My feet were nourish'd on her breasts all night.

Though the images may seem similar, Lawrence probably felt that placing feet on the breasts was perverse and led to the degradation rather than the exaltation of the man.

In "The Song of the Man Who Has Come Through," which provides the title of Frieda's autobiography, the angels who appeared to Abraham in Genesis 18:2 and announced "Sarah thy wife shall have a son" (they also appear in "Lady Wife") suggest that "we shall find the Hesperides." In "One Woman to All

Women" Frieda proclaims the glad doctrine that "his separate being liberates me / And gives me peace!" The satirical "People" and "Street Lamps" express his contempt for the unenlightened, mechanical "Ghost-flux of faces" that pass through the streets of London without reason or meaning because they have not experienced his own self-awareness and self-fulfillment.

"She Said As Well To Me," "New Heaven and Earth," "Elysium" and "Manifesto" are didactic poems. In the first, Frieda celebrates the beauty of Lawrence's body, as Connie Chatterley later does with Mellors. The second promises a resurrection, which is achieved in "Elysium." In the fourth poem, Lawrence acknowledges his vital debt to Frieda:

> She stood before me, like riches that were mine.
> Even then, in the dark, I was tortured, ravening,
>   unfree. . . .
> What many women cannot give, one woman can;
> So I have known it.

"Manifesto" also explains how Lawrence achieved the kind of self-transcendence that Birkin and Ursula were striving for in *Women in Love:*

> Then, we two shall be two and distinct, we shall have
>   each our separate being.
> And that will be pure existence, real liberty. . . .
> It is in pure, unutterable unresolvedness, distinction
>   of being, that one is free,
> not in mixing, merging, not in similarity. . . .
> two of us, unutterably distinguished, and in
>   unutterable conjunction.

In the novel, Birkin's ideal is "an equilibrium, a pure balance of two single beings:—as the stars balance each other."[19] The didactic poems (the opposite of passionate experience) cast important light on the meaning of Lawrence's novels, but fail artistically because they preach doctrine instead of allowing the meaning to evolve directly from the experience of love.

The sequence concludes with three poems of late 1916. "Autumn Rain" (with its allusions to the War) leads, by way of "Frost Flowers" (Lawrence's satiric description of the "ice-rotten" Londoners) to a "Craving for Spring"—with the "rush of creation" and the hope of rebirth as the promise of "Moonrise" is achieved.

II

The poems in *Birds, Beasts and Flowers* (1923) were written mainly in Tuscany and Sicily during 1920–21; continued in Austria, Germany, Ceylon, and Australia; and completed in New Mexico in 1923. Lawrence rightly thought it was his "best book of poems." According to Jessie Chambers, the young Lawrence was in primal sympathy with wild things and "a living vibration passed between him and them."[20] He retained this power in manhood and used it "to realise the tremendous *non-human* quality of life . . . the tremendous unknown forces of life, coming unseen and unperceived." For Lawrence, the scent of wildflowers was "really a communication direct from the source of creation—like a breath God breathed into Adam"; for him, as for his beloved Etruscans: "every man, every creature and tree and lake and mountain and stream, was animate, had its own peculiar consciousness."[21]

Lawrence's description of fruits is essentially symbolic; he is more interested in what they represent than in what they actually are. But the heart of *Birds, Beasts and Flowers*—the poems on creatures and reptiles—is intensely realistic and reflects the same brilliant success that he had with his fictional animals: the rabbit Bismarck, the Fox and St. Mawr. Unlike Goethe, who pitied animals "as masked and muffled creatures unable to express their feelings intelligibly and appropriately,"[22] Lawrence communicates with them as if they possessed the power of speech, penetrates their "peculiar consciousness" and presents an imaginative realization of what it is like to be an animal. He probes beneath their feathers, scales, skins, shells and hides, and gets much closer to "pure, passionate experience" than in *Look!* He conveys intimations of other modes of existence, explores the essence of natural creatures and transmutes animal energy into poetic feeling.

With woman in *Look!* and with animals in *Birds, Beasts and Flowers,* Lawrence experiences conflict, feels isolation and attempts reconciliation. His persona is important in both volumes. He connects the secret power of animals with the mysterious force of sex, and his penetration of the strange being of beasts helps him to understand the essentially alien nature of woman. His attitude toward creatures varies (as it did with woman) between curiosity and envy, admiration and rivalry, sympathy and hostility. He is interested in what animals reveal about himself, man's nature and moral understanding, and the human condition itself.

He fights with the mosquito, fish and snake; and his encounters have the dramatic quality of a short story. But his desire for connection with them remains unacknowledged and unfulfilled, and reveals the gulf between men who are "aware of being aware of being"[23] and animals who inhabit their own closed world. In poems like "Mountain Lion" he reverses King Lear's humanistic lament: "Why should a dog, a horse, a rat, have life, / And thou no breath at all?," and suggests that animal life is as valuable—perhaps even more valuable—than human existence.

"What is remarkable in Lawrence's 'nature' poems," writes Joyce Carol Oates, "is his fierce, combative, occasionally peevish relationship with birds, beasts, and flowers—he does them the honor, as the Romantic poets rarely did, of taking them seriously."[24] Unlike the symbolic Skylark of Shelley or the Nightingale of Keats, Lawrence's volume belongs to the great tradition of realistic animal poems that runs from Burns' "To a Mouse," Clare's "Badger," Whitman's "Dalliance of the Eagles" and Rilke's "The Panther" to Moore's "The Pangolin," Jeffers' "Hurt Hawks," Roethke's "Snake," Bishop's "The Fish," Jarrell's "Bats" and Hughes's "The Jaguar." The closest visual analogy to Lawrence's poems are Gaudier's sharp-lined ink-drawings of animals: the high-shouldered wolf, recumbent lion, square-jawed Egyptian cat, fierce serrated cock, heavy-haunched eland and swirling stag.

Lawrence declared: "In the tension of opposites all things have their being."[25] The conflict in the four sequential poems—"Mosquito," "Fish," "Bat" and "Snake"—expresses the essential polarity of man and beast, rather than the compassionate connection portrayed in Burns' "To a Mouse":

> I'm truly sorry Man's dominion
> Has broken Nature's social union,

> An' justifies that ill opinion,
> Which makes thee startle,
> At me, thy poor, earth-born companion,
> An' *fellow-mortal!*

Unlike Donne's Flea, who joins the lovers' blood and whose death encourages their union, Lawrence's mock-heroic Mosquito is a menacing gadfly, treated with cautious aggression. The poem opens with a series of rhetorical questions and exact observations that define the physical and moral nature of the insect. The weightless translucent phantom has thin wings and high streaming legs that make him seem a "nothingness"; yet he is diabolical in his tricks and (as Winged Victory) triumphs over man.

The "streaky sorcerer," evasively stalking and prowling the air, numbs Lawrence's mind with his filthy magic: "Invisibility, and the anaesthetic power / To deaden my attention." He lands on Lawrence, aware that he is seen, and then lurches off sideways in a game of bluff that reveals the power struggle between man and mosquito. The parasite's strafing buzz—dangerous but uncontrollable—outrages Lawrence even more than his cheekiness. When he strikes at the scalp and sucks the forbidden liquor—

> I behold you stand
> For a second enspasmed in oblivion,
> Obscenely ecstasied
> Sucking live blood,
> My blood—

a vital connection is established (as in Donne) between the tiny vampire and his host. Drunk and staggering with his "obscenity of trespass," the freighted victor derisively wafts away "on the very draught [a pun on drink and air] my anger / makes in its snatching." But the poet pursues and kills the winged blood-drop—and drowns with his own blood "the infinitesimal faint smear of you!" Though Lawrence wins the unequal contest, the moral victory belongs to the crushed mosquito whose "nothingness" has become something to take seriously. Donne's criticism of his mistress applies with equal force to Lawrence: "Cruel and sudden, hast thou since / Purpled thy nail, in the blood of innocence."

Like "Mosquito," "Fish" is a series of intense visual perceptions that reflects Lawrence's ambiguous attitude, ends in conflict and death, but does not achieve resolution. "So little matters" to the cold-blooded fish, who is completely at one with his protective (though sometimes threatening) element. He never has to emerge from the water, as man does, or fear floods that cover the earth. Lawrence's alliterative lines give a vivid sense of its swift spurts of motion, chromatic scales and mechanical air slits:

> Your life a sluice of sensation along your sides,
> A flush at the flails of your fins, down the whorl of
>   your tail,
> And water wetly on fire in the grates of your gills.

Though the fish is dehumanized—"No fingers, no hands and feet, no lips"—and detached from the female in sex and in shoals, Lawrence envies its *noli me tangere* attitude and its attractive enwombed state, which resembles a contented foetus. The fish knows hunger, fear and the joy of curvetting, but not love—though the element moves under him like a lover and he merges with the water after leaping for a fly: "Loveless, and so lively!" Lawrence tries to make an intuitive identification, but fails as the fish remains "forever apart." Lawrence "didn't know his God" because the ancient, mysterious, pre-Christian creature was "Born before God was love" (1 John 4:8) and seems to know a prehistoric life that the poet can never know.

So Lawrence (remembering his Italian vision of a water serpent swimming in the Anapo River near Siracusa) makes a violent physical connection with line and hook, disturbs the natural order, and pulls the "lucent fish from below" as if he were probing his own subconscious. But the "horror-tilted eye" leads to self-accusation and to a denial of Protagoras' dictum: "Man is the measure of all things"—for the fish has its own measure. Lawrence is guilt-stricken when the "pure lacquer-mucus comes off in [his] hand, / And the red-gold mirror-eye stares and dies." By killing the fish he has also destroyed something valuable in himself. He wanted to prove his superiority and acquire the power of the fish, but he failed to discover its secret. At the end of the poem the unknowable, loveless fish is negatively identified with the passive and detached figure of Jesus:

> In the beginning
> Jesus was called The Fish. . . .

> And in the end.

This ambiguous conclusion is clarified in *Etruscan Places,*
where Lawrence ignores the mystical significance of the acro-
nym ΙΧΘΥΣ (Jesus Christ, Son of God, Savior) and associates
Jesus with the element of the fish: "The fish is the *anima,* the
animate life, the very clue to the vast sea, the watery element
of the first submission. For this reason Jesus was represented
in the first Christian centuries as a fish . . . the *anima* of the
vast, moist ever-yielding element."[26]

"Bat," more concentrated but less compassionate than
"Man and Bat," attempts an exorcism rather than a connection.
The highly visualized poem, rooted in the Italian landscape,
opens in a contemplative mood. Lawrence sits on a Florentine
terrace watching the sun set on the mountains of Carrara and
on the Arno flowing under the arches of the Ponte Vecchio. At
first he sees "things flying," then wrongly identifies them as
swallows and finally realizes, with a shock, that the elastic
shudders of serrated wings are—Bats!   ·

Randall Jarrell's "Bats"—hanging by their toes, wrapped
in brown wings and bunched together—are cosy and even tender:

> Their sharp ears, their sharp teeth, their quick sharp
>   faces
> Are dull and slow and mild.
> All the bright day, as the mother sleeps,
> She folds her wings about her sleeping child.

But as the "vindictive" *pipistrelli* swoop madly overhead, Lawrence feels an uneasy creeping in his scalp. Their tiny shrieks
and umbrella wings awaken subconscious fears of rodents,
werewolves, vampires; blindness, bites, rabies; and what Baudelaire called "The wind of the wing of madness":

> Creatures that hang themselves up like an old rag, to
>   sleep;
> And disgustingly upside down.

Though Lawrence, in a moment of cultural relativism, generously acknowledged that "In China the bat is a symbol of happiness" (because "the word for bat, *fu,* has the same sound as the word for happiness"[27]), he violently rejects it. The force of the poem lies not, as with "Mosquito" and "Fish," in the attempt to identify with the creature, but in the powerful imaginative associations that lead to physical revulsion.

"Snake," the best-known poem in the volume, contrasts the vitality and indifference of the reptile with the morality and awareness of the poet. The poem lacks unity because Lawrence, who feels both reverence and hostility, is much better at describing the snake than in analyzing the reasons for his fearful and malicious response to it. He is acutely aware of the distance between the consciousness of man and beast; and would agree with Roy Fuller's "The Giraffes":

> I
> Saw evidence that these were animals
> With no desire for intercourse, or no
> Capacity,

and with Robert Frost's "To a Moth Seen in Winter":

> [I] know the hand I stretch impulsively
> Across the gulf of well nigh everything
> May reach to you, but cannot touch your fate.

The familiar tone and fluid rhythm that characterize Lawrence's animal poems immediately establish his hospitable and deferential attitude (tinged with curiosity and fear) toward the mysterious, yellow, straight-mouthed, silent snake. It drinks at his water-trough at noon on a hot Sicilian summer day, flicks its devilish tongue, looks vaguely at Lawrence as if he does not exist and, like the smoke from Mount Etna, comes "from the burning bowels of the earth."

When Lawrence pulls the lucent fish from the water his heart accuses itself. And when he sees the snake, the voice of education (false learning) destroys his intuitive response to the poisonous creature and insists: "He must be killed." Lawrence realizes that the snake arouses feelings of cowardice, perversity and fear. But he submits to his inner voice, and expresses an ambiguous envy and repulsion toward the sexual power of the phallic snake:

> As he put his head into that dreadful hole,
> And as he slowly drew up, snake-easing his
>   shoulders, and entered farther,
> A sort of horror, a sort of protest against his
>   withdrawing into that horrid black hole,
> Deliberately going into the blackness, and slowly
>   drawing himself after,
> Overcame me now as his back was turned.

Theodore Roethke's "Snake" conveys a similar desire to connect with the vital power of an elusive serpent:

> It turned; it drew away;
> Its shadow bent in half;
> It quickened, and was gone.
> I felt my slow blood warm.
> I longed to be that thing.

But Lawrence reacts violently and hurls a log at the snake whose body, as if in orgasm, "convulsed in undignified haste."

The last part of the poem, which comments on the dramatic action and repeats what is already clear, should surely have been omitted. Lawrence regrets his vulgar response, blames his cursed education and condemns himself. He thinks of Coleridge's Ancient Mariner, who "inhospitably killed the pious bird of good omen," and wishes the snake would return so he could reestablish their intimacy and discover its secret power. For the snake seemed, like Pluto, a god of dark forces. Lawrence missed his chance to understand "one of the lords / Of life" and must, like the Ancient Mariner, do penance for his petty act and learn to love "Both man and bird and beast."

"Lui et Elle" is the most significant of the six poems that were written in San Gervasio, outside Florence, in September 1920, published separately as *Tortoises* in 1921 and then included with "Snake" in the "Reptiles" section of *Birds, Beasts and Flowers.* In these poems Lawrence convincingly projects man's sexual experience in the unlikely form of sluggish, cold-blooded tortoises. He uses them to express his sexual anguish and illuminates the difficulties he had experienced in *Look!*

"Lui et Elle" is a comic ironic portrait of the large, slovenly Frieda and her small, tidy husband as erotic "French" reptiles:

> She is large and matronly
> And rather dirty,
> A little sardonic-looking, as if domesticity had
> driven her to it.

She lays her eggs in an offhand manner, tolerates her husband and is unaware of Lawrence when he feeds her. Unlike Connie and Mellors who experience tenderness when they feed the pheasant chicks in *Lady Chatterley's Lover,* Lawrence feels the female tortoise is cruel:

> She has no qualm when she catches my finger in her
> steel overlapping gums,
> But she hangs on, and my shout and my shrinking
> are nothing to her.

The dapper male seems ridiculously small. He has a laconic yet fiery eye, a skinny neck, long striving legs and an obstinate "horizontal persistence." Instead of food, he concentrates on *her:* "Parting his steel-trap face, so suddenly, and seizing her scaly ankle." Yet he looks a fool, "enveloped in isolation," and is masochistically degraded because he cannot bear to be alone. The core of the poem is an astonishingly naked expression of Lawrence's own sexual torments, described as a crucifixion without a resurrection:

> Alas, the spear is through the side of his isolation.
> His adolescence saw him crucified into sex,
> Doomed in a long crucifixion of desire, to seek his
> consummation beyond himself,
> Divided into passionate duality,
> He, so finished and immune, now broken into
> desirous fragmentariness,
> Doomed to make an intolerable fool of himself
> In his effort toward completion again.

Birkin considers the same problem in *Women in Love* and exclaims: "On the whole, he hated sex, it was such a limitation. It was sex that turned a man into a broken half of a couple, the woman into the other broken half. And he wanted to be single in himself, the woman single in herself. He wanted sex to revert to the level of the other appetites, to be regarded as a functional process, not as a fulfilment."[28] This is Lawrence's interpretation of the Platonic theory of physical love. In *The Symposium* Aristophanes explains Love by supposing that "the primeval man was round and had four hands and four feet, back and sides forming a circle, one head with two faces," and was subsequently divided into two. After the division, the two parts of man, each desiring the other half, came together, and threw their arms about one another, eager to grow into one. Plato's theory is appealing because it explains the attraction of the sexes and shows that the union of masculine and feminine complements is a return to original wholeness. But in Lawrence's version there is no return to wholeness, and the polarized broken half, much more "pestered and tormented" than the female, is doomed to make a "fool of himself / In his effort toward completion." At the end of the poem Lawrence repeats the crucifixion image as the male tugs at the female's vulnerable, nail-studded skin while she bites him, as she bit Lawrence, "pulls herself free, and rows her dull mound along." The female crudely rejects the sexually aroused male, who is both enraged and humiliated by her indifference and her power.

The strange opening of "He-Goat," who represents pure unsatisfied libido—"See his black nose snubbed back, pressed over like a whale's blow-holes"—is clarified by Lawrence's essay on Melville: "What then is Moby Dick? He is the deepest blood-being of the white race; he is our deepest blood-nature."[29] The sea imagery continues when Lawrence describes the ram as a ship with rancid cargo (his testicles), rowing through the herd of females but, however often he mates with them, never arriving at his journey's end.

The slit-eyed, nerve-urged, rock-hammering goat seems godlike as he engages in sexual combat with his rivals:

> In a rush from the shrieking duct of his vertebral
>   way
> Runs a rage drawn in from the ether divinely
>   through him
> Towards a shock and a crash and a smiting of horns
>   ahead.

But when he defeats his enemy he is left with his lust—"an egoist, aware of himself . . . full of malice prepense, and overweening"—and becomes a devil. As in the tortoise poem, Lawrence subtly shifts the emphasis from animal to human nature, and admits that the goat persona never quite penetrates to the core of the female. She makes certain that he experiences sexual satisfaction before she does, and remains amused by and indifferent to his futile efforts:[30]

> It is over before it is finished.
> She, smiling with goaty munch-mouth, Mona Lisa,
>   arranges it so.

The Don Juanesque goat, driven by an irresistible urge, has an inexhaustible series of orgasms. But he can never "overleap and surpass" the female and is finally frustrated. Unlike the soft voluptuous cat, who does not knock bone against bone but pierces to the depths "where will gives out, like a sinking stone that can sink no further," the goat is driven and trapped by "selfish will and libidinous desire." Like modern man, he has become domesticated by females and has lost his divine potential. Lawrence finds no solution to this crucial sexual conflict in any of the animal poems. But he "corrects" the problem in his last two novels by forcing his heroines to submit to male dominance. In *The Plumed Serpent* Kate renounces her orgasm to satisfy Cipriano's "column of blood"; and in *Lady Chatterley's Lover* Connie (like Ursula in the "Excurse" chapter of *Women in Love*) achieves her sexual apotheosis with the potent Mellors in animal-like anal intercourse.

In "The Spirit of Place" Lawrence proclaims: "Every great locality expresses itself perfectly, in its own flowers, its own birds and beasts, lastly its own men, with their perfected works."[31] Lawrence's meditations in these poems celebrate his zest for the Italian spirit in fruits (pomegranate, peach, medlar, fig, grape), trees, flowers, creatures, reptiles and animals; exalt the sea, light, landscape, heat, wine, sensuality that made "living in Sicily after the war years like coming to life again." As Horace Gregory observes: "In the early sections of *Birds, Beasts and Flowers,* we are given the best and yet most fleeting of his Italian journeys, the very heart of idyllic Italy which is recreated in *The Lost Girl.*"[32]

6

The Lost Girl

LIKE *A Passage to India, Ulysses, Remembrance of Things Past* and *The Magic Mountain, The Lost Girl* was started before 1914, interrupted by the War and finished after the conflict. Lawrence began the novel as "The Insurrection of Miss Houghton" (other titles were "Mixed Marriage" and "The Bitter Cherry") in Gargnano in 1913, when he wrote about 200 holograph pages, revived it after his journey to Italy in November 1919, and concluded it while living in Taormina. The original manuscript has not survived; and the extant novel, entirely rewritten between March and May 1920, is probably a very different kind of book from the 1913 version. As John Worthen writes: "There is simply no way of telling how far he had got with the story from the extant novel. . . . Anything we can say about the 1913 'Insurrection' has to be inspired guess-work."[1]

My guess, based on internal evidence, is that the first five chapters—which have an intrusive narrator and a bright, racy, satiric style—were originally written before the War. For Mr. May, based on Maurice Magnus, whom Lawrence met in November 1919 and was deeply embroiled with as he completed the book, first appears in chapter six. In Lawrence's essay on Magnus he mentions travelling past Montecassino, which he later visited in February 1920, en route from the Abruzzi to Capri in December 1919: "My wife and I were due to go into the mountains south of Rome, and stay there some months . . . . But it was so icy cold and snowy among the mountains, it was unbearable. We fled south again, to Naples, and to Capri. Passing, I saw the monastery crouching there above, world-famous."[2]

Lawrence's landlord in Taormina was Francesco "Ciccio" Cacopardo, and Alvina Houghton's lover Francesco "Ciccio" Marasca is introduced in chapter seven. This evidence is not conclusive, since these characters could have been changed in the later version. But the *terminus ad quem* of the lost 1913 manuscript is the end of chapter ten, for at the beginning of chapter eleven Lawrence describes the malicious spying on the Indian troupe that both recalls his wartime persecution in Cornwall and anticipates the "Nightmare" chapter of *Kangaroo:* "All the repulsive secrecy, and all the absolute power of the police authorities. The sense of a great malevolent power which had them all the time in its grip, and was watching, feeling, waiting to strike the morbid blow: the sense of the utter helplessness of individuals who were not even accused, only watched and enmeshed!"[3]

The declaration of War on August Bank Holiday, 1914, is also mentioned in chapter eleven; and the last three chapters, which describe Lawrence's journey to Picinisco in the Abruzzi, could have been composed only after the War. In the prewar chapters of the novel Alvina is dominated by her father; in chapter six she becomes the "almost inseparable" companion of Mr. May; in chapters seven to thirteen she falls in love with and marries Ciccio; and in the last chapters she is subjected to the oppressive influence of Italy.

The Lost Girl, which lacks the imaginative depth and symbolic resonance of its great predecessors *The Rainbow* and *Women in Love,* has been dismissed or condemned by critics.[4] But they have ignored its crucial importance as a transitional novel that appeared exactly halfway through Lawrence's literary career. The book is both a postscript and a prelude that recalls past themes and anticipates future ones: the attraction of a lady to a passionate working-class man in *The White Peacock;* the constrictive mining village in *Sons and Lovers;* the peasant's longing for America in *Twilight in Italy;* the disappointment with a barbaric landscape in *Sea and Sardinia;* the re-creation of a past life in *Etruscan Places;* the portrayal of Magnus in the Introduction to his *Memoirs;* the attraction to primitivism in the translations of Verga; the lacerating sexual conflict in *Look! We Have Come Through!;* the animal imagery in *Birds, Beasts and Flowers;*[5] the conflict of generations and sexual rebellion in *The Rainbow;* the destruction of love by war in *Women in Love;* the escape to Italy (which recalls the elopement with Frieda) in *Women in Love, Aaron's Rod* and *Lady Chatterley's Lover;* the use of pure travelogue in *Kangaroo;* the sacrifice of woman in a wild landscape in "The Princess" and "The Woman Who Rode Away"; the Indian mumbo-jumbo in *The Plumed Serpent;* the homosexual motif in *The White Peacock, Aaron's Rod, Women in Love* and *The Plumed Serpent;* the submission of woman to a dominant male in *The Virgin and the Gipsy, The Plumed Serpent* and *Lady Chatterley's Lover;* and the resurrection theme in *Lady Chatterley's Lover* and *The Man Who Died.*

The Lost Girl raises two questions that are central in Lawrence's work: "What is one's own real self?" and "How does one realize one's true nature?" Lawrence insists that "extraordinary people [have] extraordinary fates" and that Alvina *"was her own fate."* At the very end of the novel, as she urges Ciccio to come back from the War, she exclaims: "We have our fate in our hands."

Alvina's impressive ability to determine her own fate resolves the novel's secularized paradox, expressed in Matthew 10:39: "He that loseth his life for my sake shall find it." At various times in the novel Alvina is mentally, morally, physically and geographically lost. She loses her parents, her friends, her fiancés, her social position, her career, her inheritance, her self-respect, her virginity, her reputation, her security, her language and her country. She is "lost to Woodhouse, to Lancaster, to England . . . cut off from everything she belonged to." Ciccio feels he cannot bear to lose her; she fears she will lose him—in the War, or afterwards. Despite these formidable difficulties, her attitude remains: "All for love, and the world well lost." She finds salvation not of the soul, but of the flesh.

Each phase and major experience of Alvina's life prefigures Ciccio and prepares her for Italy. She comes from an ugly, provincial, class-constricted, mining town; from a family declining in both health and fortune. Her mother (like Proust's Tante Léonie) is a professional invalid, her father a frantic failure, Miss Frost and Miss Pinnegar rather cold and bitter examples of spinsterhood. The lives of the women in the household provide a grim warning about Alvina's future just as their deaths release her from a repressive life. She has nothing to gain by remaining "buried alive" in Woodhouse, and almost any other mode of existence appears more promising.

The five disastrous business ventures of James Houghton (which resemble the dismal careers of Simon Dedalus) parallel the five suitors of Alvina, foreshadow her fate and force her toward Ciccio. Houghton is a flamboyant but unrealistic draper who organizes sensational exhibitions in his shop window on Friday nights when the miners get their pay, and "hovered in the back-ground like an author on his first night in the theatre." He then fails as a Klondyke brick manufacturer, a Throttle Ha'Penny colliery manager, a would-be proprietor of a Private Hotel and finally—encouraged by the persuasive impresario Mr. May—the owner of a shabby, ill-situated cinema and music-hall.

Each of Alvina's five beaux—Australian, English, South African emigrant, American and Scotsman—anticipate an aspect of the Italian Ciccio. The passionate receptivity of Alexander Graham, who has strong teeth and dark blood, "dark in colouring, with very dark eyes, and a body which seemed to move inside his clothing," overwhelms Alvina as Ciccio does. Though she cannot bring herself to marry him, Graham's love gives her the confidence to leave home.

Alvina, who (like Connie Chatterley) has been visibly fading away, blooms as a maternity nurse (a symbol of her commitment to life) and flirts with all the physicians. Dr. Young, her second suitor, with his "deep, half-perverse knowledge of the other sex," touches, kisses and rouses her. But her inflexible virginity prevents her from yielding to him.

Alvina is genuinely attracted to the married plumber Arthur Witham. His "vulnerable hairy, and somehow childish leg" reveals the kernel of the real man beneath the workman's trousers, as he passes her hand over his broken shin after an accident in the chapel. But she is courted by his brother Albert, whose Oxford education makes him brittle and flat. Albert prefigures Ciccio's shallow "little modern education" that oppressed his natural instinct and "made money and independence an *idée fixe.*"

The fourth beau, the plump and perky Mr. May, is not as brilliantly drawn as the real Magnus in Lawrence's Introduction to his *Memoirs,* but he is still the liveliest character in the book. He is sensitive, dainty, manicured, fastidious; sports immaculate clothes and silk underwear (he later dresses as a girl to act with the Indian troupe); stays at the best hotel, though down-at-heel; has a quick but pedestrian mind; is evasive and unscrupulous. He has been a journalist and managed "for Miss Maud Callum [Isadora Duncan], the *danseuse.*" Mr. May introduces Alvina to the music-hall world and the Indian troupe. She must free herself from his influence, after they quarrel about money while playing cards and drinking, before she can fully commit herself to Ciccio. Mr. May, in an ironic twist of the plot (for his model, Magnus, had been pursued by detectives throughout Italy), pretends to concern himself with Alvina's virtue, curries favor in Woodhouse, and takes revenge by sending detectives to determine if she is involved in White Slave Traffic.

The last suitor, Dr. Mitchell, is a domineering male who hates to be thwarted. In a brilliant tragi-comic scene, he brutally flings Alvina against the wall when she refuses to kiss him—just as Ciccio does ("he seemed to throw her down and suffocate her") when he first has sex with her. And Mitchell's astonishing abasement, when he falls to his knees and begs forgiveness and love, recalls Alvina's slavish degradation with Ciccio.

Alvina's character predetermines her impulsive acts and unconventional behavior. This very proper and well-bred young lady's eyes are sardonic and mocking, her tone mad and jeering, her expression deliberately derisive, her "ancient sapience . . . deeper than Woodhouse could fathom." She scorns protection, is reckless, fascinated by the outlawed look of navvies and seems as knowing as a prostitute. Her employment as a maternity nurse and music-hall piano player makes her *déclassé* even before she meets Ciccio.

The descent into her father's mine is an exploration of her own subconscious desire for sexual as well as social experience. For the subterranean creatures, swooning in the drafts of darkness, suggest "something for ever unknowable and inadmissible." The miners "brought with them above ground the curious dark intimacy of the mine, the naked sort of contact . . . [and] preferred to take life instinctively and intuitively."[6] They make Alvina realize that she wants "a Dark Master from the underworld."

The peripatetic pattern of Alvina's life also prepares her for Ciccio and the flight to Italy. She escapes from Woodhouse (Lawrence's Eastwood) to become a nurse in London and to join the Indian troupe in Sheffield (after searching for them in Cheshire, Stockport and Chinley). She runs away from the troupe to meditate in Scarborough and becomes a nurse in Lancaster. She finally escapes from her enforced engagement to Dr. Mitchell, meets Ciccio in Scarborough, and lives with him in London before leaving for Italy.

Alvina's passion for Ciccio is the crux of the novel. He is physically attractive, with yellow-tawny eyes and gleaming teeth, muscular, graceful, sensual, passionate, exciting, an expert horseman. But his negative qualities are dominant. He is, Lawrence emphasizes, stupid, inarticulate, childish, common, loutish, crude, violent, servile and surly. In sex (his strongest card) he is emotionally unresponsive, insensitive, heartless, domineering, brutal and even bestial—though Alvina seems to like this. He is also mercenary and exploitive, and uses Alvina to gain wealth and social status. Ciccio's love for Geoffrey, the French actor in the troupe, seems stronger than his love for Alvina, though his passion for her is greater.

Despite these formidable faults, Alvina is instinctively attracted to Ciccio and establishes "an implicit correspondence between their two psyches." She must learn to respond to his sensual nature without losing her self-respect and becoming degraded. Soon after they first meet Alvina, who had noticed his Mediterranean hand, "prehensile and tender and dusky," reaches for him in the dark outside her house and meets his groping fingers. After Ciccio fights with the actor Max and stabs him with a stage knife, Alvina kisses the offending hand and convinces him to rejoin the troupe.

Immediately after her father's death, Alvina declares her love for Ciccio, "and smiling, he kissed her, delicately, with a certain finesse of knowledge." The conjunction of death and love is not ironic, as in the funeral-wedding sequence of *Antigone* and *Hamlet* (Lawrence refers to "The funeral tea, with its baked meats"), but suggests the kind of acceptance of death and affirmation of life, both part of the same process, that Lawrence so admired in Etruscan culture. As he wrote in *Apocalypse:* "The dead may look after the afterwards. But the magnificent here and now of life in the flesh is ours, and ours alone, and ours only for a time."[7] Her mother's illness encouraged Alvina to break her engagement to Alexander Graham just as her father's opposition prevented her marriage to Ciccio. Only after she quarrels with Miss Pinnegar and Mr. May, and breaks the last bonds with the people who influenced her maiden life, is she physically and emotionally free to give herself to Ciccio.

Their first sexual encounter occurs after Alvina has escaped the domineering benevolence of Woodhouse and joined the absurd Indian troupe—inspired by Lawrence's early reading of the novels of Fenimore Cooper.[8] She is on probation with the troupe (just as she had been on her first nursing job) and unwittingly adopts the obscene name of Allaye, which is derived through association with the Italian and French words *Viale, Voie, Petit Chemin, Allée,* and suggests vagina. Though Madame Rochard promised to protect Alvina (who had previously said she did not mind being unprotected), she acts as procuress and gives Ciccio the key to Alvina's lodging house room. "So he took her in both arms, powerful, mysterious, horrible in the pitch dark . . . and made her his slave. But the spell was on her. . . . How she suffered no one can tell." After he treats her brutally and enslaves her, she cried hysterically and "turned her face to the wall, feeling beaten. . . . She lay inert, as if envenomed." After sleeping with Ciccio she is torn between desire and humiliation, and forced to bribe her inquisitive landlady. Ciccio simply ignores her and wears an ugly, jeering expression.

Alvina's second sexual encounter is even more brutal than the first. It takes place in her parents' bed, as if to exorcise the spirits of her family, Miss Frost and Miss Pinnegar, when she returns to Woodhouse with Ciccio to consult her lawyer and settle her father's affairs. Once again he takes her brutally, against her conscious will, and tears away her defense and dignity: "She struggled frenziedly. But almost instantly she recognized how much stronger he was, and she was still, mute and motionless with anger. . . . Recklessly, he had his will with her—but deliberately, and thoroughly, not rushing to the issue, but taking everything he wanted of her, progressively, and fully, leaving her stark, with nothing, nothing of herself— nothing." She responds to this treatment by fighting her slavish desire to fall at his feet (she is dumbfounded and disgusted when Dr. Mitchell later does this after she rejects his proposal) and becomes ridiculously happy. She clearly takes masochistic pleasure in being reduced to nothingness by Ciccio as punishment for her sexual guilt. When friends see her in the street immediately afterward, they cheerfully remark how well she looks: "A change does you good."

When Alvina learns she is to receive virtually nothing from her father's estate, she realizes she must endure both the insolent contempt of Madame Rochard and the officious yet ineffectual patronage of the Woodhouse magnates. So she leaves the troupe, gets a second job as maternity nurse, suffers the rather repulsive courtship of Dr. Mitchell and nurses the pregnant Mrs. Tukes. In an extraordinarily contrived moment of the plot, Ciccio turns up in Lancaster as suddenly as he had in Woodhouse, when he played his "wildly-yearning Neapolitan songs" under her window after taking her virginity. Now he plays the mandolin under the window of Mrs. Tukes with a despairing, "clamorous, animal sort of yearning." As Alvina goes downstairs to meet him, he becomes the active suitor for the first time, declares his love and begs her to come with him to Italy. Ciccio's wails somehow induce Mrs. Tukes's labor, and an implicit connection is made between sexual desire and (its inevitable consequence) the pain of parturition. Mrs. Tukes is drawn to Ciccio because, she says, they are both tormented by the flesh: "I'm howling with one sort of pain, and he's howling with another." In a birth-love scene that parallels the death-love scene when James Houghton dies, Mrs. Tukes invites Ciccio into her bedroom, presumably to distract her from her agony. Wildly clutching at her sheets, she begs her husband to go away. The would-be composer Tommy Tukes is virtually annihilated by the instinctive music of Ciccio, whose life force and animal brutality seem more powerful, during emotional extremity, than art and intelligence.

Despite her instinctive sympathy with Ciccio, Lawrence does not allow Alvina an easy and obvious choice, or insist that she has made the right decision by submitting to Ciccio. She constantly courts him, though he fails to respond to her on any but the sexual level, and chooses him despite his obvious defects. Alvina is like the woman in Ezekiel 19:5: "When she saw that she had waited, and her hope was lost, then she took another of her whelps, and made him a young lion." The great weakness of *The Lost Girl* is that Lawrence does not make Alvina's love for Ciccio convincing (" 'and I can hardly bear it that I love you so much,' she said, quavering, across the potatoes") or persuade us that Ciccio, though better than her five unsatisfactory lovers, is the right man for her. The theme of the novel is Alvina's inability to find a man who has both passion and intellect, and her willingness to choose the former if she cannot have both. Lawrence creates three types of characters: the sensitive intellectual (Paul Morel, Rupert Birkin, Richard Somers), the passionate animal (Annable, Ciccio, Mellors) and the strong leader (Rawdon Lilly, Ben Cooley, Ramón Carrasco). But the ideal hero, who combines all these qualities, is never realized in his fiction.

Ciccio is even more strongly attracted to Italy than Alvina, and that country becomes their goal and destiny. It pulls him away from England, the troupe and their little playlet in which he is repeatedly crushed by the bear ("I am tired of being dead, you see"). Both Ciccio and Alvina realize that she cannot live in England as the wife of a "dirty Eyetalian" and that in Italy she will legally be his property—helpless even if he beats her.

They travel to Italy soon after their marriage, and the novel becomes more lively, intimate, immediate in the last three chapters. They enter a world more fierce and barbaric than Verga's. It is much more like the threatening Alps of *Twilight in Italy* and the conclusion of *Women in Love* than the romantic promise of Naples and the castles, cactus, almond trees, rocks, bays and glittering water of the classic Mediterranean that Alvina glimpses when they reach Genoa. The actual journey to the Abruzzi, where Lawrence had an introduction to Orazio Cerni (Pancrazio), who had been an artist's model for the father of his friend Rosalind Popham, took place just before the composition of the novel in early 1920. Though Lawrence spent only seven days in the Abruzzi and three in Montecassino, Picinisco, like the monastery, provided a shock of inspiration.

"This is what is so attractive about the remote places," Lawrence writes in *Sea and Sardinia,* "the Abruzzi, for example. Life is so primitive, so pagan, so strangely heathen and half-savage."[9] But both Alvina and Ciccio decline in Italy as it changes from a symbolic (as it was in England) to an actual country. The wild and savage landscape and new mode of life reflect the difficulties of Alvina's marriage and force her to examine her innermost self. The house is crude and filthy (but soon scrubbed in characteristic Lawrencean fashion), the cold is piercing, the sun seems extinguished, the atmosphere is strange and hostile, the people are "watchful, venomous, dangerous," the "fetish-worship" in the church is repulsive, there is a constant threat of war.

Critics of the novel have seen the Abruzzi as an "opposite

pole to England"; have stated: "Alvina escapes the frustrations of conventionality, and briefly finds a new 'life' in the under-world"; and have insisted: "An Italian man and the Italian landscape emancipate 'the lost girl' from England and set her face toward a new destiny."[10] But this is not true. The great irony of *The Lost Girl,* like *Sea and Sardinia,* is that Alvina is profoundly disappointed in the primitive landscape and that Califano, though apparently very different, has the same re-strictive features as Woodhouse. Both houses (the largest in the place) are "gloomy miserable holes." In both towns the people are money-grubbing, Alvina is fearful of gossip and scandal, subject to an almost oriental surveillance, threatened by finan-cial insecurity and faced with an apparently hopeless future. Both Alvina and Ciccio are intensely miserable, as eager to flee from Califano as they were to escape from England. As Gudrun tells Ursula at the end of *Women in Love:* "Isn't it really an illu-sion to think you can get out of it? After all, a cottage in the Abruzzi, or wherever it may be, isn't a new world."[11]

The one hope is Alvina's pregnancy (thematically related to her maternity nursing), which follows extreme despair, fore-shadows the coming of new life in the spring and symbolizes her love for Ciccio: "And even as he turned to look for her, she felt a strange thrilling in her bowels: a sort of trill strangely within her, yet extraneous to her. . . . She knew how he loved her—almost elementally, without communication. . . . It seemed to her she was with child."

This particular aspect of the novel, in which Lawrence (like Verga) tries to convey a sense of elemental life and primi-tive emotions (both the pregnant Mrs. Tukes and the amorous Ciccio howl with pain), provoked an angry response from the more subtle Katherine Mansfield, who objected to his visceral mode of expression. She intended to review *The Lost Girl* for Middleton Murry's *Athenaeum* in December 1920, and sent Murry her notes on the novel when she became seriously ill:

Lawrence denies his humanity. He denies the powers of the Imagination. He denies Life—I mean *human* life. His hero and heroine are non-human. They are animals on the prowl. . . . They submit to the physical response and for the rest go veiled—blind—*faceless—mindless.* This is the doctrine of mindlessness. . . .
Take the scene where the hero throws her in the

kitchen, possesses her, and she returns singing to the washing-up. It's a *disgrace*. Take the rotten rubbishy scene of the woman in labour asking the Italian into her bedroom. All false. All a pack of lies! . . .

Don't forget where Alvina feels *"a trill in her bow-els"* and discovers herself with child. A TRILL—What does that mean? And why is it so peculiarly offensive from a man? Because it is *not on this plane* that the emotions of others are conveyed to our imagination. It's a kind of sinning against art.[12]

Though Mansfield had formerly praised Lawrence's vital response to life, she now feels that he denies life and has descended into a kind of crude mindlessness that degrades women to the level of animals. Mansfield, who had portrayed the gruesome details of childbirth in her *German Pension* stories, had been through a miscarriage and an abortion that prevented her from having the children she so desperately wanted. She therefore has little tolerance for Lawrence's ignorance of female physiology, and condemns as false his description of Mrs. Tukes in labor and of Alvina's discovery that she is pregnant.

The malicious letter that Alvina receives from Dr. Mitchell (which recalls Ernest Weekley's spiteful missives to the adulterous Frieda), and Ciccio's farewell to Geoffrey in the Paris railway station, represent the final break with their life in England and their commitment to each other. Ciccio is drawn away from Alvina and forced into military service when Italy enters the War in May 1915. His love must be tested and annealed by the army as hers was by the raw experience of Italy. Though *The Lost Girl* ends with characteristic inconclusiveness, Ciccio promises that he will come back to his wife and child, if he survives the War; and both he and Alvina believe America holds hope of a new life.

7

Fascism and the Novels of Power

I

LAWRENCE, like most writers of his generation, came to political awareness after 1914. The development, changes and contradictions in his political ideas were influenced not only by the War, but also by four traumatic personal events: the violent quarrel with Bertrand Russell in September 1915; the suppression of *The Rainbow* in November 1915; the harrowing medical examinations described in the "Nightmare" chapter of *Kangaroo;* and the expulsion from Cornwall in October 1917. Lawrence's political ideas and the novels of power were also influenced by his direct experience with the rise of Fascism in Italy, which intensified his authoritarian tendencies.

Lawrence's first reaction to the War was horror and shock at "the ghastliness and mechanical, obsolete, hideous stupidity." His previous knowledge of Germany made him aware that the War was not a glorious adventure, but the sign of a collapsing civilization in Europe. In the midst of that first winter, plagued as always by poverty and poor health, and wandering from house to house, he imagined himself as a Christ-like cadaver, wrapped in the cerements of the tomb: "I feel very sick and corpse cold, too newly risen to share yet with anybody, having the smell of the grave in my nostrils, and a feel of grave clothes about me. The War finished me: it was the spear through the side of all sorrows and hopes."[1]

Lawrence, who rejected patriotism and propaganda, opposed the War, not on pacifist principles, but because it was meaningless: fought "for the sake of Allies who gloat and feed like enormous rats on [England's] dismemberment." All this, however, did not prevent him from being possessed by a murderous loathing of Germany: "Soon we in England shall go fully mad, with hate. I too hate the Germans so much, I could kill every one of them. Why should they goad us to this frenzy of hatred, why should we be tortured to bloody madness? . . . I am mad with rage myself. I would like to kill a million Germans—two millions."[2]

The War led Lawrence to deny the "Christian-democratic principle," for the masses had blindly elected politicians who betrayed the tenets of Christianity and led Europe to chaos and destruction: "Our leaders have not loved men: they have loved ideas, and have been willing to sacrifice passionate men on the altars of the blood-drinking ever-ash-thirsty ideal."[3]

Lawrence had, with considerable difficulty, escaped from the proletarian mass; he knew its defects and feared that he might slide back to his lower-class origins. He therefore asserted his own individuality and condemned militarism as "a decadence, a degradation, a losing of individual form and distinction, a merging in a sticky male mass." In January 1915 Lawrence still called himself a democrat in politics and favored the *"Liberté-Égalité* business" in the State. By July, while still opposing tyranny, he announced: "I don't believe in the democratic electorate. The working-man is not fit to elect the ultimate government of the country. And the holding of office *shall not* rest upon the choice of the mob: it shall be almost immune from them. . . . Unless real leaders step forward, to lead in the light of a wide-embracing philosophy, there will be another French Revolution muddle. . . . There must be an elected aristocracy. . . . The whole must culminate in an absolute *Dictator.* . . . Every man shall vote according to his understanding, and the highest understanding must dictate to the lower understandings."[4] Lawrence was specific in his opposition to foolish democracy, but characteristically vague about defining the true leaders and the new philosophy.

Though Lawrence despaired, he was not entirely without hope, however naive and idealistic. The new future could still be built on the ruins of the past: "One must speak for life and growth, amid all this mass of destruction and disintegration. ... The fact of resurrection, in this life, is all in all to me now ... whether we dead can rise from the dead and love, and live, in a new life, here." One hopeful possibility was the founding of a new community, Rananim, which would start a brave new life "in which the only riches is integrity of character. So that each one may fulfill his own nature and deep desires to the utmost."[5] The destruction of prewar society coincided with Lawrence's acceptance of his new roles as husband and writer; his belief in Rananim suggests that he hoped to re-create society around himself rather than in relation to the dominant culture of England. He wanted to forge a new prose style, new novelistic forms and new social values according to his personal vision.

In February 1915 an introduction to Bertrand Russell, who combined prestige of birth, learning and power, led Lawrence to believe that Rananim could arise in England's grey and somber land. In March, Russell invited him to Cambridge to meet J. M. Keynes and G. L. Dickinson; but Lawrence felt uneasy with these homosexual reformers—"they are our disease, not our hope"—and could not "bear the smell of rottenness, marshstagnancy. I got a melancholic malaria."[6] In June Lawrence planned to collaborate with Russell on a series of public lectures about social reconstruction. But Lawrence's vehement and absolute condemnation of Russell's synopsis deeply wounded Russell and drove him to contemplate suicide. Russell and Lawrence were both temperamentally and ideologically opposed, and their partnership was doomed from the start. Russell was an intellectual aristocrat who advocated democracy, Lawrence a passionate proletarian who believed there must be "an elected King, something like Julius Caesar." In September, Lawrence terminated their friendship with a violent blast: "The enemy of all mankind, you are, full of the lust of enmity. It is *not* the hatred of falsehood which inspires you. It is the hatred of people, of flesh and blood. It is a perverted, mental blood-lust."[7]

Lawrence had supported Socialism, unemployment insurance and pensions in February 1915: "The land, the industries, the means of communication and [oddly] the public amusements shall all be nationalised. Every man shall have his wage till the day of his death, whether he work or not, so long as he works when he is fit." But three years later, in February 1918, he was prepared to lay a mine under the whole foundation of the establishment: "I feel that nothing but a quite bloody, merciless, almost anarchistic revolution will be any good for this country, a fearful chaos of smashing up."[8] All these radical changes were to be achieved by an unshakeable faith in "the creative unknown"—his own creative power.

Lawrence rightly believed that his opposition to the War was sane and salutary, and that he suffered in his heart and mind as much as any combatant at the front. He felt that the suppression of *The Rainbow,* the military examinations and the expulsion from Cornwall were due to personal persecution rather than the exigencies of war. These disastrous quarrels with British officials led Lawrence to shift from a collective to an individualistic answer to the problem of political authority and to a belief in a powerful leader. The ideas that grew out of the War were certainly anti-democratic, for Lawrence was an elitist who despised the ignorant masses. But they were not Fascist: that totalitarian, nationalistic and racist movement, founded in Milan in 1919, did not yet exist when Lawrence first formulated his ideas.

II

After the War Italy had very grave problems: a huge national debt, rising inflation, high unemployment, economic collapse, a mass of dissatisfied veterans. These conditions caused serious riots, and in 1919 many Communist risings and counter-revolutionary reprisals took place. In September 1919 Gabriele D'Annunzio captured Fiume, which had been awarded to Yugoslavia by the Paris Peace Conference, and was driven out by the Italian navy, which bombarded the Adriatic city in December 1920.[9] The harvest failed in 1920 and serious agrarian strikes continued throughout the year.

During 1920–22 a civil war raged in Italy between the Fascists and Socialists, in which 300 of the former and 3000 of the latter were killed in riots. After a no-confidence vote, the nation had no government for several weeks in July 1922. When a general strike was declared the following month, the Fascists aligned themselves with the police and public opinion, which called for authoritarian rule. The successive governments—

weak, confused, paralyzed—could not control the economic chaos or the civil war, and took no action when the Fascists mobilized their cohorts. The March on Rome in October 1922 was neither a revolution nor a *coup d'état.* Denis Mack Smith writes that it was actually "a comfortable train ride, followed by a petty demonstration, and all in response to an express invitation from the monarch."[10]

Mussolini, born two years before Lawrence in 1883 and named after the Mexican revolutionary Benito Juárez, had emigrated to Switzerland in 1902 to avoid the draft—like the exiled workers described in *Twilight in Italy.* Mussolini, whose supporters were particularly brutal in Tuscany, believed that a violent minority insurrection could achieve authoritarian rule. "Under the pretense of saving the country from bolshevism, the fascists were thus able to attack governmental authority and create anarchic conditions which would make people long for authoritarian government."[11]

Fascism boasted of being a movement, not a doctrine; its program was always changing and inconsistent. An article in the *Enciclopedia italiana* of 1931 vaguely proclaimed: "The fascist conception of the state is all embracing, and outside of the state no human or spiritual values can exist, let alone be desirable." Despite, or perhaps because of this, Mussolini, who had only 7 percent of the deputies in November 1922, gained 65 percent of the votes in the last free election of April 1924. He was supported by such notable Italians as D'Annunzio, Pirandello, Marinetti, Puccini, Marconi and Croce (who later recanted), and by Englishmen like Churchill and Shaw. The dictatorship—which became increasingly tasteless, corrupt and inefficient—was absolute by January 1925, and the anti-Fascist movement had disappeared by 1926. Mack Smith concludes: "The success of Fascism in 1919–22 was due less to any interior logic or merit of its own than to the vacuum left by the failure of other parties."[12]

It is essential to remember that Lawrence lived in Italy from November 1919, when he finally escaped from England, until February 1922, when he sailed for Ceylon; and that he remained outside Italy from February 1922 until he returned from America in November 1925. Thus, he was there during the postwar breakdown of government authority and the civil war between Socialists and Fascists, when there was a real need for strong rule. But he was away during the March on

Rome (October 1922), the brutal consolidation of Fascist power (1922–24), and the murder of the Socialist deputy, Giacomo Matteotti (June 1924). By the time he returned in November 1925, the opposition had been destroyed, the dictatorship was absolute and civil order had been restored.

The Epilogue (written in 1925) to Lawrence's school text-book, *Movements in European History,* expresses his angry response to the bullying and violence that he experienced in postwar Italy. He blamed this entirely on the Socialists (who were then in power), and described these conditions both in *Aaron's Rod* and in the transposition of Italian politics to Australia in *Kangaroo:* "By 1920 prices had gone up three times, and socialism was rampant. Now we began to be bullied in every way. Servants were rude, cabmen insulted one and de-manded treble fare, railway porters demanded large sums for carrying a bag from the train to the street, and threatened to attack one if the money were not paid. . . . In the summer of 1920 I went north, and Florence was in a state of continual so-cialistic riot; sudden shots, sudden stones smashing into restau-rants where one was drinking coffee, all the shops suddenly barred and closed."[13]

Lawrence's letters from postwar Italy reflect the violence (particularly disturbing to a foreigner who desires stability and is not especially concerned with the kind of government that provides it), the prospect of revolution and the need for authori-ty. The chaotic aspect of politics in Italy, like the revolutions he later experienced in Mexico, frightened Lawrence and made him feel insecure. In January 1920, two months after he arrived, Lawrence was less interested in the crisis in Fiume than in his foodstuffs and mail: "Italy is a ridiculous kingdom, politically, governs itself so badly, that one becomes indifferent to all political fates—Fiumes, Jugo-Slavakias, and such like my-eye, and merely curses because there's no coffee and no post." In 1921 Lawrence, who mentions railway strikes and po-litical riots, half-expected a revolution in Italy, though he was confused about what form it would take. In January the para-doxical firebrand wanted to join the revolutionary Socialists and take part in the real struggle, though he admits he is nei-ther interested in politics nor competent in revolution: "If I knew how to, I'd really join myself to the revolutionary social-ists now. I think the time has come for a real struggle. That's the only thing I care for: the death struggle. I don't care for politics. But I know there *must* and *should be* a deadly revolution very soon, and I would like to take part in it if I knew how."[14]

In March Lawrence rightly predicts a long civil war followed by a gradual (rather than sudden) disintegration of government authority: "I think Italy will not revolute or bolsh any more. The thing will settle down to a permanent *socialisti v. fascisti* squibbing—the old Italian faction, Guelph and Ghibellini—and so the house will come to bits. It will have no one smash, like Russia. . . . I shouldn't wonder if before very long they effected a mild sort of revolution here, and turned out the king. It would be a clergy-industrial-socialist move— industrialists and clergy to rule in the name of the people. Smart dodge, I think. If the exchange falls again they'll effect it."[15]

The threat of revolution prompted Lawrence to restate the anti-democratic ideas he had first formulated during the War: "I don't believe either in liberty or democracy. I believe in actual, sacred, inspired authority: divine right of natural kings: I believe in the divine right of natural aristocracy, the right, the sacred duty to wield undisputed authority."[16] But Lawrence is once again vague about precisely who the natural kings are and how they will rule. The opposition of the aristocracy and the masses, the emphasis on unity, leaders, heroism, will, responsibility, authority, rule and power frequently recur in Lawrence's works of the early 1920s, which were written in postwar Italy: *Movements in European History* (1921), *Fantasia of the Unconscious* (1922), *Aaron's Rod* (1922), "Hibiscus and Salvia Flowers" (1923) and also "Blessed Are the Powerful" (1925).[17]

The breakdown of order in England and Italy led Lawrence to journey round the world in quest of a solution to postwar chaos; and the failure to convince either Russell or his own disciples of the validity of his political beliefs led directly to the imaginative expression of these ideas in the novels of power. It was both ironic and inevitable that Lawrence found in democratic Australia during 1922 and in revolutionary Mexico during 1923–25, the settings of *Kangaroo* and *The Plumed Serpent,* the same violent conflict between Left and Right that he had fled in Europe. "Labour is very strong and very stupid," he wrote from Australia in June 1922, condemning the crude materialism of that new country and equating strikes with Socialism. "The more I see of democracy the more I dislike it. It just brings everything down to the mere vulgar level of wages and prices, electric light and water closets, and nothing else. . . . The working people [are] very discontented—always threaten more strikes—always more socialism." In Mexico, the political situation was even worse: more violent, more threatening and more meaningless. The masses were more savage than in Australia and after numerous revolutions of Bolshevists and Fascists everything remained the same: "The Indians are queer little savages, and awful agitators pump bits of socialism over them and make everything just a mess. It's really a sort of chaos."[18]

Lawrence always sought to define himself in response to external nature and society. So his travels in Australia and Mexico and residence in Italy, which provided dazzling natural surroundings and a society that was psychologically comfortable because he did *not* belong to it, also stimulated his intensely subjective attempt to formulate a new social order in terms of his own relation to foreign places and alien societies.

III

Aaron's Rod (1922), which begins in England on December 24, 1919 and ends in Florence a year later in November 1920, reflects Lawrence's first postwar journey to Italy in November 1919, his brief stay at Sir Walter Becker's villa in Turin and his three weeks in Florence, during November and December, when he renewed his friendship with Norman Douglas and first met Maurice Magnus. Like Alvina in *The Lost Girl,* Aaron leaves his family in the Midlands, takes a different job in another town, has sexual relations with a hot-blooded foreigner and journeys to a new life in Italy. Most of the English scenes take place at night (the first daylight does not appear until chapter 8), and though Aaron arrives at Novara in the evening, the Italian scenes are suffused with brilliant sunshine.

Aaron's Rod—like *The Sun Also Rises* and *Tender is the Night*—shows the influence of the War on expatriates, just as *Women in Love* shows the effect of the War on civilian life. The English homosexuals in Florence—satirized in the portraits of Angus and Francis, the precious Mr. ffrench, James Argyle and Algy Constable (Norman Douglas and Wilde's friend Reggie

Turner)—make Aaron distinctly uncomfortable. But Aaron shares their misogyny, and is homosexually as well as politically attracted to Lilly.[19]

Aaron, whose flute and union activities combine art and politics, goes to Italy to find Lilly. (The lily is the flower of Florence.) And in Italy he becomes more intensely alive—"[It's] a new world to me. I feel I've come out of myself"—and more politically astute. Though he dismisses the Duomo of Milan as "a grey-purple sea-urchin with many spines," he is exhilarated by the snow-streaked peaks of the Dolomites and by the splendid squares that recall the glorious history of Florence: "He felt that here he was in one of the world's living centres, here, in the Piazza della Signoria. The sense of having arrived—of having reached a perfect centre of the human world: this he had. . . . Here men had been at their intensest, most naked pitch, here, at the end of the old world and the beginning of the new. . . . Aaron felt a new self, a new life-urge rising inside himself. Florence seemed to start a new man in him."[20] But he must learn to use this new vitality to escape from his cul-de-sac and to direct his artistic and political energy toward a purposive goal.

The fourth sentence of the novel—"A man felt the violence of the nightmare [of War] released now into the general air"—expresses the dominant theme, symbolized by the splashing explosion of the blue ball of glass, which belonged to Aaron's childhood and foreshadows the detonation of the bomb at the end of the book. Robert Cunningham and Jim Bricknell in the Midlands, Herbertson (who tells atrocity stories) in Covent Garden, the Colonel and the Major in Novara, Angus in Milan, were all officers in the War—that "huge obscene machine" which Lilly refused to join. Sir William Franks' house was a hospital during the War, and he surprises Aaron by serving port in "those bleak, post-war days." Argyle is proud of his old suit of beautiful English cloth, made before the War. The Marchesa stopped singing during the War, though she is revived by Aaron's flute. Just after the War, when foreigners were rare and poor folk with prewar notions stayed packed in third-class carriages, a large man with a fat neck (who prefigures the insolence and hostility of the working class) refused to give back Aaron's seat in the train to Florence and ordered him to take a place in the first-class carriage. Lilly says the postwar "world is coming to pieces bit by bit." Men, houses, drink, suits, song, comfort, stability and order have all deteriorated as a result of the War.

The release of violence also threatens to lead to civil war and revolution. Josephine Ford (Aaron's mistress) longs for a bloody revolution that would bring the world to an end. Jim Bricknell, "a red-hot revolutionary of a very ineffectual sort," sees Lilly as his savior. But when Lilly, annoyed by Jim's flirtation with his wife Tanny, mocks his belief in love, Jim foreshadows the theme of violence and the relation of love and power by punching Lilly in the stomach. Lady Franks dreams of the working class of Novara rushing up from the town to ransack her house. And Aaron watched a riot take place during a Communist procession in Milan: "In utmost amazement he saw the sturdy, greeny-grey carabinieri, like a posse of foot-soldiers, rushing thick and wild and indiscriminate on the crowd, with a frenzied excitement which must have been based on fear: a sudden, new, excited crowd in uniform attacking the civilian crowd and laying about blindly, furiously with truncheons." A similar riot breaks out in Florence when the Socialists are demonstrating against the imprisonment of the railway strikers and an Anarchist shoots a mounted carabiniere, who tries to bar the way down a street paved with loose cobblestones: "Then there was hell let loose, the carabinieri fired back, and people were bolting and fighting like devils. . . . If you let loose the dogs of war you mustn't expect them to come to heel again in five minutes."

Lilly's fanatical response to these revolutionary outbursts is to attack Christian-democratic idealism and call for strong authority: "The ideal of liberty, the ideal of the brotherhood of man, the ideal of the sanctity of human life, the ideal of what we call goodness, charity, benevolence, public spiritedness, the ideal of sacrifice for a cause . . . [have all] gone putrid, stinking." He deplores bullying and thinks every man is a sacred and holy individual, but immediately contradicts these principles by calling for the extermination of all opposition. He believes this will lead to a healthy slavery, enforced by permanent power, and "a real committal of the life-issue of inferior beings to the responsibility of a superior being." But Lilly's political lecture is interrupted by the explosion of a bomb in the Florentine café, and he never persuades the sceptical Aaron to accept his ideas.

Lawrence's beliefs are more personal than political, and the revolutionary struggle is analogous to the fight for power between men and women. Lilly announces to Aaron: "there are only two great dynamic urges in *life:* love and power," and the novel attempts to work out the complex relation between them. At the beginning of the book, Aaron abandons his three children and his nagging, bitter, disembodied and ultimately unreal wife (he hears her voice from another room and twice observes her through glass from outside the house), who rightly accuses Aaron of withholding himself from her. Aaron's flight raises the crucial issue of personal—and ultimately political—responsibility: not only of the British for their Indian subjects (discussed by the doctor at the pub), but also of Aaron for his family, of Julia Cunningham for her husband Robert (whom she eventually leaves for Cyril Scott), of Josephine Ford for her fiancé Jim Bricknell (whom she abandons for Aaron), of the Marchesa for her husband del Torre (whom she betrays with Aaron), of Argyle for his late wife (whom he smashed up along with their marriage), and finally of Lilly for Aaron, and Aaron for his "own soul's self." In each case, emotional impulse triumphs over social responsibility.

The theme of responsibility is also related to the conflict between dependence and isolation. Aaron needs a woman, but is smothered by sex; he craves singleness, but longs for male friendship. His submission to Lilly is analogous to the masses' submission to a leader. Both Jim Bricknell and Aaron seem to prove Josephine's thesis that "Men are simply afraid to be alone." For Jim seeks out his former wife and girlfriend after Josephine leaves him; and Aaron has disastrous relations with two American women, Josephine and the Marchesa, after leaving his wife. After sleeping with Josephine, he speaks of his influenza as if he had contracted venereal not viral disease. And he blames the theft of his wallet on his affair with the Marchesa: "If I hadn't exposed myself: if I hadn't got worked up with the Marchesa, and then rushed all kindled through the streets without reserve: it would never have happened."

Lawrence believes that the struggle for sexual dominance results in destructive violence, and that the masses must submit to the authority of a leader in the same way that women must yield their willful defenses and submit to men. When Aaron's rod is shattered by the Anarchist bomb, the four different but complementary meanings of the main symbol—rod, flower, flute and penis—fuse into a significant whole. When the bomb destroys the flute and Aaron "has to live without a rod," he must submit his sexual will to Lilly, who allows him to retain his "sheer, finished singleness." He would rather yield "to the peculiar mastery of one man's nature than to the quicksands of woman or the stinking bog of society."

The title of the last chapter, "Words," recalls the sixth chapter, "Talk," and subtly undermines the validity of Lilly's didactic harangue. His purely personal urge for power in love is based on the idea of male superiority and directed mainly against women; but it has very little to do with political leadership. For he repeats his earlier condemnation of Tanny, who refused to "submit to a bit of healthy individual authority" and forced him to "do a grovel" before a woman: "The woman must now submit, but deeply, deeply, and richly! . . . There will be a profound, profound obedience in place of this love-crying, obedience to the incalculable power-urge. And men must submit to the greater soul in a man, for their guidance: and women must submit to the positive power-soul in man, for their being."

The novel ends inconclusively, with Aaron unconvinced by Lilly's arguments and uncommitted to a movement or a leader. The novel makes no distinctions between Fascists, Socialists, Communists and Anarchists; and there is no prospect of a political—as opposed to a personal—solution. The isolated Lilly is clearly not the man to resolve the postwar chaos.

IV

Kangaroo (1923), which has a great deal in common with its predecessor, develops the personal and political themes of *Aaron's Rod.* Both books describe the hero's response to a new country and contain significant sections of travel writing. Struthers is the name of a painter in *Aaron's Rod* and a Labour leader in *Kangaroo;* and the composer Cecil Gray appears in both novels: first as Cyril Scott and then as James Sharpe. Both novels describe Anarchist bomb explosions and riots between Fascists and Socialists. Both novels concern the conflict between love and power, and express disdain for "grovelling wife-worshippers." Both Lilly and Somers refuse to join the army and unleash a violent attack on idealism. Both Aaron and Somers have a homosexual attraction to the rather deflated leader—Lilly is punched in the belly and Kangaroo shot in the stomach—but finally renounce him for individuality and isolation.

Somers, who is sick of the horrible staleness and trite consciousness of over-upholstered Europe, escapes to Australia. But as soon as he arrives there he begins to long for Italy: "Florence, with Giotto's pale tower: or the Pincio at Rome. . . . Or the tall corn under the olives in Sicily." He misses Italian violets and Sicilian honey, dreams of Italy and finds the Australians more foreign than the Latins. There are also enormous differences between the political situation in chaotic Italy and in calm Australia, where "Nobody seemed to bother, there seemed to be no policemen and no authority, the whole thing went by itself, loose and easy, without any bossing. . . . There is a great relief in the atmosphere, a relief from tension, from pressure." Tedlock is quite wrong to claim: "Authoritiless, the country is on the verge of anarchy."[21] But the raw, slovenly democracy makes Somers anxious and frightened of the mob; and he reverts to his hatred of anarchy and instinct for authority, based on the aristocratic principle of Europe.

In *Kangaroo,* Lawrence emphasizes the superficial similarities of Italy and Australia rather than the profound differences. Somers' description of politics in Italy—the insolence, the threat of revolution, the weakness of the Socialists and corresponding rise of the Fascists—applies with equal force to his experience in Australia. "When I left Europe it seemed to me socialism was losing ground everywhere—in Italy especially," Somers remarks. "In 1920 it was quite a living, exciting thing, in Italy. It made people insolent, usually, but lifted them up as well. Then it sort of fizzled down, and last year there was only the smoke of it: and a nasty sort of disappointment and disillusion, a grating sort of irritation. Florence, Siena—hateful! The Fascisti risen up and taking on airs, all just out of spite."

Several unconvincing attempts have been made to show a close connection between Australian politics of the early 1920s and the political events of *Kangaroo.*[22] There are certain similarities between the nationalistic Returned Servicemen's League and the Diggers (the Australian word for war veterans),[23] between the agitation within the Labour Party and Struthers' Socialist movement, between Sir John Monash—a Jewish lawyer and engineer who became commander of the Australian forces in the Great War—and Kangaroo,[24] between the name of a contemporary Labour leader Jim Dooley and the (not very Jewish-sounding) name of Kangaroo, Ben Cooley.[25] But the Australian Fascist movement, the New Guard, did not exist until a decade *after* Lawrence's visit to the country and there were no Fascist-Socialist riots in Australia while he *was* there.[26] Lawrence transposes Italian Fascism to the suggestive foundation of Australian politics, contrasts it to distasteful Australian democracy, and uses it to symbolize the frightful emptiness of the uprooted people and wild landscape.

The Diggers are led by Kangaroo, but their fascistic principles are more accurately represented by Somers' neighbor, the ex-officer Jack Callcott. He explains their military organization, their revolutionary aims and their ambition to seize political power, while the thunderous ocean nearly drowns his words. Jack insists that authority, discipline and obedience are needed to oppose the rotten politicians and the exploded ideal of democratic liberty. The old soldiers, returned from the War, "chaps with some guts in them," are secretly sworn to keep silent, obey the leaders and wait for the moment to strike. The well-equipped Diggers' Clubs practice martial sports, have regular military training and are indoctrinated with nationalistic ideology. There is a strong emphasis on intimate comradeship—"Men fight better when they've got a mate"—modelled on David and Jonathan, which had always been Lawrence's cherished ideal.

But there is a great difference between Jack's enthusiasm and Somers' scepticism about the Diggers, for its actual model, the Returned Servicemen's League, represented almost everything that Lawrence disliked about Australia. It was militaristic, philistine, bigoted, brutal, crude, conformist, democratic and nationalistic:

> The Returned Servicemen's League did a great deal to make the values associated with Anzac Day and the "old digger" dominant in the Australian community. Along with the virtues ascribed to the idealised digger—courage, loyalty, mateship and democratic levelling—went other less admirable characteristics. The stereotyped figure exhibited also tough, sardonic contempt for coloured people and foreigners generally, for minority views, for art, literature, culture and learning; and something not far from contempt—patronage dis-

guised as chivalrous protectiveness—for "good" women and brutal disdain for "bad" ones. He magnified "male" virtues like decisiveness, directness, physical strength, and despised "female" ones like thoughtfulness, gentleness, subtlety. The tone of most of the writing in the *Bulletin* or *Smith's Weekly* at this period exactly mirrors the prevailing ethos—levelling values, rough manners and philistine tastes as the outer form; conformity, conservatism and unquestioning Anglo-Australian patriotism as the inner content.[27]

When Somers meets Kangaroo he is struck by the unusual mixture of essential Jewish kindness and "shrewd fiendish subtlety of will"—though we never see anything of the latter. Unlike the ferocious Jack, Kangaroo favors benevolent tyranny, with humane laws and wise authority. Lawrence never makes clear why Somers thrilled to his voice "as he had never thrilled," thinks: "the man is like a god, I love him," and is homosexually attracted to the ugly, shapeless leader (modelled on S. S. Koteliansky and David Eder). Somers, who has to restrain his desire to touch Kangaroo's body, which emits a "magnetic effusion," is personally drawn to Kangaroo, but rejects his party and his ideas. But when Kangaroo presses Somers' slight body against his own big breast, squeezes so he can hardly breathe and passionately declares, "I love you so. I love you so," Somers withdraws from the willed force of this love and wishes that Kangaroo were dead.

There are a number of serious contradictions in Lawrence's portrayal of the Diggers that undermine the significance of the political theme in the novel. First, there is no motive for revolution in Australia and no real reason for the Diggers to exist, for unlike Italy, political affairs are running quite well. Somers feels that the real enemy is boredom (not democracy) and that the returned war heroes "were doing it all just in order to have something to do, to put a spoke in the wheel of the bosses, to make a change." And Jack's colleague, Jaz, admits: "You can die in Australia if you don't get a bit of excitement."

Second, there is an illogical gap between the violent methods of Jack and the idealistic love of his leader, Kangaroo; between Jack's anti-Semitic fulminations—"I hate the thought of being bossed . . . by Jew capitalists and bankers"—and his fanatical allegiance to the "physically warm love" of the orderly, clever, Jewish intellectual and savior. Third, Kangaroo's naive, high-minded and idealistic politics of love, which are much closer to Woodrow Wilson (whom Lawrence scorns) than to Mussolini, make him an extremely ineffectual leader. During the Socialist riots the defenseless Kangaroo bellows at the wild crowd while a gunman shoots him in the guts.

Jaz, who is aware of Kangaroo's defects as a political leader and has a greater grasp of *Realpolitik,* wants to start the revolution by having the Diggers join their enemies and inciting the Communists to act in Australia as they did in Russia: "Couldn't we get [Kangaroo] to use all his men to back Red Labour in this country, and blow a cleavage through the old system. . . . These Diggers' Clubs, they've got all the army men, dying for another scrap. And then a sort of secret organisation has ten times the hold over men than just a Labour Party or a Trades Union. He's damned clever, he's got a wonderful scheme ready. But he'll spoil it, because he'll want it all to happen without hurting anybody." When Somers puts this proposal to Kangaroo, the leader calls Jaz a traitor, rejects Somers and orders him to leave Australia.

Somers fares no better in his talk with the Labour leader, Willie Struthers. For Struthers, like his ideological adversary, also wants to base his political movement on Whitman's democratic-homosexual love of man for man: "He wanted this love, this mate-trust called into consciousness and highest honour. He wanted to set it where Whitman tried to set his Love of Comrades. It was to be the new tie between men, in the new democracy. It was to be the new passional bond in the new society." It is significant that Somers reacts to Struthers, as he did to Kangaroo, on the physical level ("I don't like him physically—something thin and hairy and spiderish") and rejects his offer to edit a Socialist newspaper because he is repelled more by his person than by his ideas.

After the complementary interviews with Struthers and Kangaroo, the action of the novel is interrupted and the climax delayed by the most lively and interesting part of the book. The retrospective and autobiographical "Nightmare" chapter describes Somers' three humiliating medical examinations, his persecution by the military authorities who ransacked his house and accused him of spying, and his expulsion from his cottage on the Cornish coast. Though Graham Hough declares that the "Nightmare" is "almost wholly irrelevant to the progress of the narrative,"[28] this chapter is, in fact, crucial to the structure and meaning of the novel.

The "Nightmare," which seems to provide a contrast between England and Australia, actually reveals the fundamental similarities of the two countries. The chapter shows the evils of mass rule in the army, which tried to compel Somers to serve a dead ideal, and in Australia, where he felt a similar dread of the democratic mob. In *Mornings in Mexico,* Lawrence compares himself to his servant Rosalino, who refused to join the army and has "a horror of serving in a mass of men, or even of being mixed up with a mass of men."[29] This fear of the army and the mob explains Somers' refusal to join the militaristic, authoritarian, violent and fascistic Diggers, who helped to create in Australia the kind of world he had just escaped in England. For Somers, who had been falsely accused of spying before the War in Germany and during the War in England, is again called a spy by Jack Callcott after the War in Australia.

Somers' dearest friend in Cornwall, John Thomas Buryan (whose Christian names are slang for penis), is based on William Henry Hocking. This Cornish farmer inspired Lawrence's homosexual treatise, "Goats and Compasses," which he burned in the great fire of all his old manuscripts just before he left Cornwall. The passionate friendship with Buryan, whom Somers connects with the Cornishman Jaz, explains why Somers is so strongly attracted to male comradeship in the political movements of *Kangaroo.*

Finally, the "Nightmare" chapter reveals why Somers left his own country: "England had lost its meaning for him. The free England had died, this England of the peace was like a corpse." It also explains why he came to Australia in search of a new mode of life and why he had to leave Australia when its oppressive politics reminded him of the morbid atmosphere in England.

The climax of the novel occurs when Struthers makes a speech to a packed Canberra Hall on the solidarity of labor, the core of Diggers count him out and annihilate him "by their moral unison," and an Anarchist bomb explodes. The chaotic mass, "struggling with the Diggers, in real blood-murder passion," inspires Somers with a blind—but ludicrously vague— urge to kill: "small as he was, [he] felt a great frenzy on him, a great longing to let go. But since he didn't *really* know whom he wanted to let go at, he was not quite carried away." Guns are fired, Kangaroo is shot, and Somers escapes to a remote Diggers' Club. There he meets Jack, who gleefully describes how, with an iron bar, he bashed out the brains of the man who shot Kangaroo. He then draws a revolting analogy between sex and power: "There's *nothing* bucks you up sometimes like killing a man—*nothing.* You feel a perfect *angel* after it. . . . Having a woman's something, isn't it? But it's a flea-bite, nothing, compared to killing your man when your blood comes up"—as in an erection. The newspaper accounts of the riot, in which three people were killed, blame the Labour incendiaries and cautiously praise Jack Callcott ("the well-known V.C."), who is neither tried nor punished for murdering two men.

When Somers visits Kangaroo, who emits a sickening smell (rather than a "magnetic effusion"), the dying leader ironically claims "Perfect love casteth out fear" (1 John 4:18) and begs Somers to save him from death, by love. Somers, who willed Kangaroo's death during their previous interview, once again rejects the Christian doctrine of love and "kills" Kangaroo: "I don't love him—I detest him. He can die. I'm glad he is dying."

Somers had always insisted: "I never take part in politics at all. They aren't my affair." Though he longs for a smash-up of the social-industrial world, he considers love and benevolence to be as dangerous and unreal as riots and revolutions. He loathes both the politicians and the working class, holds himself back from both Jack and Jaz, denies the appeals of Struthers and Kangaroo, and remains "the most forlorn and isolated creature in the world, without even a dog to his command." Somers thus resolves the conflict between artistic and political commitment more conclusively than Aaron by firmly rejecting both Fascism and Socialism. As John Worthen writes: "Somers is wooed by two conflicting political parties to be their spokesman and guide; he shows no aptitude for such a job, and they both show appalling political naivety in asking him to consider it. But Lawrence is concerned to have his hero faced by those two appeals, as any European in the twenties was faced by the rival claims of Socialists and *Fascisti.* "[30] At the end of the novel, Somers' vague and completely irrelevant commitment to the greater mystery of the dark gods—"This dark, passionate religiousness and inward sense of an inwell-

ing magnificence, direct flow from the unknowable god"—
undermines the significance of the political themes.

Jack and Victoria Callcott have tempted Somers with
power and love, threatened his marriage with political and sexual involvement. But he finally chooses individuality within
marriage. Harriet Somers prevails with her convincing criticism of his vain attempts to succeed in the world of men and
his inevitable return to the protective security of the love of
woman: "It only angered her when he thought these other
things—revolutions or governments or whatnot—higher than
their essential marriage. But then he would come to himself
and acknowledge that his marriage *was* the centre of his life,
the core, the root." For Somers, as for Lawrence, political activity is meaningless.

V

The Plumed Serpent (1926) is much closer to the historical
reality of Mexican politics than *Kangaroo* is to Australian.[31]
Lawrence's third novel of power portrays violent Mexico—
"Blackened under a too-strong sun, surcharged with the heavy
sundering electricity of the air, and tormented by the bubbling
of volcanoes away below the feet"[32]—as ripe for yet another
revolution. The country is ugly, squalid, nauseous, oppressive,
gruesome, cruel, evil, destructive, dangerous, doomed, hopeless; subject to Bolshevism, banditry, murder and outrage. Almost anything that would provide an "escape from a world
gone ghastly" seems better than this "sterility of nothingness."
Lawrence's response and solution to this intolerable chaos
evolves from his experience with Italian Fascism and is essentially the same as *Aaron's Rod* and *Kangaroo:* scorn for the de-
generate mob, hatred of Socialism and revolution, belief in
discipline, respect for authority, and admiration for a strong
and physically attractive leader.

Lawrence's grim picture of Mexico, which makes Naples
seem debonair by comparison, provides a negative contrast to
Italy; for life in Mexico certainly does not permit *dolce far
niente.* There is no animation in a Mexican market as there
is in a Mediterranean one; no gentle ceremonials or mysterious
holiness in the cheap and cynical churches as there are in Ital-

ian cathedrals. Even the moon is not lovely or friendly, as in Italy. Throughout the novel Kate Leslie is torn between her fascination with the primitive and repellent aspects of Mexico and her longing to return to the familiar civilization of Europe.

Lawrence was thoroughly familiar with the contemporary political situation in Mexico, and his novel is based on a political reality which the mythology attempts to transcend and redeem. His personal reaction to revolutionary violence was fear, tempered by a fascination with primitive power, and this is reflected in his letters as well as in *The Plumed Serpent.* In a letter to Knud Merrild on April 21, 1923, just after he arrived in Mexico City, Lawrence writes with alarm and anger: "In these states almost *every* hacienda (farm) is smashed, and you can't live even one mile outside the village or town: you will probably be robbed or murdered by roving bandits and scoundrels who still call themselves revolutionaries." Two months later, on June 27, he writes to Merrild with ironic bravado: "One could easily get a little place. But now they are expecting more revolution, and it is so risky. . . . If I can't stand Europe we'll come back to Mexico and spit on our hands and stick knives and revolvers in our belts—one really has to—and have a place here."[33] These observations appear again in the novel as Lawrence describes the "broken walls, broken houses, broken *haciendas,* along the endless desolation left by the revolutions." Kate is depressed because the fear of banditry and murder prevents her from walking out into the country; and at the bullfight the narrator remarks, "You don't elbow your neighbor if he's got a pistol on his hip and a knife at his belly."

Lawrence felt "put out by the vibration of this rather malevolent continent . . . this dark, dangerous Mexico." As Ramón tells Kate: "Whenever a Mexican cries *Viva!* he ends up with a *Muera!* When he says *Viva!* he really means *Death for Somebody or Other!* I think of all the Mexican revolutions, and I see a skeleton walking ahead of a great number of people, waving a black banner with *Viva la Muerte!*" Luis Quintanilla writes perceptively of Lawrence's ambivalence toward the country: "He was fascinated by Mexico's colorful personality and, at the same time, frightened by the dramatic events of the Mexican Revolution. He simply could not stand violence, noise, and least of all death. And there was plenty of that during the Revolution that shook the social structure of Mexico. So, Mexico's beauty enchanted Lawrence, but the Mexican political situation horrified him."[34]

Lawrence believes that Socialism is primarily responsible for the political horrors, and he hates and fears the ideology that was associated with the two revolutionary generals—Pancho Villa and Emiliano Zapata. Lawrence usually equates Mexican Socialism with personal danger, although the government of President Plutarco Calles had made some remarkable achievements.[35] Writing to Middleton Murry from Oaxaca on November 15, 1924, Lawrence reports: "The country is always unsettled. They've spread such an absurd sort of socialism everywhere—and these little Zapotec Indians are quite fierce. . . . Everything is so shaky and really so confused. . . . The Spanish-Mexican population just rots on top of the black savage mass. And socialism here is a farce of farces: except very dangerous."[36]

Lawrence's political reaction to Socialism and revolution is twofold: a desire to keep the Indian masses in the purity of their primitive innocence, and the wish for a powerful leader who will tame the Revolution and maintain the status quo. He insists, with a frightened vehemence: "Give them injustice and oppression—more and more oppression. That's the only thing that's likely to help Mexico!"[37]

In order to suppress dangerous agitators, Lawrence believes that the masses must unite "round one great chosen figure, some hero who can lead a great war, as well as administer a wide peace. . . . Men have got to choose their leaders, and obey them to the death. And it must be a system of culminating aristocracy, society tapering like a pyramid to the supreme leader." But, as Lawrence nervously warns Frieda, the leadership knife cuts both ways—especially in Mexico: " 'It's never God's will to kill a master, Frieda, until men themselves make it God's will. And they'll do it. There'll be a leader, like Villa or Zapata, or somebody stronger.' His face became intense. 'And once they have a strong leader, these people will be strong too. They'll be as merciless to their masters as their masters have been to them.' "[38] This, in brief, is a paradigm of the Mexican Revolution.

Kate Leslie, who craves strong and despises weak men (the foreign-educated Cipriano and Ramón provide a powerful contrast to her homosexual friends, Bud and Owen), unconsciously associates the Quetzalcoatl movement with her dead husband Joachim, a sacrificial leader in the fight for Irish independence. The deification of personal terror and sexual slavery near the "sperm-like" lake (which symbolizes a release of sexual energy and gigantic ejaculation of semen) obliterates Kate's sexual identity, and betrays both her personal and political ideals. Kate's role in the Quetzalcoatl pantheon is never made clear, but her abject deference to Cipriano—she kisses his feet and abandons the pleasure of orgasm—leads to a complete loss of her individuality. With Cipriano she regresses to a state of virginity, which effectively eliminates her two husbands and two children, and satisfies his overweening ego. Kate's marriage to Cipriano thus parallels the sultan-slave marriage of Ramón and Carlota (whom he calls a "stale virgin") and of Ramón and his second wife Teresa, who loves him "with a wild, virgin loyalty."

The Plumed Serpent, like *Aaron's Rod,* expresses an overwhelming need to dominate, and even extinguish, the sexual power of women. As Cipriano's atrocities increase, Kate's desires diminish: "as the sex is exhausted, gradually, a keener desire, the desire for the touch of death follows on. . . . [Then come] fatal wars and revolutions which really create nothing at all, but destroy, and leave emptiness."[39]

The novel charts "the death of her individual self," the degeneration of Kate from a woman who is revolted by the cruelty of the bullfight to one who is indifferent to Cipriano's bloody executions; from the wife of Joachim Leslie who *"can* only love a man who is fighting to *change* the world, to make it freer, more alive," to one who marries Cipriano, a "sinister to her, almost repellent" general who suppresses rebellions to preserve the interests of the conservative landowners; from "a modern woman and a woman in her own right" who states, "I'm not going to submit. . . . Why should one give in," to one who believes that "Without Cipriano to touch me and limit me and submerge my will, I shall become a horrible, elderly female. I ought to *want* to be limited. I ought to be *glad* if a man will limit me with a strong will." What Lawrence intends to be Kate's sexual apotheosis is merely her sexual degradation.

The execution scene, a savage regression to the elaborate ritual of death when "the Aztecs raised their deity to heights of horror and vindictiveness," is related to Cipriano's subjugation of Kate. When Cipriano plunges his knife into a helpless victim, he experiences "the clutching throb of [sexual] gratification as the knife strikes in and the blood spurts out!"[40] For Cipriano's "dark and powerful instinct" is actually a cruel desire to dominate Kate and make her submit to his will—the triumph of unnatural authority, of power over love. The violent events in the novel are the political manifestation of Cipriano's struggle for sexual domination, and he suppresses the rebellions of peons as well as of Kate.

The Quetzalcoatl movement, which hopes to bring back the Aztec gods and "take up the old, broken impulse that will connect us with the mystery of the cosmos," is religious rather than political. It does not attempt to inspire a traditional revolution, but a revolution in consciousness. Though Ramón is authoritarian—"There is no such thing as liberty. . . . All we can do is to choose our master"—his movement has no educational aims, social goals or political ambitions. The only Fascists in the novel are two minor characters, both condemned by Lawrence. Jésus, the eldest son of Kate's maid, wears "a black Fascisti shirt, he had the queer animal jeering of the socialists"; Don Antonio, Kate's fat landlord, "was a great Fascista, the reactionary Knights of Cortes held him in great esteem."

Ramón, in contrast to the Fascists, wants to save his country's soul and is determined to keep free from the taint of politics: "I must stand in another world, and act in another world.—Politics must go their own way, and society must do as it will." Far from doctrinaire, he vaguely insists: "I shall be First Man of Quetzalcoatl—I know no more. . . . Only the Natural Aristocrats can rise above their nation. . . . Leagues and Covenants and International Programmes. Ah, Cipriano! it's like an international pestilence." General Cipriano Viedma, who commands the Guadalajara division and backs Ramón with his army, is even less political than his idol. He blindly follows Ramón and slips "back into [the role of] the inevitable Mexican General, fascinated by the opportunity for furthering his own personal ambition and imposing his own personal will."

Though Lawrence despises the landowning class (as well as the peons and priests) and calls them depraved, corrupt and cowardly (the *hacendado* "is such a brave man, that while the soldier is violating his wife on the bed, he is hiding under the bed"), Ramón, the hero of the novel, belongs to this class. (In the same way, Lawrence condemns Mexican generals but glorifies Cipriano, a law-and-order soldier who suppresses revolutions.) Like the *hacienda* of the Bishop of Oaxaca, Ramón's large estate had been decimated by the Revolution. The irrigation aqueducts were destroyed, the water supply cut off, the land taken away, divided among the peons and reduced to a mere three hundred acres. A powerful longing for pre-revolutionary days is an important theme of the book, which is reactionary but not Fascist.

Ramón's high-minded motives for leading the anti-Christian Quetzalcoatl movement are convincingly attacked by his fanatically religious wife, Carlota. She maintains that his primary motives are male vanity, a wicked lust for power and a desire to be worshipped. Cipriano's godfather, the Bishop of Oaxaca (based on the actual Archbishop Gillow), agrees that Ramón is "smitten with the madness of pride." And even Kate, in a moment of rare lucidity, exclaims: "I loathe the very sound of Quetzalcoatl and Huitzilopochtli. I would die rather than be mixed up in it any more. Horrible, really, both Ramón and Cipriano. And they want to put it over me, with their high-flown bunk." Ramón's ceremonial hymns are not likely to appeal to "the stone-heavy passivity of resistance in the demonish," illiterate, exhausted and impoverished peons, who crave more substantial attractions. When Ramón solemnly proclaims: "I am the living Quetzalcoatl," he does not bring back the dark gods: he merely impersonates them.

Ramón's principal aim is to exploit the country's anti-ecclesiastical tradition, destroy the Catholic Church and have President Montes, backed by the army, declare Quetzalcoatl the state religion of Mexico. At the end of the novel this ambition is achieved; for the old Church is declared illegal and Quetzalcoatl becomes the national religion of the Republic.

The success of the fantastic Quetzalcoatl movement, a rebellion from the Right and against the Right, is realistically based on the long and powerful anti-clerical tradition in Mexico, on the ecclesiastical depredations during the Revolution, and on the moribund state of the Church in the 1920s. Lawrence writes that "In the revolutions, many of the churches in Mexico have been used for stables and for barracks. . . . The convents and the monasteries are most of them barracks for the rag-tag-and-bobtail soldiers." And his portrayal of the debilitated Church is an accurate account of its contemporary condition: "The Church in Mexico has to move gingerly; it is not popular, and its claws are cut. The priest may not ring the church bells for more than three minutes. Neither priests nor monks may wear any habit in the street. . . . Nevertheless, he still has influence. Processions in the streets are forbidden, but not sermons from the pulpit, nor advice from the confessional. Montes, the President, had no love for the Church, and was meditating the expulsion of all foreign priests."[41]

Even more interesting than Lawrence's precise knowledge of Church-State relations is his prediction of the religious wars that began in 1926, the year his novel was published. The reverential removal and incineration of ecclesiastical images in the Auto de Fé is not only an ironic parody of the Spanish Inquisition and a reenactment of the kind of religious procession that can still be seen on Catholic feast days, but also an accurate prophecy of future events.[42]

The Church, then, weak and vulnerable, easily succumbs to a hostile force, and its moribund condition is symbolized by Carlota (the name of the wife of the hated French Emperor Maximilian, executed—as in Manet's painting—in 1867), who crawls on her knees to the steps of the altar in a final, pathetic attempt to save the dying gods, and expires at the same time as they do. But the Church retaliates by excommunicating Ramón and Cipriano, a religious war breaks out between the followers of Quetzalcoatl and the Catholic Knights of Cortes, and the fate of the neo-Aztec movement remains uncertain.

The radical flaws of *The Plumed Serpent* are Lawrence's lack of concern for the human dignity of "the black savage mass"; his inability to create a meaningful social or religious alternative to the frightening revolutionary reality that he knew so well; and his failure to conceive the political destiny of a nation: "These old civilisations down here, they never get any higher than Quetzalcoatl. And he's just a sort of feathered snake. Who needed the smoke of a little heart's-blood now and then."[43]

VI

When Lawrence returned to Italy at the end of 1925, after his near-fatal illness in Mexico, it was immediately clear that Fascism did not provide the political solution he had been searching for. He had not supported Fascism in the early twenties, and now mocked Mussolini when he saw the results of his three years of power. When an Englishwoman, Violet Gibson, shot a bullet through the "dear heroic" Dictator's nose in 1926, Lawrence advised Lieutenant Ravagli to "put a ring through it": "Mussolini says, *Vivi pericolosamente!* and then makes millions of laws against anybody who takes a pot shot at him." Lawrence felt Fascism was not natural to the Italians, who (like the tourists) were irritated by the government. He was disgusted by Italy's lack of freedom and by its tastelessness: "Italy, humanly, isn't very interesting nowadays. Fascism, whatever it does, spreads the grand blight of boredom."[44]

The radical change in Lawrence's political beliefs—his renunciation of faith in political action and his criticism of authoritarian rule—resembles the severe disillusionment of Leftwing intellectuals at the end of the thirties. This change becomes apparent in the works he wrote during the last five years of his life. In 1925 he maintained: "I know now, it is no use trying to do anything—I speak only for myself—publicly. It is no use trying merely to modify present forms."[45] Two years later he added: "I've hated democracy since the war. But now I see I'm wrong calling for an aristocracy. What we want is a flow of life from one to another."[46]

In *The First Lady Chatterley* (written 1927), Parkin becomes a leader of factory workers and expresses hope in a Communist future. But in *John Thomas and Lady Jane,* the second version of the novel that was written immediately afterwards, Parkin advocates withdrawal and isolation, and tells Connie: "I shouldn't care if the bolshevists blew up one half of the world, and the capitalists blew up the other half, to spite them, so long as they left me and you a rabbit-hole apiece to creep in, and meet underground." She replies that she is glad he has left the factory (in contrast to the first Parkin) lest he "deteriorate into a socialist or a fascist, or something dreary and political."[47] In *Lady Chatterley's Lover* (the third version), when Clifford insists (as Lawrence did during the War and afterwards) that the masses have been ruled since time began and will have to be ruled till time ends, Connie, who has been having an affair with the proletarian gamekeeper, contradicts him and remains sceptical.

In the 1925 Epilogue to *Movements in European History,* Lawrence recants his earlier belief in the need for "one great chosen figure" and returns to his faith in the rights of the individual: "Fascism and Law and Order [are] only another kind of bullying. . . . [Fascism] degrades both the bully and those who are bullied." In *St. Mawr* (also 1925), he exposes the corruption beneath the orderly surface of Fascism when the heroine, Lou Carrington, ironically says: "Try fascism. Fascism would keep the surface of life intact, and carry on the undermining business all the better. All the better sport. Never draw blood. Keep the haemorrhage internal, invisible. And as soon as fascism makes a break—which it is bound to, because all evil works up to a break—then turn it down. With gusto, turn it down."[48]

In 1927 Lawrence condemned the Nietzschean Will and brute force of the Fascists by comparing them to the Imperial Romans who destroyed the civilization of the Etruscans. In March 1928 he told Rolf Gardiner, a disciple of the fascistic John Hargrave who had founded the Kibbo Kift movement: "One can ignore fascism in Italy for a time. But after a while, the sense of false power forced against life is very depressing."[49] Lawrence's last—and perhaps most important—political statement was made that same month in a letter to Witter Bynner, his travelling companion in Mexico. Lawrence renounced his belief in a strong military leader and turned to the new mode of thought that he expressed in *Lady Chatterley's Lover,* published in Florence later that year: "About *The Plumed Serpent* and the 'hero.' On the whole, I think you're right. The hero is obsolete, and the leader of men is a back number. After all, at the back of the hero is the militant ideal: and the militant ideal, or the ideal militant, seems to me also a cold egg. We're sort of sick of all forms of militarism and militantism, and *Miles* is a name no more, for a man. On the whole I agree with you, the leader-cum-follower relationship is a bore. And the new relationship will be some sort of tenderness, sensitive, between men and men and men and women, and not the one up one down, lead on I follow, *ich dien* sort of business."[50]

VII

Just as Lawrence's political ideas evolved during a particular moment of history, so the criticism of these ideas grew directly out of the Leftist opposition to Fascism during the 1930s and the Second World War. The Communist John Strachey expressed the first significant criticism of Lawrence's politics in *Literature and Dialectical Materialism* (1934): "The parallel between Lawrence's terminology and that of the Nazis has often been pointed out. Lawrence was a typical—indeed, the archetypal—member of the school of 'the fascist unconscious.' "[51] Since this argument was frequently repeated during the next thirty years, it is worth exposing its logical fallacy *(post hoc, ergo propter hoc)*. Lawrence, who was either unaware of Hitler or ignored him entirely, died three years before the Nazis came to power in January 1933. The parallels in terminology—not in belief or in action—must therefore be unconscious; and if Lawrence was unaware of the similarities, he cannot be blamed for them.

Emile Delavenay's dissertation, written in 1932 but not published until 1968, states: "His search for a new society and for disciples with whom to found it leads to concepts closer to those of fascism than to democratic socialism; the mental attitudes which it reveals are those on which the twentieth-century dictatorships were able to establish themselves in the minds of men."[52] Though Lawrence's concepts were "closer to" Fascism than Socialism, he never supported that totalitarian system. And the vague "mental attitudes" of Lawrence were very far from Hitler's, as Delavenay should have realized after a lifetime of studying Lawrence's works.

Another French scholar, Ernest Seillière, who published his book in 1936 (the year Hitler remilitarized the Rhineland), claimed to find the sources of Lawrence's thought in German Romanticism. Like Strachey, he discovered analogies between Lawrence's belief in a strong leader and Nazi ideology; and though there was no direct connection between the two, Seillière found Lawrence guilty of "anticipating" Hitler: "C'est surtout dans *la Fantaisie de l'inconscient* que s'accumulent les appels (spengleriens) au chef, au César de demain. Et voici un programme d'avenir à peu de choses près hitlérien: ce serait à croire que l'auteur avait pu lire *Mein Kampf* par anticipation."[53]

In 1939 William York Tindall's *D. H. Lawrence and Susan His Cow,* which William Empson called "a repulsive little book," charged: "His yearning for authority and obedience, his hatred of socialists, Catholics and international financiers, his national religions with their pagan rites, his propaganda, symbols, and storm troopers, his attitude toward women and laborers, his desire to think with his blood, and the other ways in which he anticipated Hitler appear to justify those who have regarded Lawrence as a proto-fascist." But even Tindall (who later recanted his views and wrote favorable introductions to *The Plumed Serpent* and *The Later D. H. Lawrence*) is forced to admit: "Lawrence wanted dictatorship, to be sure, but he was critical of every totalitarian system with which he was acquainted. For every favorable comment upon Mussolini and Italian fascism, Lawrence made several unfavorable comments."[54] Yet Tindall's charge cannot be accepted, despite his lenient concession, for he overstates his case and makes no distinction between the imaginary politics of *The Plumed Serpent* and Lawrence's actual political ideas. Lawrence—who chose to live most of his adult life in a Catholic country, expressed admiration for Montecassino and praised the Church in *Kangaroo*—did not hate Catholics. He died before Hitler's storm troopers became a political reality, and never commented favorably on Mussolini or Fascism.

Unlike the previous critics of Lawrence's politics, Stebelton Nulle was an American Fascist who praised Lawrence's "Fascist" tendencies in an essay of 1940. Nulle naively believed the guiding principle of Fascism is "to live intensely and fully" and that "the spirit of fascism is nowhere better expressed than in [Lawrence's] work. . . . One might say that Adolf Hitler is bringing into Western consciousness something of the insight and idealism of D. H. Lawrence."[55] Such bizarre logic needs no refutation.

The composer Cecil Gray, who lived near Lawrence in Cornwall in 1917 and was mildly satirized in *Aaron's Rod* and *Kangaroo,* had scant reason to be sympathetic. In his autobiography, *Musical Chairs* (1948), he repeats the "anticipated Hitler" argument and draws a parallel between the character of Lawrence and of Hitler:

He was, indeed, the stuff of which Hitlers are made, especially at that time [1917] when his gifts were unrecognized and he was on the verge of penury. Unsuccessful and thwarted artists are the most common type of the revolutionary politician; such, it should be remembered, was not only Hitler, but also Goebbels; not only Mussolini, but also Ciano—all of them artists *manqués.* . . . Lawrence, in fact, could easily have become a British

Hitler. Apart from many striking similarities of doctrine between them, which have become increasingly
evident in the passage of the years, there was in Lawrence also the same dark, passionate, fanatical power,
the same capacity for casting spells and captivating the
sympathies and imagination of the common people.[56]

It is of course absurd for the obscure Cecil Gray, who is largely
known through his association with Lawrence, to call the latter
an "unsuccessful and thwarted artist" and to compare him, as
a failed artist, to Hitler and Mussolini. Since Lawrence showed
no interest in political activity and had no capacity for leadership, it is extremely unlikely that he "could have become a British Hitler." This passage is, in fact, pure malice.

Though Bertrand Russell's attack on Lawrence, like Cecil
Gray's, was influenced by personal animosity and by Lawrence's satiric portrayal of Russell as Sir Joshua Matheson in
Women in Love, it was extremely damaging. For Russell, who
was dismissed from his position at Trinity College, Cambridge,
had his library seized, was refused a passport to America and
was imprisoned for four months in 1918, rightly felt he had suffered far more than Lawrence for his opposition to the War. In
the second volume of his *Autobiography* (1968), Russell, with
heavy irony and unusual vagueness, traced the origins of Lawrence's ideas to Frieda: "Somehow, she imbibed prematurely
the ideas afterwards developed by Mussolini and Hitler, and
these ideas she transmitted to Lawrence, shall we say, by blood-
consciousness." The *Autobiography* reprinted the bitterly hostile chapter on Lawrence which Russell wrote in *Portraits
From Memory* (1953). He accused Lawrence of having a passionate hatred of mankind (thus reversing Lawrence's charge
against Russell), of being a positive force for evil and of believ-
ing "that when a dictatorship was established he would be the
Julius Caesar." The "bloodless" Russell first repeats Strachey's
"anticipation" theory ("He had developed the whole philosophy of fascism before the politicians had thought of it"), next
condemns Lawrence's belief in blood-consciousness ("This
seemed to me frankly rubbish, and I rejected it vehemently")
and then abandons all logic to draw a wild inference ("though
I did not then know that it led straight to Auschwitz").[57] Despite
the absurdity, Russell's immense prestige and reputation for
intellectual clarity have led serious critics like John Harrison

to repeat this condemnation and connect Lawrence with the dictators: "In politics, the casting off of mental consciousness leads straight to the mass hysteria of the regimes of Hitler and Mussolini. Belief in the power of a natural leader, in the 'dark gods,' in irrationalism and racialism, had disastrous results in the 1930s, when Nazism gave them perverted political forms."[58]

Despite the difference in their political beliefs, the criticism of Strachey, Delavenay, Seillière, Tindall, Lehmann, Nulle, Gray, Russell and Harrison—who all base their arguments on the same unquestioned assumptions—have a great deal in common. None distinguishes between fictional creations and political reality. None attempts to show that Mussolini or Hitler were aware of Lawrence's ideas, but all try to blame Lawrence for the atrocious events that occurred after his death: the dictatorship of Hitler, storm troopers, Auschwitz. Most important, none takes into account Lawrence's renunciation of his belief in leadership and authority, and the radical change in his political ideas from 1925 to his death in 1930.

The vague style and frequent contradictions in Lawrence's political ideas, which matched the deliberate obscurity of Fascist doctrine and were often expressed in furious letters that were not intended for publication, permitted distorted interpretations of what he actually meant. Though Lawrence criticized democracy, he did not support Fascism, which was absolutely opposed to his profound belief in spontaneity and individuality.

Lawrence did not take part in political activities, though he had ample opportunity to do so while living in Italy and Germany in the 1920s. The ideas expounded in Lawrence's letters and novels were purely theoretical and had no relation to his actual life, for Lawrence was no leader of men. He could not find more than one person to follow him to America, could never establish his long-sought Rananim, was deceived by both his wife and his closest friend. As E. R. Dodds said of Yeats: "He admired men of action and would have liked to be one, but his outspoken contempt for the ordinary man disqualified him from any sort of national leadership."[59]

In the novels of power, Aaron refuses to follow Lilly, Somers rejects Kangaroo, and though Kate submits to Cipriano, her choice is more personal than political. In each of the novels the ideas about authority and leadership are constantly attacked by a solid woman—Tanny Lilly, Harriet Somers, Kate Leslie—who opposes political fantasies with practical reality. Lawrence, always vague about the actual details of politics, is never able to formulate a consistent and convincing solution to the problem of postwar chaos.

Until 1925 Lawrence was a determined authoritarian who disliked democracy and socialism. He advocated strong leadership that would ensure a peaceful and stable society in which artists and intellectuals led a privileged existence. He therefore aligned himself with the source of power that controlled the ignorant masses, and agreed with Wyndham Lewis' aristocratic belief: "Instead of the vast organization to exploit the weaknesses of the Many, should we not possess one for the exploitation of the intelligence of the Few?"[60] After 1925 Lawrence rejected his belief in a powerful leader and turned to the tenderness of *Lady Chatterley's Lover* and the resurrection theme.

8

The Paintings

BETWEEN 1926 AND 1928 Lawrence painted the twenty-five pictures that were exhibited at the Warren Gallery, London, in June 1929. During the same period he wrote his major works on the resurrection theme: "Sun" (1926), *The Man Who Died* (1928) and the three versions of *Lady Chatterley's Lover* (1928); brought out the Florentine edition of his controversial novel; visited the archeological sites and composed his book, *Etruscan Places;* and translated Verga's *Cavalleria Rusticana* (1928). When he was living outside Florence at the Villa Mirenda in early November 1926, a single imaginative impulse inspired both his painting and his novel. On November 11 he told the Huxleys: "I've already painted a picture on one of the canvases," and four days later he wrote his publisher Martin Secker: "I have begun a novel in the Derbyshire coal mining districts— already rather improper." The same spark recurred six months later in May 1927, when he informed Mabel Luhan: "I've finished the 'Resurrection,' also a story on the same theme."[1] *Resurrection* is analogous to *The Man Who Died* just as *The Lizard* is to "Sun" and *Boccaccio Story* to *Lady Chatterley's Lover.* The paintings are a visual representation of the themes Lawrence was simultaneously expressing in his writing: the triumph of pagan over Christian values—of the flesh over the spirit—and the resurrection of paganism in the landscape and people of Italy.

Though Lawrence loved folk art and seemed relieved when there were no Peruginos to see in Nuoro, he was a knowledgeable if eccentric art critic and an accomplished painter. He had always loved pictures, and as a young man trained himself as an artist by making copies of great Italian paintings: "I think the greatest pleasure I ever got came from copying Fra Angelico's 'Flight into Egypt' and Lorenzetti's big picture of the Thebiad, in each case working from photographs and putting in my own colour; or perhaps even more a Carpaccio picture in Venice. . . . None of [the Dutch masters] gave me the deep thrill of the Italians, Carpaccio, or the lovely 'Death of Procris' in the National Gallery, or that 'Wedding' with the scarlet legs, in the Uffizi, or a Giotto from Padua. I must have made many copies in my day, and got endless joy out of them."[2]

Lawrence was a successful art teacher in the Davidson Road School, Croydon, in 1909. He made Greiffenhagen's *The Idyll* (Liverpool), which he frequently copied and gave to his girls as a present, the symbolic center of his first novel, *The White Peacock*, and used Fra Angelico's *The Last Judgement* to provide a visual representation of the themes of *The Rainbow*.[3] Paul Morel in *Sons and Lovers* is an accomplished painter who wins a prize in the annual Nottingham Castle exhibition; Tom Brangwen in *The Rainbow* and Loerke in *Women in Love* are both professional artists.

Lawrence's painter-friend Knud Merrild reports that "A constant item in Lawrence's travelling outfit was a small portfolio of coloured prints, chiefly of Renaissance and primitive Italian paintings. Although he did not care to possess things, here was something he seemed to treasure very much." Lawrence planned to write a *History of Italian Painting* for children, though that project never materialized. And in the essay on Maurice Magnus he described the view from Montecassino as it was portrayed by Renaissance painters: "Roads, river, streams, a world in accurate and lively detail, with mountains sticking up abruptly and rockily, as the old painters painted it. I think there is no way of painting Italian landscape except that way—that started with Lorenzetti and ended with the sixteenth century."[4] Lawrence perceptively discussed the works of Botticelli, Correggio, Raphael and Michelangelo (as well as those of Boccioni and the Italian Futurists) in the "Study of Thomas Hardy."

In Lawrence's middle years, when the desire to paint was

quiescent, he became close friends with a number of talented painters—Mark Gertler, Dora Carrington, Earl Brewster, Dorothy Brett, Jan Juta and Kai Gotzsche—was painted by the last three and sculpted by Jo Davidson. He was eager to acquire their expertise and to compete with them in their own medium of expression. The patient Brett reports (as if speaking to Lawrence directly) that in Oaxaca in 1925 Lawrence, who believed formal art training obstructed direct vision, grabbed her paint brush and "improved" her work: " 'Do look at the mountain. It has great bare toes, where it joins the desert. Here, let me have a try.' Down you sit, and with delicate finger-touches, you proceed to give the mountain its toes. You roughen fir-trees on the mountain and darken the blue of the sky. 'You are dumb, Brett; you don't look at things; you have no eyes.' "[5] He later collaborated with Brett and Frieda on *The Kiowa Ranch,* a painting of riders in a vast New Mexican landscape.

Maria Huxley provided the immediate stimulus for Lawrence's paintings of November 1926 when she drove up to the Villa Mirenda and presented him with four rather large and very tempting stretched canvases, which had been abandoned in her house. Lawrence responded immediately and found: "It's rather fun, discovering one can paint one's own ideas and one's own feelings—and a change from writing." But it was also a complementary means of expression. Lawrence, who waited for the moment of inspiration and sometimes dashed off novels in a few months, made no preliminary studies or sketches. He believed the creation of a painting was similar to writing and "comes clean out of instinct, intuition and sheer physical action. . . . The picture itself comes in the first rush, or not at all. It is only when the picture has come into being that one can struggle and make it *grow* to completion. . . . [There must be] concentration of delight or exaltation of visual discovery."[6]

Lawrence's paintings confirm Baudelaire's belief: "It is one of the characteristic symptoms of the spiritual condition of our age that all the arts aspire, if not to take one another's place, at least reciprocally to lend one another new powers." Lawrence believed there was an inherent relationship of the arts. His "interest in painting," writes Mervyn Levy, "though clearly incidental to the main body of his work, is nevertheless fundamental to an embracing understanding of his evolution as a man, and writer."[7]

The novel is essentially a linear art which presents a temporal sequence of events, while painting fixes reality and produces a simultaneity of experience. Lawrence's paintings attempt to transcend the limitations of fiction and to transform successive moments into immediate images. The correspondence between his painting and writing helps to explain how he shapes his vision of the world and enforces his way of seeing on the observer, for, as Proust maintains: "Painting can pierce to the unchanging reality of things, and so establish itself as a rival of literature."[8]

The most direct and powerful influence on Lawrence's paintings are not Cézanne and the Post-Impressionists, whom he later discussed in "Introduction to These Paintings," but rather the tomb paintings of the ancient Etruscans. Though Lawrence did not visit the Etruscan towns until April 1927, he had seen their art in museums like the Villa Giulia in Rome and described the "sensitive-footed, subtly-smiling Etruscans" in his poem "Cypresses," written in Tuscany in 1920. Lawrence, like the Etruscan painters of the dancing *Masker* (which he copied in embroidery) and of the birds and fish in the fresco of *Four Men Fishing*,[9] loved dance and ritual and delighted in natural creatures. Both Lawrence and the Etruscans emphasized the sexual organs of their highly stylized rust-colored figures. Lawrence praised "the subtlety of Etruscan painting . . . [which] lies in the wonderfully suggestive *edge* of the figures. It is not outlined. It is not what we call 'drawing.' It is the flowing contour where the body suddenly leaves off, upon the atmosphere."

Lawrence also related the color of the Italian peasants to his imaginative conception of the ancient people: "Men are nearly always painted a darkish red, which is the colour of many Italians when they go naked in the sun, as the Etruscans went."[10] He was attracted to their mysterious, primitive and violent quality; and tried to recapture an art that was exotic, dynamic and vital; sensuous, spontaneous and passionate; lyrical, joyous and free. Etruscan paintings like the *Wrestlers,* which foreshadows Lawrence's *Renascence of Men,* and the lively *Red-Figured Stamnos,*[11] whose brilliant color prefigures *Red Willow Trees,* portray the kind of dramatic action that Lawrence admired and re-created in his own art. The obliteration of many Etruscan paintings made the remnants seem even more precious: "Fragments of people at banquets, limbs that dance without dancers, birds that fly in nowhere, lions whose devouring heads are devoured away! Once it was all bright and dancing: the delight of the underworld; honouring the dead with wine, and flutes playing for a dance, and limbs whirling and pressing. And it was a deep and sincere honour rendered to the dead and to the mysteries."[12] The Etruscans' obsessive concern for the fate of the dead made their art a constant meditation on the nature and end of death, and their paintings were a "material communion between the living and the dead."[13]

John Russell has summarized the defects of Lawrence's paintings (Brewster reports that he sometimes used his thumb instead of a brush), which lack subtlety and are weak in draftsmanship: "He had almost no natural gift, his acquired skills were few and insufficient, and his subject-matter was simplistic to the point of absurdity."[14] But this judgment is too severe. It misses the essential effect of Lawrence's art which, he believed, must "hit deep into the senses" and, like Van Gogh's landscapes, make a "violent assault on the emotions."[15] For Lawrence, who disliked abstract painting because it was removed from life, preferred a picture that expressed passion and appealed to "the whole sensual self: as such it must have a meaning of its own, and a concerted action." Lawrence was more Etruscan than Greek; and as Herbert Read observes, "was an expressionist, an extreme example of that type of artist who seeks a direct correspondence between feeling and representation, to the neglect of the more sophisticated values of proportion and harmony."[16]

The most striking aspect of Lawrence's paintings, and of *Lady Chatterley's Lover,* was the desire to provoke, to shock, to challenge the repressive attitude toward sex and to release this "rather lovely and almost holy" aspect of pagan life from the deadly stranglehold of Christianity. He announced his aesthetic credo to the gentle Buddhist, Earl Brewster: "I put a phallus, a lingam you call it, in each one of my pictures somewhere. And I paint no picture that won't shock people's castrated social spirituality. I do this out of positive belief that the phallus is a great sacred image; it represents a deep, deep life which has been denied in us, and still is denied." Yet Lawrence recognized the powerful opposition and hostility to his art, and wanted to execute a basilisk-painting that would slay with its stare the cowardly, the repressed and the timorous: "I feel that people *can't even look* at them. They glance, and look quickly away. I wish I could paint a picture that would just *kill* every cowardly and ill-minded person that looked at it. My word, what a slaughter!"[17]

Lawrence's most provocatively sexual pictures—*The Rape of the Sabine Women* (which he well-named "A Study in Arses"), *Leda* (a crude version of a subject with a great iconographic tradition), *Fight with an Amazon* (a rape scene in which jackal-like dogs encourage the satyr to assault the woman and put his foot in her crotch), *Close Up: Kiss* (with its thick-lipped lecherous lovers) and *The Mango Tree* (where the man squeezes the woman's flaccid breasts)—are his least successful works of art. He is much more effective when he introduces humor, tenderness, harmony and mystery into his paintings of naked men and women. Lawrence wryly called the charming *A Holy Family,* his first painting of 1926, "the 'Unholy Family,' because the *bambino*—with a *nimbus*—is just watching anxiously to see the young man give the semi-nude young woman *un gros baiser.*"[18] The nude figures in *Family on a Verandah* convey a feeling of reverence as the crouching man admires his reclining wife and their children play in the foreground. The nude figures are similar in the two companion pieces: *The Lizard,* where their mysterious communion is expressed through the magnetic Mediterranean saurian; and *Under the Hay-Stack,* where the muscular man rests his head and back against the cheek and breast of the seated woman.

Lawrence's major paintings fall into three main groups: direct depictions of the Italian landscape and people, which are analogous to *Twilight in Italy* and *Sea and Sardinia;* the closely related pagan scenes, which are similar in style and feeling to *Etruscan Places;* and the works on the resurrection theme, which are connected to his writings of 1926–28 and to *Apocalypse,* and reveal the triumph of paganism over Christianity.

The early and purely conventional watercolor, *Italian Scene with Boat* (1913), is executed in Lawrence's tame prewar style and provides a useful standard of comparison for his later works. The delicate pastel colors and sophisticated composition of *Italian Landscape* (1928) provide a spectacular contrast to the seascape. The scene suggests Taormina, for in the background a church stands on a high red cliff, overlooking the pale blue sea which is sharply separated from the yellow sky. In the foreground and leaning toward the curve of the hills, a dark

Gauguin-like peasant woman, with hair pulled straight back and a stylized, almost Byzantine face, tends two black goats who are nibbling at the fruit of a cactus plant.

Boccaccio Story is one of Lawrence's largest and most ambitious paintings. Richard Aldington notes that Boccaccio, "who is the very essence of country Tuscany, was one of the few authors he always loved, a man filled with that warm instinctive life Lawrence wanted so much to see around him." And in "Pornography and Obscenity" (1929), Lawrence urged that Boccaccio be used as a healthy antidote to obscene art: "Today Boccaccio should be given to everybody young or old, to read if they like. Only a natural fresh openness about sex will do any good, now we are being swamped by secret or semi-secret pornography."[19]

The painting is based on the first story of the third day of *The Decameron* (c. 1350) and concerns the peasant Masetto di Lamporecchio who pretends to be mute, becomes a gardener in a convent and sleeps with all the nuns. The story refutes the naive idea that a nun "is no longer a woman and is no longer sensible of feminine appetites," for the nuns, who wish to taste the fabled delights of men, sleep secretly with Masetto and think they are safe with him. But after lying with the Abbess, he breaks his forced silence and complains that he cannot continue to service nine nuns. They then make him bailiff, and his profitable job ensures his secrecy.

The painting portrays the moment in the garden when the Abbess finds the handsome Masetto, exhausted from both his agricultural and sexual labors. He is "stretched out asleep under the shade of an almond-tree" as the wind lifts his clothes and reveals his sexual parts. Masetto's sprawling pose is modelled on that of the sleeping peasant in Brueghel's *The Harvesters* (1565); and the lines from the deeply furrowed field and from the V of his massive open thighs all converge on his penis. The long file of fascinated nuns, "in frocks like lavender crocuses," large bibs and wide flat hats, passes through the orchard of fruit trees and stares fixedly at their somnolent lover. Lawrence called it a "nice improper story, that tells itself."[20]

In *Contadini* the powerful head (with its helmet of hair, deep-set eyes, Roman nose and heavy moustache) and the muscular nude torso (seated and looking downward to the left, with genitals in view) are modelled on Pietro Pini, who lived near the Villa Mirenda. Harry Moore notes that the figure also seems like an idealization of the young Lorenzo. In his review of the Warren Gallery exhibition, Frank Rutter wrote in the *Sunday Times:* "Technically his best exhibit is the half-length male nude entitled *Contadini,* in which we feel there has been a genuine personal search for form as well as colour."[21]

The four pagan paintings combine the bodies of the modern Italian *contadini* with the spirit of the ancient Etruscans. Lawrence described *Fauns and Nymphs* as "a nice canvas of sun-fauns and sun-nymphs laughing at the Crucifixion—but I had to paint out the Crucifixion,"[22] which left an empty space in the background. In the center of the picture a bearded, bronze-skinned Lawrence, with a lecherous grimace, embraces a large-breasted Frieda-figure, who stares up at him wistfully. The head of another dark faun looks out from the bottom of the painting, while a nymph and faun gaze down at Lawrence from the left. Though the skin tones are warm and glowing, the mood is strangely static.

Unlike the somber American Indians in *Mornings in Mexico,* who "with bodies bent a little forward, shoulders and breasts loose and heavy, feet powerful but soft, tread the rhythm into the centre of the earth," the Dionysian participants in *Yawning, Fire Dance* and *Dance Sketch,* stretch backward, fling their arms in the air and dance belly to belly. In *Yawning* the dancers are watched by a seated woman, who puts up her hair as her feet dangle in a circular pool of flowing water. In *Fire Dance* the ecstatic couple swirl around a tall phallic fire, surrounded by a sinister grove of tree trunks with branches stripped of leaves. And in *Dance Sketch* the ruddy male and pallid female, elongated like dancers in Matisse, are joined by a spritely goat who dances on his hind legs. The effect of this overtly pagan grey-yellow painting, in which the slim tree trunks are bent to echo the whirling vortex of their bodies, is more dreamlike than realistic. These figures, like the Etruscans and the Indians, are "experiencing a delicate, wild inward delight, participating in the natural mysteries."[23]

In *Renascence of Men,* the first picture in the resurrection group—where renewal is achieved in the *flesh*—one naked man kneels with his head between the feet of his seated friend, who leans forward to embrace him. The painting bears a close affinity to the wrestling scene in *Women in Love,* where Birkin hopes that "the swift, tight limbs, the solid white backs, the physical junction of two bodies clinched into oneness,"[24] will help him to achieve a mental and spiritual intimacy with Crich.

Throwing Back the Apple, in which "Adam and Eve [are] pelting the Old Lord-God with apples, and driving him out of paradise," is thematically tied to *Flight Back into Paradise,* "a nice big canvas, Eve dodging back into Paradise, between Adam and the Angel at the gate, who are having a fight about it—and leaving the world in flames in the far corner behind her." In *Throwing Back the Apple* the three figures are extremely awkward: Adam, his back to the viewer; Eve, crouching and facing him; God, wide-hipped and white-bearded, receiving the missile. Though Eve has sinned, Adam, on behalf of future mankind, refuses to accept the penalty of sin and death, and flings the offensive fruit back at the Deity, who arranged their fall from grace. *Flight Back into Paradise* suggests that God refused to accept the apple and drove them from the Garden of Eden. In this apocalyptic picture the red-haired Eve, wired for mechanical efficiency and attached to a tall-chimneyed factory in the modern world, flees from industrial captivity and attempts to return to paradise. Philip Trotter, who credits Lawrence with more sensitivity and significance than the picture reveals, notes "the compacted tragedy, pathos, and satire in the poignant face, struggling form, and huddled figure of the machine-shackled Eve."[25] She is helped by a black-bearded, pot-bellied Adam, who restrains the flaming sword of the archangel Michael, which cuts through the yellow blades of fire that fall from the sky at the end of the world.

"I finished my 'Resurrection' picture," Lawrence irreverently informed Earl Brewster, "and like it. It's Jesus stepping up, rather grey in the face, from the tomb, with his old ma helping him from behind, and Mary Magdalen easing him up towards her bosom in front." The painting is actually more like a Deposition of Christ from the cross than a triumphant Resurrection from the tomb, for there is nothing in the Gospels about "helping" Christ; he has risen before the women arrive, and they find the tomb empty. Lawrence suggests "Jesus stepping up" by the raised right knee in the foreground rather than by a powerful surge of his body. The emergence of the pallid, bearded, snout-nosed Lawrence-figure in the center of the painting is painful and almost involuntary; he still wears the doomed and distant expression of the Crucifixion. The Virgin, with red kerchief and long black-striped toga, has the intent look of a nurse handling an invalid; the red-haired Magdalen, her face hidden by Christ, wears a red and green belted gown that leaves her right breast exposed. The *Resurrection* does not portray the glorious rebirth of Christ, but rather the Christian repression of man's vital life. It expresses Lawrence's deeply felt belief: "We have lost the cosmos. . . . The great range of responses that have fallen dead in us *have* to come to life again. It has taken two thousand years to kill them. Who knows how long it will take to bring them to life?"[26]

The exhibition of paintings that opened at the Warren Gallery on June 14, 1929 was a popular success and drew 12,000 visitors, partly because Lawrence had again become notorious after the confiscation in England of privately printed copies of *Lady Chatterley's Lover.* But the combination of blasphemy and indecency was too provocative, and on July 5 the gallery was raided by the police. "You have heard of the catastrophe, of course," Lawrence wrote to Maria Huxley, "13 pictures seized and in gaol—yours among them—and threatened to be burnt—*auto-da-fe.*" *Boccaccio Story* and *Fight with an Amazon* precipitated the crisis and every painting with pubic hair was instantly seized. The fact that a copy of Blake's *Pencil Drawings* was also impounded on the same charge did not soften the blow.

Dorothy Warren wanted to fight the case. But Lawrence, who had been through the costly suppression of *The Rainbow* in 1915 and was under attack for *Lady Chatterley's Lover,* was weary of the martyr's role. He was now an older, a wiser—and a dying man. He feared another disaster, wanted above all to rescue his paintings and urged her to accept the authorities' offer to give back the pictures in return for a promise that they would never again be exhibited in England:

I think it's a mistake to want to go to High Court. What to do? prove that the pictures are not obscene? but they are not, so how to prove it? And if they go against you there, then more is lost than will be got back in years. No, no, I want you to accept the compromise. I do not want my pictures to be burned, under any circumstances or for any cause. The law, of course, must be altered—it is blatantly obvious. Why burn my pictures to prove it? There is something sacred about my pictures, and I will not have them burnt.[27]

On August 10, two days after the court hearing at Great Marlborough Street, Lawrence told Pino Orioli that the volumes of reproductions that accompanied the exhibition were going to be destroyed: "I had telegrams to say: Pictures to be returned, books to be burned. Let them burn their own balls, the fools. This has given me a great sickness of England."[28] Lawrence expressed his outrage in three poems—"13,000 People," "Innocent England" and "Give Me a Sponge"—which were published in *Nettles,* just after his death in 1930:

> But it can't be so, for they behaved
> like lunatics looking, they bubbled and raved
>
> or gloated or peeped at the simple spot
> where a fig-leaf might have been, but was not. . . .
>
> Virginal, pure policemen came
> and hid their faces for very shame,
>
> while they carried the shameless things away
> to gaol, to be hid from the light of day. . . .
>
> Ah, my nice pictures, they are fouled, they are
>   dirtied,
> not by time, but by unclean breath and eyes
> of all the sordid people that have stared at them
>   uncleanly
> looking dirt on them, and breathing on them
>   lies.[29]

Lawrence's paintings are interesting both in themselves and as the work of a literary genius. The aim of all his art was to change people's ways of thinking and feeling, and to make the "dirty" seem holy. But his long residence abroad had put him out of touch with the morality of contemporary England; and after the hostile response to his Florentine novel, it was naive to imagine that his didactic and egoistic paintings would be well received. Lawrence was determined to shock the English public, but surprised when the self-willed disaster took place. England was not yet ready to receive his pagan revelation, and he was not redeemed until 1960, at the successful trial of *Lady Chatterley's Lover.*

9

The Resurrection Theme

I

THE THEME OF RESURRECTION originates in Lawrence's early exposure to evangelical Christianity. It is complicated by his simultaneous identification with and rejection of Christ: his view of himself as prophet and redeemer, martyr and messiah of a decaying civilization, and his hostility to the elements of Christianity he thought repressive and life-denying. Lawrence's ambivalent attitude to Christianity became especially significant in his work in February 1925, just after completing *The Plumed Serpent,* when he became gravely ill in Oaxaca and had to confront the likelihood of his own death. The doctor confirmed Frieda's greatest fears when he told her: "Take him to the ranch; it's his only chance. He has T.B. in the third degree. A year or two at the most."[1] After this nearly fatal experience, Lawrence abandoned his faith in a strong leader and his hope for a political solution to the problems of postwar chaos, which he had explored in the novels of power during 1921–25. He returned to his prewar belief in the regeneration of society through the personal relations of men and women, and portrayed characters who defied disease and experienced, in Italy, a rebirth in *this* life.

Lawrence, brought up in a strict evangelical tradition, recalled that the Bible permeated his consciousness and "became an influence which affected all the processes of emotion and thought." He often used resurrection imagery, identified himself with Christ and felt a personal mission to redeem society. Contrasting England and Italy during a brief trip to London in December 1923, he wrote: "It's all the dead hand of the past, over here, infinitely heavy, and deadly determined to put one down. It won't succeed, but it's like struggling with the stone lid of the tomb." Lawrence was especially sensitive to Good Friday, and in 1927 he told Mabel Luhan: I'm "suffering from a change of life, and a queer sort of recoil, as if one's whole soul were drawing back from connection with everything. This is the day when they put Jesus in the tomb—and really, those three days in the tomb begin to have a terrible significance and reality to me. And the Resurrection is an unsatisfactory business—just *noli me tangere* and no more."[2]

Yet Lawrence's relation to Christianity was essentially negative, for he disapproved of its dreary repression and used its imagery in an attempt to lead society back to a pre-Christian, pagan awareness of vital possibilities. He preached the radical limitations of Christ to his own disciple, Dorothy Brett: "Christ was a rotter, though a fine rotter. He never *experienced* life as the old Pagan Gods did. His merit was that he went through with his job: but that was soft, squashy and also political—a labor leader. He never knew animals, or women, from a child—never. He held forth in the temple and never *lived.* He was out to die, that's what makes his preaching disastrous." In *Phoenix* he exclaimed, even more forcefully: "The history of our era is the nauseating and repulsive history of the crucifixion of the procreative body for the glorification of the spirit, the mental consciousness." And in *Apocalypse* he maintained: "What man passionately wants is his living wholeness and his living unison. . . . Man wants his physical fulfilment first and foremost, since now, once and once only, he is in the flesh and potent."[3] To Lawrence, the survival of the spirit was not enough: there must also be a resurrection of the body. He was determined to transform the Christian myth—maintaining its images but abandoning its renunciation—and to achieve the promise of salvation while on earth.

The resurrection theme was Lawrence's personal and artistic response to the threat of death. He had been an invalid throughout his life; and in 1930, when he lay dying in Vence, he told Frieda: "I have had bronchitis since I was a fortnight old." As early as June 1913 David Garnett noticed that after a fit of coughing Lawrence's handkerchief was "spotted with bright arterial blood." While living at the Villa Mirenda in July 1927 Lawrence had a massive hemorrhage: "He called from his room in a strange, gurgling voice," Frieda wrote. "I ran and found him lying on his bed; he looked at me with shocked eyes while a slow stream of blood came from his mouth."[4] In January 1930, Dr. Andrew Morland, the tuberculosis specialist who came from London to Bandol to examine Lawrence, stated he "had obviously been suffering from pulmonary tuberculosis for a very long time—probably 10 or 15 years."[5] After Lawrence's death Aldous Huxley said that for the last two years of his life Lawrence had been like a flame that miraculously burned on though it had no fuel to feed it.

The poignant letters that Lawrence wrote during the last months of his life reveal his brave but hopeless fight against tuberculosis. Always reluctant to face the reality of his illness, he at first blamed the winter climate and decaying atmosphere of Europe: "This winter makes me know I shall just die if I linger on like this in Europe any more; and what's the good of my dying! And anyhow it's so wearying and painful being ill. . . . I do want to do something about my health, for I feel my life leaving me, and I believe it's this old moribund Europe just killing me."[6] In February 1929, when he weighed only ninety pounds, he emphasized the disease of his bronchials, belly and liver rather than his lungs, and still refused to recognize the immediate danger of death: "The lung has moved very little since Mexico, in five years. But the broncs are awful, and they have inflamed my lower man, the *ventre* and the liver. I suppose that's why I've gone so thin—I daren't tell you my weight—but I've lost a lot this winter, can't understand why. . . . The lung trouble is slight, but the bronchial-asthma condition very bad, it uses up my strength—and I've lost my appetite. . . . I'm not in any sudden danger—but in slow danger." And at the end of his last month—he died on March 2, 1930—he finally admitted: "I am rather worse here—such bad nights, and cough, and heart, and pain decidedly worse here—and miserable. Seems to me like *grippe,* but they say not. It's not a good place—shan't stay long—I'm better in a house—I'm miserable."[7]

Frieda shared Lawrence's belief that the depressing routine of a clinic would stifle his creative genius, and felt that her own marvellous power could resurrect and cure—or at least strengthen and revive—the man who had nearly died. Huxley explains this mysterious dependence on Frieda in a fascinating letter of October 1932: "Lawrence was, in some strange way dependent on her presence, physically dependent, as one is dependent on the liver in one's belly, or one's spinal marrow. I have seen him on two occasions rise from what I thought was his death bed, when Frieda, who had been away, came back after a short absence."[8] Lawrence asked Frieda to stay with him one night in February 1930, and she later described her inability to strengthen him: "One night he asked me: 'Sleep with me,' and I did ... all night I was aware of his aching inflexible chest, and all night he must have been so sadly aware of my healthy body beside him ... always before, when I slept by the side of him, I could comfort and ease him ... now no more. . . . He was falling away from life and me, and with all my strength I was helpless." Yet Lawrence never entirely gave up hope that he would recover: " 'Come when the sun rises,' he said, and when I came he was glad, so very glad, as if he would say: 'See, another day is given me.' "[9]

The resurrection theme had often been evoked at the conclusion of Lawrence's works. In *Sons and Lovers,* Paul Morel rejects the direction of darkness after his mother's death and "walked towards the faintly humming, glowing town, quickly." In *The Rainbow,* Ursula "saw in the rainbow the earth's new architecture, the old, brittle corruption of houses and factories swept away, the world built up in a living fabric of Truth, fitting to the over-arching heaven." *Look! We Have Come Through!* celebrates a rebirth in the flesh after his mother's death and Frieda's moribund marriage. And in *The Lost Girl* and *Aaron's Rod,* Alvina and Aaron find a new life in Italy after escaping from England.

Virtually all the works that Lawrence wrote after the Mexican illness and during the last five years of his life concern the resurrection theme: "The Woman Who Rode Away," *St. Mawr, The Virgin and the Gipsy,*[10] "The Flying Fish" (all 1925); *The Plumed Serpent* and "Sun" (both 1926); *Etruscan Places* (written 1927); *Lady Chatterley's Lover* and *The Man Who Died* (both 1928); "The Risen Lord," "Bavarian Gentians," "The Ship of Death" and *Apocalypse* (all 1929). These thematically unified works were Lawrence's final response to the despair of the War years as well as to his own death—which was always immanent during this period. In "The Flying Fish," which "was written so near the borderline of death, that I have never been able to carry it through, in the cold light of day," he declared: "Even as the flying fish, when he leaves the air and recovereth his element in the depth, plunges and inevitably rejoices. So will tall men rejoice, after their flight of fear, through the thin air, pursued by death."[11]

The three works of 1926–28 that are most clearly connected to Lawrence's paintings and to the resurrection theme that dominated the last phase of his career and was realized in Italy are the story "Sun" and the novel *Lady Chatterley's Lover* —both of which reveal the characteristic movement from illness to health, from an arty society at the beginning of the work to a sensual cure at the end—and the novella *The Man Who Died.* Finally, Lawrence's greatest poem, "The Ship of Death," directly inspired by his vision of the Etruscan tombs, transforms the resurrection theme into pagan terms and expresses his acceptance of death.

II

"Sun," Lawrence's only Italian story, was written in Spotorno in December 1925 and set in Taormina. The pagan element was influenced by the sun worship in Taos and related to "The Woman Who Rode Away" (the title story of a 1928 volume that included "Sun"), in which the woman is sacrificed when the red setting sun sends its ray through a column of ice. Lawrence's sun worship was more theoretical than practical, for he knew that intense sunlight was bad for tuberculosis and wrote from Taormina in March 1921: "The sun is dangerous these months—it has a radio-chemical action on the blood which simply does for me. I avoid it. The thing is to keep *cool*— not get hot at all." Yet toward the end of his life, when he was desperate for any form of vitality, he said: "I don't think I could live in a sunless country any more," and advocated the sun cult in *Apocalypse:* "We can only get the sun by a sort of worship. . . . By *going forth* to worship the sun, worship that is felt in the blood. . . . Start with the sun [he concluded], and the rest will slowly, slowly happen."[12]

The pagan aspect, the seasonal cycle, the ritual and the fable of regeneration in "Sun" all foreshadow *Lady Chatterley's Lover* and *The Man Who Died.* Like Juliet's, Connie Chatterley's "body was flattening and going a little harsh. It was as if it had not had enough sun and warmth; it was a little greyish and sapless." Like Juliet's doctor, Michaelis urges Connie: "Come to Sicily with me, it's lovely there just now. You want sun! You want life! Why you're wasting away!"[13] Connie's naked dance in the rain is like Juliet's naked immersion in the sun.

The opening injunction—"Take her away, into the sun"— echoes the command of Lawrence's doctor in Mexico in 1925: "Take him to the ranch; it's his only chance." And the couple's gloomy separation on the New York dock recalls Frieda's bitter departure from Lawrence in the summer of 1923. Mabel Luhan reports, with some satisfaction: "I had heard that he and Frieda had gone to New York to sail for England, but that they had quarrelled at the last moment and he had let her sail alone. . . . She told me, long afterwards, that she thought they had come to a final separation."[14]

Standing in opposition to this disease and dreariness—as Mellors' wood and Venice oppose Wragby Hall and Clifford's mines in *Lady Chatterley*—is Lawrence's idealized description of a lush and fragrant Sicily that alludes to Fontana Vecchia and Mount Etna:

> She had a house above the bluest of seas, with a vast garden, or vineyard, all vines and olives steeply, terrace after terrace, to the strip of coast-plain; and the garden full of secret places, deep groves of lemon far down in the cleft of the earth, and hidden, pure green reservoirs of water; then a spring issuing out of a little cavern, where the old Sicules had drunk before the Greeks came; and a grey goat bleating, stabled in an ancient tomb, with all the niches empty. There was a scent of mimosa, and beyond, the snow of the volcano.[15]

After dismissing her nagging, citified mother, Juliet watches the naked sun rise like an erection and surrenders her naked self to the personified penetrating sun, who connects with and flows into her body, and *"knew* her, in the cosmic carnal [sun-woman] sense of the word." Her little boy, who rolls a sun-like orange across the red tiles of the terrace, also becomes acclimatized and transformed from his grey father's to his golden mother's son. Like Juliet, he no longer fears the sun, emerges from his shell, sheds his civilized tension and accepts even the poisonous gold-brown snakes (as Lawrence failed to do in the Sicilian poem "Snake") as a natural part of the harmonious environment.

Her ritual is shattered by the unexpected appearance of her grey-faced, grey-garbed husband, who contaminates the Eden of Italy with the lifeless world of America. He is led down the twisty path to his wife, standing, erect and nude, by her servant, "the old woman of Magna Graecia," who saw at once that he was "not a man, poor thing." The monastic husband, "dazed with admiration, but also, at a deadly loss," is frightened by Juliet's hostility and does not know how to respond to her strange behavior. (His son, now playing with bitter lemons, ignores his feeble greeting.) Juliet immediately places the burden of responsibility on him and vaguely demands: "What are you going to do about it, Maurice?" Maurice, grey from earning money to support his solar wife and child, finds it difficult to follow her example and impossible to compete sexually with the sun. Apparently defeated, he submits to her wishes and agrees that she can do anything she likes.

Juliet, who walks through the fields completely naked (an impossibility in a Mediterranean country), then directs her attention to the local peasant who has been aroused by the spectacle of her body. His animal vitality, quick energy, generous blood and *farouche* shyness (the full range of Lawrencean qualities) provide a striking—if unfair—contrast to her lifeless husband. When the peasant sees her, "A flame went over his eyes, and a flame flew over her body, melting her bones." Her bold thought: "Why shouldn't I meet this man for an hour, and bear his child?" anticipates Connie's feeling about Mellors.

But this parable, unlike most of Lawrence's works, ends in bitter irony, for Juliet's resurrection is still incomplete—she has had a physical but not a mental change. She acts dishonestly by submitting to her husband, who has remained indifferent to the Sicilian sun and "smelled of the world, and all its fetters and its mongrel cowering. . . . Her next child would be Maurice's. The fatal chain of continuity would cause it."

The original, unexpurgated ending of "Sun," published in Paris by Harry Crosby's Black Sun Press in 1928 and paid for magnificently with the Queen of Naples' snuffbox and three pieces of gold, is more explicit and more crude. Lawrence explains that Juliet "had not enough courage, she was not free enough," though she felt "the rousing of [the peasant's] big penis against his body—for her, surging for her." But she submits to the etiolated body of her city-branded husband, who "would possess her, and his little frantic penis would beget another child in her."[16] In both versions of the story the fiery, sun-soaked peasant, who has no children of his own, rouses the lust that is slaked by her husband in precisely the same way that Lawrence himself once awakened the passion in his lover Alice Dax (Clara Dawes in *Sons and Lovers*), which led to an undesired pregnancy with her husband. Alice later told Frieda: "How I resented his snobbery and his happiness [with Frieda] whilst I was suffering in body and sick in soul, carrying an unwanted child which would never have been conceived but for an unendurable passion which only *he* had roused and my husband had slaked. So—life!"[17]

III

Harry Moore describes the composition of *Lady Chatterley's Lover,* which was written and published in Tuscany: "Lawrence sometimes wrote in the Villa Mirenda's tower, which looked out on orchards and olive trees towards the distant scrawl of Florence, and sometimes on the sunny terrace of the villa, but most often behind the small church of San Polo (sometimes Paolo), where, on days when the weather was gentle, he sat in a little wood of umbrella pines." Lawrence's mode of writing is portrayed in the novel when "Constance sat down with her back to a young pine-tree, that swayed against her with curious life, elastic, and powerful, rising up. The erect, alive thing, with its top in the sun!" The Tuscan wood is transformed, in Lawrence's imagination, into the wood that becomes Connie's refuge and sanctuary; and Oliver Mellors, whose name suggests Mediterranean olives and the Italian word for best *(meglio),* is modelled not only on Lawrence's father and on himself but also on the Italian peasant "in velveteen corduroys, bandolier, cartridges, game-bag over his shoulder, and gun in his hand,"[18] who sometimes passed by when Lawrence was writing. Mellors is the essence of the Italian spirit, transposed to and expressed in England.

Lawrence finished the novel in March 1928; and in April he was busy buying paper, correcting proofs and designing the phoenix rising from the nest in flames, which he had printed on his *Way of All Flesh*. The first edition of 1000 copies was published in July 1928 at a cost of £300 in "a nice little printing shop, all working away by hand—cosy and bit by bit, real Florentine manner—and the printer doesn't know a word of English—nobody on the place knows a word—where ignorance is bliss! Where the serpent is invisible! They will print on nice hand-made Italian paper—should be an attractive book. I do hope I'll sell my 1000 copies—or most of 'em—or I'll be broke. I want to post them direct to purchasers." Unlike the English, the Italians—exemplified by the Florentine printer who when told about certain words in the novel replied: "O! *ma!* but we do it every day!"[19]—accepted sex as a natural part of ordinary life. The book did well, and a second edition of 200 copies was brought out in November 1928.

The notorious novel was stopped by the American customs officials almost immediately. Though there was a fortunate delay in obstruction by the English authorities, Lawrence reported in February 1929: "Lately they have been making a great fuss over *Lady C.* Scotland Yard holding it up—visiting my agents—sort of threatening criminal proceedings—and holding up my mail—and actually confiscating two copies, MS. copies of my poems, *Pansies.*"[20] Since the book was not protected by copyright, five pirated editions—which paid Lawrence no royalties—had appeared by April 1929. The following month, in order to undersell them and regain his rights, Lawrence published a third edition of 3000 copies in Paris, photo-printed from the Florentine edition. This was also sold out and reprinted in August, by which time Lawrence's profits had amounted to £1616. It was the only Lawrence novel that sold briskly and earned considerable money during his lifetime.

Frieda was attracted to Lawrence's working-class background just as Connie was to Mellors': "That he came of the common people was a thrill to me. It gave him his candour, the wholesomeness of generations of hard work and hard living behind him, nothing sloppy, and lots of guts."[21] After Lawrence's death Frieda, who never valued fidelity, revealed that Lawrence had become sexually impotent toward the end of 1926 and that she had slept with Lieutenant Angelo Ravagli, who had been their landlord in Spotorno, while Lawrence was in France in October 1928.[22]

Frieda later wrote: "The terrible thing about Lady C. is that L. identified himself with both Clifford and Mellors; that took courage, that made me shiver."[23] Clifford Chatterley's sexual impotence and unfaithful wife are thus a bravely honest portrayal of Lawrence's own impotence—due to his wasting disease—and Frieda's adulterous liaison with Ravagli. Connie wants the child that Lawrence could never give Frieda, whose own three children were the main cause of her early quarrels with Lawrence. Mellors agrees to have a child "provided it doesn't touch your love for me. If it would touch that, I am dead against it." Connie's transfer of loyalty from the impotent Clifford to the virile Mellors is an important aspect of the resurrection theme.

The biographical connection between Lawrence and Mellors is even more significant; and Mark Schorer is quite mistaken when he asserts: "Connie and Mellors are *not* Frieda and D. H. Lawrence."[24] Like the young Lawrence, Mellors was a clever lad who had learned French and won a scholarship to an urban grammar school. The photograph of Mellors taken when he was married at twenty-one, which he destroys to show his loyalty to Connie, reveals him for what he was: "a young curate" and "prig." This description refers to the photograph of Lawrence at twenty-one, which (he said) shows him as a "clean-shaven, bright young prig in a high collar like a curate."[25] Mellors' description of his early love affairs is clearly based on Lawrence's relations with Jessie Chambers and Helen Corke just as his "bringin' her her breakfast in bed sometimes" refers to his practice with Frieda. Connie's first, unsuccessful sexual encounter with Mellors recalls Lawrence's wedding night with Frieda, described in the poem "First Morning." Mellors' loathsome and messy divorce—"I hate those things like death, officials and courts and judges. . . . Couldn't one go right way, to the far ends of the earth, and be free from it all?"—reflects Lawrence's squeamish response to Frieda's divorce after their scandalous elopement.

Most important, Mellors' pneumonia—which he caught during army service and which left him ill and coughing, with weak heart and lungs—shows Lawrence's courage to confront his own disease and mortality. Connie brings him back to life just as Frieda did Lawrence. Mark Schorer points out that "In the first version [of *Lady Chatterley*, Mellors] is physically strong; in the second, not so strong; in the third, sometimes rather frail." Mellors' extreme exhaustion after pushing Clifford's broken wheel chair up the hill—"his heart [was] beating and his face white with the effort, semi-conscious"—is similar to Knud Merrild's description of Lawrence's fatigue after chopping wood in New Mexico: "Lawrence did his share. Although he tired quickly, he stubbornly kept on. . . . It had hurt us to see him strain himself. He did not have the strength to be efficient."[26] Mellors' narrow escape from death and damaged health—"It seems to me I've died once or twice already"—connects him with Lawrence, who also came back from the dead, and with the resurrection theme in the novel.

In "A Propos of *Lady Chatterley's Lover*," Lawrence expresses the idea that provides both a thematic and structural unity to the work, which begins in autumn and follows the seasonal cycle to spring: "The greatest need of man is the renewal forever of the complete rhythm of life and death, the rhythm of the sun's year, the body's year of a lifetime, and the greater year of the stars, the soul's year of immortality."[27] Tommy Dukes, who prepares Connie for Mellors' revolutionary beliefs, states the theme of temptation and the fortunate fall that leads to rebirth: "Once you start the mental life you pluck the apple. You've severed . . . the organic connection. And if you've got nothing in your life *but* the mental life, then you yourself are a plucked apple. . . . [And] it's a natural necessity for a plucked apple to go bad." Later he demands the resurrection of the body and describes cerebration and money as the stone on the tomb. Soon after meeting Mellors in March, Connie walks in the wood, quotes Swinburne's attack on the "pale Galilean" in the "Hymn to Proserpine," recalls the Christian adage of the grain of wheat that dies only to spring forth from the ground (John 12:24) and remembers Persephone-Proserpine (the central myth in "Bavarian Gentians") rising from Hell to a new life on earth.

Just as Clifford seems ironically "to be re-born" when a new sense of power flows through him and he transforms the mines in the manner of Gerald Crich, so Mellors, after his first sexual experience with Connie, exclaims that he too has begun life again. When Clifford casuistically insists that the life of the body is merely the life of animals, Connie, revitalized by her sexual experience, sharply contradicts him: "With the Greeks [the body] gave a lovely flicker, then Plato and Aristotle killed it [by idealizing love], and Jesus finished it off. But now the body is coming really to life, it is really rising from the tomb."

Mellors' programmatic plea for men who could sing and

swagger and wear bright red trousers (pp. 205, 281) as a way
to replace money with manhood may seem an absurd residue
of *The Plumed Serpent.* But this scheme for rebirth has deep
roots in the regenerative idealism of Ruskin and William Morris as well as in Lawrence's youthful ideas about miners'
schools. "What they ought to do," he told Jessie Chambers, "is
recreational work. Teach the adolescents to sing and dance and
do gymnastics, and make things they enjoy making." Mellors'
plea is also connected to Lawrence's admiration for the scarlet
legs in Bernardo Strozzi's *Parable of the Wedding* (mentioned
in "Making Pictures") and to the brilliant clothing worn by
imaginative folk in the Italian Renaissance: "In the really great
periods like the Renaissance, the young men swaggered down
the street with one leg bright red, one leg bright yellow."[28]

In *Lady Chatterley's Lover,* Connie is urged by her sister
Hilda and Mrs. Bolton to go to Italy, by Michaelis to leave Clifford, and by Lady Bennerley, her father and Clifford himself
to find a lover. The considerable criticism at the beginning of
the novel of intellectualism and smart talk about sex (which
resembles the sterile conversations in *Aaron's Rod*) prepares
Connie to respond to the inarticulate animalism of Mellors.
Later, his rather brutal conversation with Hilda—whose will,
like Connie's, must be broken—shows that he also has a good
mind and can argue forcefully.

It is essential to recognize that the sexual rebirth is developed through and subservient to the maternal theme. Clifford
urges her to have a child by another man—as if emotion and
procreation could be separated; Connie comforts the sobbing
gamekeeper's daughter, Connie Mellors, whose name will
eventually be her own; she holds "the soft little arms, the unconscious cheeky little legs" of Mrs. Flint's baby; and discovers
the charming old family cradle of rosewood in the lumber room
of Wragby.

The maternal theme is superbly evoked in the scene when
Connie feeds the pheasant chicks—who are destined to be
slaughtered by Clifford's friends as soon as they reach maturity
(like the soldiers in the War). Like Miriam in *Sons and Lovers,*
Connie is afraid of the fierce pecks of the protective mother
hen, and "drew back startled and frightened." Then Mellors,
in a subtle mixture of sexual exploration and midwifery, "slowly, softly, with sure gentle fingers, felt among the old bird's
feathers and drew out a faintly-peeping chick in his closed

hand." As Connie holds the soft baby bird and begins to cry, the maternal is linked to the sexual theme. Mellors comes to life and is suddenly "aware of the old flame shooting and leaping up in his loins, that he had hoped was quiescent forever." He caresses Connie, establishes his authority by commanding her to lie down and makes love to her for the first time as sex transcends class through the "democracy of touch."

Lawrence holds the contradictory belief: "One is swindled out of one's proper sex life, a great deal. But it is nobody's individual fault: fault of the age: our own fault as well."[29] He therefore places strong emphasis on simultaneous orgasm and is careful to show how Connie progresses from a kind of clitoral masturbation with her prewar German lover and again with Michaelis, to early sex with Mellors where only he is satisfied, to vaginal and then to simultaneous orgasm. Finally, we learn that the road to excess does not lead to the palace of wisdom. For Mellors recklessly burns out the last shame, "stripped her to the very last, and made a different woman of her" in the only sexual act that is not made explicit in the novel: the strange apotheosis of anal penetration. "How could anything that gave one satisfaction be excluded," Gudrun asks in *Women in Love.* "Degrading things were real, with a different reality. . . . Why not be bestial, and go the whole round of experience?" One can only agree with André Malraux's sceptical response to Lawrence's belief that the body is wiser than the mind: "I am suspicious of the guarantees one must look for in the most profound regions of flesh and blood."[30]

Malraux's hero T. E. Lawrence, who appears in *Lady Chatterley's Lover* as Colonel C. E. Florence, is also perceptive when he explains D. H. Lawrence's themes of integrity and freedom. But he reveals more about himself than about D. H. Lawrence by claiming that the novelist's work is essentially therapeutic and advocates a sublimation of sex into beauty:

What D. H. Lawrence means by *Lady Chatterley's Lover* is that the idea of sex, & the whole strong vital instinct, being considered indecent causes men to lose what might be their vital strength and pride of life—their integrity. Conversely, the idea of "genitals being beauty" in the Blakian sense would free humanity from its lowering and disintegrating immortality [sic] of deed and thought.

Lawrence wilted & was made writhen by the 'miners-chapel-dirty little boy, you' environment: he was ruined by it: and in most of his work he is striving to straighten himself, and to become beautiful. Ironically, or paradoxically, in a humanity where "genitals are beauty" there would be a minimum of "sex" and a maximum of beauty, or Art. This is what Lawrence means, surely.[31]

Connie and Mellors, attracted by their differences of class and drawn together by threats of scandal and separation, oppose with their bodies, love and hopeful hearts the catastrophic results of the War, which Lawrence described in Spenglerian terms in the great opening sentences of the novel: "Ours is essentially a tragic age, so we refuse to take it tragically. The cataclysm has happened, we are among the ruins." As W. B. Yeats observed: "Those two lovers, the gamekeeper and his employer's wife, each separated from their class by their love, and by fate, are poignant in their loneliness, and the coarse language of one, accepted by both, becomes a forlorn poetry uniting their solitudes, something ancient, humble and terrible."[32]

At times, when they are nearly overwhelmed by this cataclysm, Mellors thinks it is wrong to bring a child into the world, longs for an apocalypse without a resurrection and happily contemplates the "extermination of the human species and the long pause that follows before some other species crops up."[33] "Lawrence's theme is a high one," Edmund Wilson wrote in 1929, "the self-affirmation and triumph of life in the teeth of all the sterilizing and demoralizing forces—industrialism, physical depletion, dissipation, careerism and cynicism—of modern English society."[34]

The emotional, as distinct from the sexual commitment of Connie and Mellors is sealed at a crucial moment: Connie's trip to Venice (mentioned thirty times in the novel) which is based on Lawrence's visits to that city during August, September and October 1920. "Venice is very lovely to look at," Lawrence wrote to Catherine Carswell, "but very stagnant as regards life. A holiday place, the only one left in Italy—but even here *écoeuré* [disheartened]."[35] In "Pomegranate" Lawrence called Venice an "Abhorrent, green, slippery city / Whose Doges were old, and had ancient eyes"; in *Sea and Sardinia* he associated Italy with tenderness, a major theme in and alternate title for *Lady Chat-*

terley: "Italy is so tender . . . soft tenderness ravelled round everything";[36] and at the very end of *John Thomas and Lady Jane* Connie suggests they both go to Italy with her money.

Connie, who had been taken to Florence and Rome as a girl and urges Clifford to travel with her to Italy, is invited to spend the summer with her father and sister at a Venetian villa. She looks forward to the visit and to bathing on the islands across the lagoon. She is pleased to escape from Clifford, but sorry about the "discipline" of leaving Mellors, though the pretense of finding a lover in Venice will account for her pregnancy with the gamekeeper. Though Clifford knows she must go on holiday, he defensively asks that "you won't go in the hopes of some love affair that you can take *au grand sérieux.*" The proposed trip at first causes friction between Connie and Mellors, who is also jealous of rival lovers; but later it intensifies their love and draws them together when (with Hilda's reluctant assistance) they spend the last night together and reach "the deepest recess of organic shame."

The journey to Venice in chapter 17, after a long anticipation, is anticlimactic. The sun shone on the city and the lagoon rippled in the light, but the gondolier rowed them "through the dark sidecanals with the horrible, slimy green walls." Their host, "a heavy, rather coarse Scotchman who had made a good fortune in Italy before the war," resembles Sir William Franks in *Aaron's Rod.* The house-guests are distinctly boring; their gondolier Giovanni is ready to sell himself for sex; and even the Piazza San Marco, Florian's café and Goldoni plays cannot compensate for the money, prostitution and deadness that had ruined the rose-colored city by 1920. Lawrence describes the hedonistic sunbathers, who are doing *en masse* what Juliet does individually, in his most severe puritanical tone:

> The Lido with its acres of sun-pinked or pyjamaed bodies, was like a strand with an endless heap of seals come up for mating. Too many people in the piazza, too many limbs and trunks of humanity on the Lido, too many gondolas, too many motor-launches, too many steamers, too many pigeons, too many ices, too many cocktails, too many men-servants wanting tips, too many languages rattling, too much, too much sun, too much smell of Venice, too many cargoes of strawberries, too many silk shawls, too many huge, raw-beef

slices of water-melon on stalls: too much enjoyment, altogether far too much enjoyment!

The journey to Venice changes Connie's relations with the most important people in her life. While there she learns that she is pregnant, like Ursula at the end of *The Rainbow* and Alvina at the conclusion of *The Lost Girl.* She also hears the scandal caused by Mellors' estranged wife and her public accusations that he liked "to use his wife, as Benvenuto Cellini says, 'in the Italian way.' "[37] Venice provides a trial separation from Clifford, a test of love for Mellors, a taste of what life would be like with Michaelis (who turns up like a bad penny) and an excuse for her pregnancy. It brings Connie under the liberating influence of her father, allows her to see England from an Italian perspective, provides Mediterranean sun and warmth. It provides a contrast to industrial ugliness, arouses opposition to her sterile life in England, provokes a revulsion against her own class, makes her long for Mellors. "Not all the sunshine of Venice had given her this inward expansion and warmth" that she feels when they are reunited in London. The news about his scandal provides the stimulus to tell Clifford that Mellors is the father of her baby and to break finally with Clifford, who has replaced Connie with Mrs. Bolton during her absence. Most significant, Connie learns that Mellors' truest role is paternal just as hers is maternal, for in the south "the act of procreation is still charged with all the sensual mystery and importance of the old past. The man is potential creator, and in this has his splendour."[38]

IV

Lawrence's attack on Christianity in *The Man Who Died* is specifically directed against St. Paul's emphasis on the division of body and spirit, and his belief that the flesh is the source of corruption: "For we know that the law is spiritual: but I am carnal, sold under sin [Romans 7:14]. . . . Meats for the belly, and the belly for meats: but God shall destroy both it and them. Now the body is not for fornication, but for the Lord; and the Lord for the body. . . . Shall I then take the members of Christ, and make them the members of a harlot? God forbid [1 Corinthians 6:13, 15]."

The most powerful modern onslaught against Paul's deviation from the Gospels is Nietzsche's *The Antichrist* (1888), which condemns, with the passionate rhetoric that Lawrence would later adopt, the degeneration of God into a force that opposed human life:

> The Christian conception of God—God as god of the sick, God as a spider, God as spirit—is one of the most corrupt conceptions of the divine ever attained on earth. It may even represent the low-water mark in the descending development of divine types. God degenerated into the *contradiction* of life, instead of being its transfiguration and eternal Yes! God as the declaration of war against life, against nature, against the will to live! God—the formula for every slander against "this world," for every lie about the "beyond"! God—the deification of nothingness, the will to nothingness pronounced holy!

Lawrence found the germ of his story in D'Annunzio's *Le Vergini delle rocce* (1895)—which he read before December 1916—for that Nietzschean sensualist wrote: "Perhaps the Jew, had his enemies not killed him in the flower of his years, would have finally shaken off the weight of his sadness, and finding a new taste in the ripe fruits of his Galilee, would have shown to his band another happiness."[39]

As early as March 1911 (after first reading Nietzsche in Croydon) Lawrence told his sister Ada: "Don't meddle with religion. I would leave all that alone if I were you, and try to occupy myself fully in the present." In *The Rainbow,* Ursula expresses Lawrence's resentment of evangelical teaching. She feels "there was something unclean and degrading about this humble side of Christianity" and is overwhelmed by horror when urged to eat the dead body of "Jesus with holes in His hands and feet."[40] In Lawrence's essay on Whitman ("I would embrace multitudes" he quotes in *The Man Who Died*), written toward the end of the War, he echoes Nietzsche and announces the theme of his story: "The Christians, phase by phase, set out actually to *annihilate* the sensual being in man." And his letters and late essay, "The Risen Lord," discuss the relation of the resurrection in the flesh to the resurgence of nature in the spring: "Church doctrine teaches the resurrection of the body; and if that doesn't mean the whole man, what does it mean?

And if man is whole without a woman—then I'm damned.
. . . He rose to become at one with life, to live the great life of
the flesh and the soul together, as peonies or foxes do, in their
lesser way. If Jesus rose as a full man, in full flesh and soul,
then He rose to take a woman to Himself, to live with her, and
to know the tenderness and blossoming of the twoness with
her."[41] Finally, Lawrence's description of the novella (which
should be read with his *Resurrection* painting in mind) shifts
from the slangy and blasphemous to the vital and responsive:
"I wrote a story of the Resurrection, where Jesus gets up and
feels very sick about everything, and can't stand the old crowd
any more—so cuts out—and as he heals up, he begins to find
what an astonishing place the phenomenal world is, far more
marvellous than any salvation or heaven—and thanks his stars
he needn't have a 'mission' any more."[42]

The Man Who Died combines the "sun" and "tenderness"
themes, which merge when the Man first becomes attracted to
the priestess of Isis: "The woman of Isis was lovely to him, not
so much in form, as in the wonderful womanly glow of her.
Suns beyond suns had dipped her in mysterious fire, the mysterious fire of a potent woman, and to touch her was like touching
the sun. Best of all was her tender desire for him, like sunshine,
so soft and still."[43] *The Man Who Died,* like "Sun" and *Lady
Chatterley's Lover,* moves—through a reawakening of the
senses—from a Christian to a pagan world and follows the
cycle of the seasons through winter to triumphant spring.

Lawrence always associated the Mediterranean with pagan
and biblical times: "Wherever one is in Italy, one is conscious
. . . of the far, mysterious gods of the early Mediterranean.
. . . Italy is like a most fascinating act of self-discovery—back,
back down the old ways of time."[44] The olive.trees remind "one
constantly of the New Testament," he wrote from Fiascherino in 1913. "I am always expecting when I go to Tellaro
for the letters, to meet Jesus gossiping with his disciples as he
goes along above the sea, under the grey, light trees."[45] The second, regenerative part of *The Man Who Died* (though apparently Levantine) is actually set, like "Sun," in a brilliant, fruitful and soothing Italian landscape, with "the steep slopes
coming down to the sea, where the olive-trees silvered under
the wind like water splashing. . . . And in the winter afternoon,
the light stood erect and magnificent off the invisible sea, fill-
ing the hills of the coast. She went towards the sun, through

the grove of Mediterranean pine-trees and evergreen oaks, in the midst of which the temple stood, on a little, tree-covered tongue of land between two bays."

The morbid stirring of the Man in the tomb—"He knew that he was awake, and numb, and cold, and rigid, and full of hurt"—is clearly connected to Lawrence's tuberculosis and gives personal poignancy to the theme of rebirth. Like the account of the raising of Lazarus (John 11:45), there is no attempt to describe what it felt like to be dead. The crowing of the cock, which awakens the Man and draws him to the peasant's house, alludes to Peter's denial—and, indirectly, to Judas' betrayal—of Christ in the Gospels (Matthew 26:34); and signifies the transformation, in Lawrence's fable, of cock into phoenix. In *Aaron's Rod,* Lilly asserts: "Judas is the real hero. But for Judas the whole show would have been *manqué.*"[46] And in the novella, the Man regrets his sacrificial mission and agrees: "I brought betrayal on myself. And I know I wronged Judas. . . . But Judas and the high priests saved me from my own salvation. . . . If I had kissed Judas with live love, perhaps he would never have kissed me with death." Like Christ in Dostoyevsky's "The Grand Inquisitor," the crucified Man realizes: "if they discover me, they will do it all over again."

The Man is twice awakened by the natural world stimulating his five senses. At the peasant's house he feels the silky wheat under his feet, hears the cock crow, tastes the figs and water, smells the aroma of strange perfumes and sees the world again as bright as glass. In Part Two, when he moves from Jerusalem to the Mediterranean coast, he sees the bright stars in the pure windy sky, smells the faint odor of goats, tastes the bread, hears the waves breaking on the shore and feels a shock of desire as the hands of the priestess soothe his wounds. This ceremony precedes sexual consummation and recalls the ritualistic massage in *The White Peacock, Aaron's Rod* and *The Plumed Serpent.*

The story progresses through a series of symbolic sensual temptations, which parallel Satan's temptation of Christ (Matthew 4:1-9), turn the Man away from his redemptive mission on earth and lead him to a regenerative sexual experience with the pagan priestess of Isis. When he sees the cock pounce on his favorite hen, "the destiny of life seemed more fierce and compulsive to him even than the destiny of death." He twice denies Mary Madeleine and "the woman who had been his mother"; and does not respond to the peasant's wife, who desires him, "though he felt gently towards her soft, crouching, humble body." The Virgin Man watches the young slave cover his mate "in the blind, frightened frenzy of a boy's first passion," which both recalls the cock's sudden mating with the hen and contrasts with his own slow "passion of tenderness" with the priestess. All this, like the spirit of Pan in the cave of goats, prepares him to respond to the priestess when she, for the first time in her life, "was touched on the quick by the sight of a man, as if the tip of a fine flame of living had touched her. . . . Men had roused all kinds of feeling in her [for she had known Caesar and Antony], but never had touched her with the flame-tip of life." Though the resurrection is complete, the Man must escape from the Romans who come to arrest him. He slips away in the night, following the current along the coast; and abandons the priestess, pregnant like so many women at the end of Lawrence's fiction, to a hopeful but uncertain future.

V

"The Ship of Death" is Lawrence's noble contribution to the *ars moriendi* and the literature of salvation. This tradition, which begins with the death of Socrates in the *Phaedo* and Cicero's *De Senectute,* reaches a peak in Taylor's *Holy Dying* (1650) and continues in Young's *Night Thoughts* (1745), Beddoes' *Death's Jest-Book* (1850) and Lampedusa's *The Leopard* (1958). Lawrence, who could speak, like Pope, of "That long disease, my life," attempts to reconcile body and soul—as he did in *The Man Who Died*—in this "act of self-mourning." The images of drowning in "the soundless, ungurgling flood" ("He called from his room in a strange gurgling voice") and "the cruel dawn of coming back to life" ("See, another day is given me") reflect the ravages of his disease and the immanence of his death.

The poem, like most of Lawrence's late works, combines pagan and Christian elements. It is inspired by the tomb in Cerveteri that "suggests Egypt" and is described in *Etruscan Places:* "Facing the door goes the stone bed on which was laid, presumably, the Lucumo [nobleman] and the sacred treasures of the dead, the little bronze ship of death that should bear him over to the other world."[47] The "long journey towards oblivion" comes from Shelley's "Epipsychidion"; "his own

quietus make / with a bare bodkin" from *Hamlet* (III.i); and
"Piecemeal the body dies, and the timid soul / has her footing
washed away, as the dark flood rises" from the opening lines
of Donne's "A Valediction: Forbidding Mourning."

The central metaphor portrays death as a journey from
physical life to spiritual peace. The ship is a way of accepting
death, not in the modern mode of fear and trembling, though
there is no religious consolation, but with a calm and stoical
resolution. The poem opens in the late autumn of 1929 as Lawrence expires in Bandol and "death is on the air like a smell
of ashes!" The falling apples are bruised (like his wounded
body) as they strike the frost-hardened earth and "exit from
themselves." He rejects the suicidal "bruise" of dagger and bullet. For violence will not provide the requisite release of "a
strong heart at peace," psychologically prepared, as the flood
rises, for the ship that carries the body on the journey "between
the old self and the new."

The turning point occurs in the middle of stanza vii when
"the fragile ship of courage, the ark of faith" that an afterlife
exists, departs "with its store of food and little cooking pans,"
rather like Lawrence and Frieda setting out for Sardinia with
their "kitchenino" and supply of English food. The process of
dying is then completed, "the body is gone" and oblivion is
reached. A thread (like Ariadne's) leads out of the darkness and
into the dawn, the flood subsides, the frail soul, "like a worn
sea-shell," steps out of the ship and the heart is renewed. The
secure unerring ship, Lawrence's consummate and convincing
symbol of the resurrection, is both a *memento mori* and a
means to achieve the peace of death and expectation of another
life.

Notes

CHAPTER 1: LAWRENCE IN ITALY

1. Edward Nehls, "D. H. Lawrence: The Spirit of Place," *The Achievement of D. H. Lawrence,* ed. Frederick Hoffman and Harry Moore (Norman, Oklahoma, 1953), p. 289. Though two books have been written on Lawrence and America, there is no work in English on Lawrence and Italy. Mary Corsani's *D. H. Lawrence e l'Italia* (Milano, 1965), a chronological and descriptive account with scant critical insight, leaves the field wide open.
2. John Haffenden, "A Conversation with Philip Larkin," *London Magazine,* 20 (April–May 1980), 88.
3. J. M. Murry, *Son of Woman* (London, 1931), p. 314.
4. Quoted in S. R. Lysaght, "A Visit to Robert Louis Stevenson," *I Can Remember Robert Louis Stevenson,* ed. Rosaline Masson (Edinburgh, 1922), p. 264.
5. D. H. Lawrence, *The Lost Girl* (New York, 1968), p. 328. See also *Kangaroo* (New York, 1976), p. 264, for a similar description when Somers leaves England.
6. D. H. Lawrence, *Collected Letters,* ed. Harry Moore (London, 1962), p. 272.
7. [Jessie Chambers], *D. H. Lawrence: A Personal Record* (London, 1935), p. 111.
8. D. H. Lawrence, "Autobiographical Sketch" (1927), *Phoenix II* (New York, 1970), p. 595.
9. D. H. Lawrence, *Apocalypse* (New York, 1966), pp. 199–200.

10. D. H. Lawrence, "Nottingham and the Mining Countryside," *Phoenix* (London, 1936), pp. 135–136.
11. Keith Alldritt, *The Visual Imagination of D. H. Lawrence* (London, 1971), p. 146.
12. Quoted in Ilsedore Jonas, *Thomas Mann and Italy* (University, Alabama, 1979), preface.
13. Lawrence, *Letters,* p. 163.
14. *Ibid.,* p. 146.
15. See Jeffrey Meyers, "D. H. and Frieda Lawrence," *Married to Genius* (London, 1977), pp. 145–173.
16. Lawrence, *Letters,* p. 180.
17. *Ibid.,* pp. 203–204.
18. *Ibid.,* p. 227.
19. *Ibid.,* p. 600.
20. *Ibid.,* p. 624.
21. *Ibid.,* pp. 632, 637, 646, 679.
22. *Ibid.,* pp. 694, 720, 814.
23. *Ibid.,* p. 881.
24. *Ibid.,* pp. 912, 920.
25. Thomas Mann, "Tonio Kröger," *Death in Venice and Other Stories,* trans. H. T. Lowe Porter (New York, n.d.), p. 106.
26. Lawrence, *Letters,* p. 1192.

CHAPTER 2: THE AESTHETICS OF TRAVEL

1. D. H. Lawrence, "Review of H. M. Tomlinson's *Gifts of Fortune,*" *Phoenix,* p. 342.
2. Quoted in Frieda Lawrence, *Not I, But the Wind* (New York, 1934), p. 223. Billy Tracy, "D. H. Lawrence and the Travel Book Tradition," *D. H. Lawrence Review,* 11 (1978), 272–293, misleadingly places Lawrence with the ethnologists (Borrow, Doughty, Belloc, Synge) and (because both books concern northern Italy) mistakenly claims that Samuel Butler's *Alps and Sanctuaries* (1881) was the model for *Twilight in Italy.* Though Tracy refers to a great number of travel writers, he fails to mention the two most important influences on Lawrence: Melville and Stevenson.
3. Herman Melville, *Typee* (London: Everyman, n.d.), p. 23.
4. D. H. Lawrence, *Studies in Classic American Literature* (London, 1924), pp. 133, 135, 137.
5. Lawrence, *Letters,* p. 713.
6. R. L. Stevenson, *Letters,* ed. Sidney Colvin (London, 1911), pp. 306–307.
7. R. L. Stevenson, *Letters to Charles Baxter,* ed. DeLancey Ferguson and Marshall Waingrow (London, 1956), p. 208; R. L. Stevenson, *In the South Seas, Works* (London: Pentland edition, 1907), p. 11; R. L. Stevenson, *An Inland Voyage* (London, 1900), p. 87.

8. R. L. Stevenson, *The Silverado Squatters, Works,* p. 277.

9. R. L. Stevenson, *Travels with a Donkey* (London, 1929), p. 57.

10. Stevenson, *An Inland Voyage,* p. 165.

11. *Ibid.,* p. 13; R. L. Stevenson, "On the Enjoyment of Unpleasant Places," *Essays of Travel* (London, 1912), p. 224.

12. Quoted in Catherine Carswell, *The Savage Pilgrimage* (London, 1932), p. 190.

13. D. H. Lawrence, *Aaron's Rod* (New York, 1961), p. 97.

14. Mark Schorer, "Lawrence and the Spirit of Place," *The Achievement of D. H. Lawrence,* pp. 282, 286.

15. Lawrence, *Letters,* pp. 177, 377.

16. *Ibid.,* p. 723.

17. *Ibid.,* pp. 743, 1155, 1218, 1221.

18. Schorer, "Lawrence and the Spirit of Place," pp. 293–294.

19. Frieda Lawrence, *Not I, But the Wind,* p. 276.

20. Quoted in Chambers, *D. H. Lawrence,* p. 49.

21. Lawrence, *Letters,* p. 311; Knud Merrild, *A Poet and Two Painters* (London, 1938), p. 251.

22. Quoted in Brian Finney, *Christopher Isherwood* (London, 1979), p. 201.

23. Lawrence, *Letters,* p. 713; Lawrence, *Phoenix,* p. 343.

24. Lawrence, *Letters,* p. 644.

25. Richard Aldington, *Portrait of a Genius, But* (London, 1950), p. 232; Richard Aldington, "Introduction" to *Sea and Sardinia* (New York, 1963), p. ix.

26. Anthony Burgess, "Introduction" to *D. H. Lawrence and Italy* (New York, 1972), p. xii; Clive James, "D. H. Lawrence in Transit," *D. H. Lawrence: Novelist, Poet, Prophet,* ed. Stephen Spender (London, 1973), p. 165; Harry Moore, *The Priest of Love* (London, 1976), p. 422. There is an interesting parallel between the naively positive readings of Lawrence's travel books and of his novels. Though Lawrence is usually praised for the triumphant expression of heterosexual love in his fiction, this love depends on male dominance and is seriously qualified by an ambivalent longing for homosexuality.

27. Burgess, "Introduction," p. vii; Paul Fussell, *Abroad* (New York, 1980), p. 149.

28. Fussell, *Abroad,* p. 157.

29. *Ibid.,* p. 164.

CHAPTER 3: MAURICE MAGNUS

1. Quoted in Carswell, *The Savage Pilgrimage,* p. 117.

2. Lawrence, *Letters,* pp. 889–890.

3. Keath Fraser, "Norman Douglas and D. H. Lawrence: A Sideshow in Modern Memoirs," *D. H. Lawrence Review,* 9 (1976), 283–295,

discusses the question of biographical truth and finds Lawrence more accurate than Douglas.

4. Lawrence, *Aaron's Rod,* pp. 211–214, 229, 234.
5. Lawrence, *The Lost Girl,* pp. 100, 117, 120.
6. Moore, *The Priest of Love,* p. 412.
7. Frieda Lawrence, *Not I, But the Wind,* p. 99.
8. Norman Douglas, *D. H. Lawrence and Maurice Magnus: A Plea for Better Manners* (Florence, 1924), p. 11.
9. Nancy Cunard, *Grand Man: Memories of Norman Douglas* (London, 1954), p. 282.
10. For a similar comparison see Jeffrey Meyers, "E. M. Forster and T. E. Lawrence: A Friendship," *South Atlantic Quarterly,* 69 (Spring 1970), 216: "Lawrence had gone to places where Forster said he 'should smash and scream in 30 seconds.' "
11. Graham Greene, "Frederick Rolfe," *Collected Essays* (London, 1969), p. 176.
12. Lawrence, *Phoenix,* pp. 327–329.
13. Douglas Goldring, *The Nineteen Twenties* (London, 1945), pp. 204–205.
14. See Jeffrey Meyers, "D. H. Lawrence," *Homosexuality and Literature, 1890–1930* (London, 1977), pp. 131–161.
15. Letter to Godwin Baynes, quoted in Edward Nehls, *D. H. Lawrence: A Composite Biography* (Madison, 1957–59), 1: 501.
16. Lawrence, *Studies in Classic American Literature,* p. 168.
17. Norman Douglas, *"Arabia Deserta," Experiments* (London, 1925), p. 16n.
18. Mark Holloway, *Norman Douglas: A Biography* (London, 1976), p. 334. For my review of Holloway's book, see *Sewanee Review,* 86 (Winter 1978), xxiv–xxvi.
19. Graham Greene, "Norman Douglas," *Collected Essays,* p. 365.
20. Lawrence, *Letters,* pp. 834, 836, 841.
21. *Ibid.,* p. 890.
22. Lawrence, "Accumulated Mail," *Phoenix,* p. 800.
23. Richard Aldington, *Life for Life's Sake* (New York, 1941), p. 376.
24. *Ibid.*
25. Norman Douglas, *Late Harvest* (London, 1946), pp. 52–53.
26. Quoted in Holloway, *Norman Douglas,* p. 334.
27. Richard Aldington, *Pinorman* (London, 1954), pp. 171–172.
28. Douglas, *Late Harvest,* p. 53.
29. Lawrence, *Letters,* p. 565.

CHAPTER 4: TRANSLATIONS OF VERGA

1. Lawrence, *Letters,* pp. 492, 668. Mary Craig translated *The House by the Medlar Tree* (New York, 1890) and *Mastro-don Gesualdo* (London, 1893) into stilted, well-laundered prose that paid full re-

spect to Victorian conventions of decorum. Alma Strettel translated six stories in *Cavalleria Rusticana and Other Tales of Sicilian Life* (London, 1893); and Nathan Dole translated six stories in *Under the Shadow of Etna* (Boston, 1896), reprinted as *Cavalleria Rusticana and Other Sicilian Stories* (Boston, 1898). Lawrence seems to have been aware of these undistinguished earlier translations, but did not consult them.

2. Thomas Bergin, *Giovanni Verga* (New Haven, 1931), p. 107.

3. Lawrence, *Letters,* pp. 670, 674.

4. D. H. Lawrence, *Letters to Thomas and Adele Seltzer,* ed. Gerald Lacy (Santa Barbara, 1976), p. 30.

5. Lawrence, "Introduction to *Mastro-don Gesualdo* by Giovanni Verga," *Phoenix II,* p. 287.

6. Lawrence, *"Mastro-don Gesualdo* by Giovanni Verga," *Phoenix,* pp. 228–229.

7. *Ibid.,* p. 230.

8. Lawrence, *Sea and Sardinia*, in *D. H. Lawrence and Italy,* pp. 3, 205.

9. Lawrence, "Note on Giovanni Verga," *Phoenix II,* p. 277.

10. In *Phoenix II,* p. 287, Lawrence seems to forget that Isabella is not Gesualdo's daughter and writes: "Diodata has his sons in her house, but Gesualdo, who has only one daughter by the frail Bianca, never seems to interest himself in his boys at all."

11. Giovanni Verga, *Mastro-don Gesualdo,* trans. D. H. Lawrence (London, 1970), p. 100.

12. *Ibid.,* p. 127.

13. *Ibid.,* p. 209.

14. *Ibid.,* p. 64.

15. See Jeffrey Meyers, "Symbol and Structure in *The Leopard,"* *Italian Quarterly,* 9 (Summer–Fall 1965), 50–70; "The Influence of *La Chartreuse de Parme* on *Il Gattopardo,"* *Italica,* 44 (September 1967), 314–325.

16. Lawrence, *"The Mother,* by Grazia Deledda," *Phoenix,* p. 264. Deledda (1875–1936) won the Nobel Prize for Literature in 1926. Lawrence wrote the Introduction for Mary Steegman's translation, published by Cape in 1928.

17. Giovanni Verga, *Little Novels of Sicily,* trans. D. H. Lawrence (Oxford, 1925), p. 58.

18. Lawrence, *"Cavalleria Rusticana* by Giovanni Verga," *Phoenix,* pp. 240–250.

19. Giovanni Verga, *Cavalleria Rusticana,* trans. D. H. Lawrence (London, 1928), p. 152.

20. Earl and Achsah Brewster, *D. H. Lawrence: Reminiscences and Correspondence* (London, 1934), p. 250. Lawrence actually sent half the book to his agent before he completed the translation.

21. *Boston Evening Transcript,* December 12, 1923, p. 6; *Dial,* 79 (July 1925), 76.

22. *Nation and Athenaeum,* 37 (May 23, 1925), 240; *TLS,* July 30, 1925, p. 507; *TLS,* March 8, 1928, p. 168.

23. Carlo Linati, "D. H. Lawrence e L'Italia," *Pegaso,* aprile 1933, pp. 386–387.

24. Giovanni Cecchetti, "Verga and D. H. Lawrence's Translations," *Comparative Literature,* 9 (1957), 343; and Giovanni Cecchetti, "Introduction" to Verga's *The She-Wolf and Other Stories* (Berkeley, 1958), p. xx.

25. Armin Arnold, "Genius with a Dictionary: Revaluating D. H. Lawrence's Translations," *Comparative Literature Studies,* 5 (1968), 393, 396.

26. Andrew Wilkin, "Review of Cecchetti's translation of *The She-Wolf,*" *Italica,* 52 (1975), 300–302.

27. Compare Cecchetti, "Verga and D. H. Lawrence's Translations," p. 337; and Andrew Wilkin, "Introduction" to Lawrence's translation of the *Little Novels of Sicily* (London, 1973), p. 12.

28. Wilkin, p. 12. Wilkin also expresses this judgment in "Sulle Traduzioni Lawrenciane delle Novelle di G. Verga," *Biologia Culturale,* 9 (settembre 1974), 123: "his translations read well as a whole: but the details show the imperfections" (my translation).

29. Corsani, *D. H. Lawrence e L'Italia,* p. 90 (my translation).

30. Lawrence, *Phoenix II,* p. 286.

31. *Ibid.,* p. 285.

32. Lawrence, *Phoenix,* p. 227. See Armin Arnold, "D. H. Lawrence, the Russians and Giovanni Verga," *Comparative Literature Studies,* 2 (1965), 249–257.

CHAPTER 5: *LOOK! WE HAVE COME THROUGH! AND BIRDS, BEASTS AND FLOWERS*

1. D. H. Lawrence, *Complete Poems,* ed. Vivian de Sola Pinto and Warren Roberts (New York, 1964), 1: 191.

2. D. H. Lawrence, "Foreword" to *Fantasia of the Unconscious* (New York, 1962), p. 57; Lawrence, "Poetry of the Present," *Complete Poems,* 1: 183–185.

3. Lawrence, "Preface to *Collected Poems*" (1928), *Complete Poems,* 1: 27; Amy Lowell, "A New English Poet," *New York Times Book Review,* April 20, 1919, p. 215; Lawrence, "Argument" to *Look! We Have Come Through!" Complete Poems,* 1: 191.

4. Lawrence, *Letters,* p. 121; quoted in Nehls, *Composite Biography,* 1: 71; Frieda Lawrence, *Not I, But the Wind,* pp. vi, 34.

5. Frieda Lawrence, *Not I, But the Wind,* pp. 40, 56–57.

6. Lawrence, *Letters,* p. 170.
7. Frieda Lawrence, *Not I, But the Wind,* p. 35; quoted in Aldous Huxley, "Introduction" to D. H. Lawrence, *Letters* (London, 1932), p. xxiv.
8. Amy Lowell, "A New English Poet," p. 215; Conrad Aiken, "The Melodic Line," *Dial,* 67 (August 9, 1919), 99; Tom Marshall, *The Psychic Mariner* (London, 1970), p. 70.
9. Sandra Gilbert, *Acts of Attention* (Ithaca, 1972), p. 98, misled by Lawrence's incorrect spelling of "Fronleichnam" (there is no "h"), or Corpus Christi, mistranslates the title as "joyful corpse."
10. *D. H. Lawrence and Italy,* pp. 57–58; Lawrence, "The Reality of Peace," *Phoenix,* p. 693.
11. Lawrence, *Fantasia of the Unconscious,* pp. 218–219.
12. Frieda Lawrence, *Memoirs and Correspondence,* ed. E. W. Tedlock (New York, 1964), p. 84.
13. Frieda Lawrence, *Not I, But the Wind,* p. 40.
14. Kenneth Rexroth, "Introduction" to *Selected Poems* (New York, 1967), p. 11.
15. Nehls, *Composite Biography,* 1: 501. This poem may be linked to the extraordinary incident of 1912 described by David Garnett in "Frieda and Lawrence," *D. H. Lawrence: Novelist, Poet, Prophet,* p. 39: "I found out that summer—Lawrence must have told me—that after they had had a row, she had gone down to the Isar and swum over to where a woodcutter was working, had made love with him and had swum back—just to show Lawrence she was free to do what she liked."
16. In D. H. Lawrence, *Women in Love* (New York, 1960), p. 18, Birkin "resembled a deer, that throws one ear upon the trail beyond, and one ear forward, to know what is ahead."
17. Quoted in Nehls, *Composite Biography,* 1: 310; quoted in John Jones, "The Prose and the Poetry," *New Statesman,* 54 (July 6, 1957), 23.
18. Lawrence, *Women in Love,* p. 257.
19. *Ibid.,* p. 139.
20. Lawrence, *Letters,* p. 737; Chambers, *D. H. Lawrence,* p. 223.
21. Lawrence, *Letters,* p. 291; *D. H. Lawrence and Italy,* p. 49.
22. Quoted in W. H. Auden, *Forewords and Afterwords* (New York, 1973), p. 150.
23. Vladimir Nabokov, *Strong Opinions* (New York, 1973), p. 142.
24. Joyce Carol Oates, *The Hostile Sun* (Los Angeles, 1973), p. 17.
25. Lawrence, *Complete Poems,* 1: 348.
26. *D. H. Lawrence and Italy,* p. 53. The same identification is made in "St. Matthew," *Complete Poems,* 1: 321.
27. John Ferguson, *Chinese Mythology,* in *The Mythology of All Races,* ed. John McCulloch (Boston, 1937), 8: 104.

28. Lawrence, *Women in Love,* p. 191.
29. Lawrence, *Studies in Classic American Literature,* p. 160.
30. See Compton Mackenzie, *My Life and Times, Octave Five: 1915–1923* (London, 1966), p. 167: "What worried [Lawrence] particularly was his inability to attain consummation simultaneously with his wife, which according to him must mean that their marriage was still imperfect in spite of all they had gone through."
31. D. H. Lawrence, *The Symbolic Meaning,* ed. Armin Arnold (London, 1962), p. 30.
32. Frieda Lawrence, *Not I, But the Wind,* p. 100; Horace Gregory, *Pilgrim of the Apocalypse* (New York, 1957), p. 63.

CHAPTER 6: *THE LOST GIRL*

1. Letter from John Worthen, editor of the Cambridge edition of *The Lost Girl,* to Jeffrey Meyers, April 11, 1977. See also John Worthen, *"The Lost Girl," D. H. Lawrence and the Idea of the Novel* (Totowa, New Jersey, 1979), pp. 105–117.
2. Lawrence, "Introduction to *Memoirs of the Foreign Legion,*" *Phoenix II,* p. 311.
3. Lawrence, *The Lost Girl,* p. 275.
4. Graham Hough in *The Dark Sun* (New York, 1959), p. 90, calls *The Lost Girl:* "the dullest and least characteristic Lawrence, the nearest thing to a pot-boiler that he ever wrote," though it is a better novel than *The White Peacock, The Trespasser* and *Kangaroo.* Julian Moynahan's *The Deed of Life* (Princeton, 1963), pp. 117–140, is the only convincing and favorable analysis of the novel.
5. The miners are described as bats; James Houghton as a bird and wagtail; Miss Pinnegar as a turkey and lynx; Arthur Witham as a dog; Albert Witham as a lemon sole; Mr. May as a pigeon and turkey; Madame Rochard as a cuttlefish, partridge and spider; Ciccio as a cat and then a leopard; the Indian troupe as swallows; Geoffrey as an ox; Dr. Mitchell as a fish; Pancrazio as a tomcat. The effect of this imagery, which links birds of a feather like Houghton and May and felines like Ciccio and Pancrazio, is satiric. Only Alvina escapes the degrading comparison with animals.
6. Lawrence, "Nottingham and the Mining Countryside," *Phoenix,* p. 136.
7. Lawrence, *Apocalypse,* pp. 199–200.
8. See Clayton Balch, "Cooper, Lawrence and the American Indian," *D. H. Lawrence and Tradition,* ed. Jeffrey Meyers (forthcoming).
9. *D. H. Lawrence and Italy,* p. 123.
10. E. W. Tedlock, *D. H. Lawrence: Artist and Rebel* (Albuquerque, 1963), p. 140; R. E. Pritchard, *D. H. Lawrence: Body of Darkness*

(Pittsburgh, 1971), p. 131; L. D. Clark, *The Minoan Distance* (Tucson, 1980), p. 65.

11. Lawrence, *Women in Love,* p. 429.
12. Katherine Mansfield, *Letters to John Middleton Murry, 1913–1922* (London, 1951), pp. 620–621. For a discussion of Lawrence's friendship with Mansfield, see Jeffrey Meyers, *Katherine Mansfield: A Biography* (London, 1978).

CHAPTER 7: FASCISM AND THE NOVELS OF POWER

1. Lawrence, *Letters,* pp. 291, 309.
2. *Ibid.,* pp. 340, 450.
3. Lawrence, *Fantasia of the Unconscious,* p. 149.
4. Lawrence, *Letters,* pp. 351, 354, 356, 456.
5. *Ibid.,* pp. 311, 369, 372.
6. *Ibid.,* pp. 330, 491.
7. *Ibid.,* pp. 356, 367. For Lawrence's quarrel with Russell, see Harry Moore, "Introduction" to Lawrence's *Letters to Bertrand Russell* (New York, 1948), pp. 1–26; James Jarrett, "D. H. Lawrence and Bertrand Russell," *A D. H. Lawrence Miscellany,* ed. Harry Moore (Carbondale, 1959), pp. 168–187; and Paul Delany, *D. H. Lawrence's Nightmare* (New York, 1978).
8. Lawrence, *Letters,* pp. 320, 542.
9. See Jeffrey Meyers, "Gabriele D'Annunzio," *A Fever at the Core* (London, 1976), pp. 89–111.
10. Denis Mack Smith, *Italy: A Modern History,* rev. ed. (Ann Arbor, 1969), p. 372.
11. *Ibid.,* p. 341.
12. *Ibid.,* pp. 410, 412.
13. D. H. Lawrence, *Movements in European History* (London, 1971), pp. 315–316.
14. Lawrence, *Letters,* pp. 617, 639–640.
15. *Ibid.,* pp. 644, 676.
16. *Ibid.,* p. 700.
17. See Lawrence, *Movements in European History,* p. 306; Lawrence, *Fantasia of the Unconscious,* pp. 123–124; Lawrence, *Complete Poems,* 1: 316; Lawrence, *Phoenix II,* pp. 436, 440.
18. Lawrence, *Letters,* pp. 705, 707, 820.
19. See Jeffrey Meyers, *"Aaron's Rod"* and *"The Plumed Serpent,"* *Homosexuality and Literature, 1890–1930,* pp. 149–161.
20. Lawrence, *Aaron's Rod,* p. 208.
21. Lawrence, *Kangaroo,* pp. 16, 21; Tedlock, *D. H. Lawrence: Artist and Rebel,* p. 161.
22. See John Alexander, "D. H. Lawrence's *Kangaroo:* Fantasy, Fact or Fiction?" *Meanjin Quarterly,* 24 (1965), 179–197; Andrew Peek,

"The Sydney *Bulletin* and D. H. Lawrence's *Kangaroo*," *Notes and Queries*, 26 (August 1979), 337–338.

23. See Geoffrey Serle, "The Digger Tradition and Australian Nationalism," *Meanjin Quarterly*, 24 (1965), 149–158.

24. See Heather Radi, "1920–29," *A New History of Australia*, ed. F. K. Crowley (Melbourne, 1974), p. 346. Moore, *The Priest of Love*, p. 445, mentions Monash as well as Koteliansky and Eder as the models for Kangaroo.

25. See Radi, "1920–29," p. 374.

26. See the Australian critics: Katharine Prichard, "Lawrence in Australia," *Meanjin Quarterly*, 9 (1950), 255; Ralph Maud, "The Politics in *Kangaroo*," *Southerly*, 17 (1956), 67; Michael Wilding, " 'A New Show': The Politics of *Kangaroo*," *Southerly*, 30 (1970), 27; Clive James, "D. H. Lawrence in Transit," *D. H. Lawrence: Novelist, Poet, Prophet*, p. 167.

27. Russel Ward, "Marking Time," *A History of Australia: The Twentieth Century, 1901–1975* (London, 1978), p. 141.

28. Hough, *The Dark Sun*, p. 104.

29. D. H. Lawrence, *Mornings in Mexico* (London, 1974), p. 42.

30. Worthen, *D. H. Lawrence and the Idea of the Novel*, p. 142.

31. See Jeffrey Meyers, "*The Plumed Serpent* and the Mexican Revolution," *Journal of Modern Literature*, 4 (1974), 55–72.

32. D. H. Lawrence, *The Plumed Serpent* (New York, 1959), p. 147.

33. Quoted in Merrild, *A Poet and Two Painters*, pp. 292, 306.

34. Lawrence, *Letters*, pp. 822–823; quoted in Nehls, *Composite Biography*, 2: 369.

35. See Frank Brandenberg, *The Making of Modern Mexico* (New York, 1964), pp. 74–75.

36. Lawrence, *Letters*, pp. 819–820.

37. Quoted in Mabel Dodge Luhan, *Lorenzo in Taos* (New York, 1932), p. 220.

38. Lawrence, *Movements in European History*, p. 306; Lawrence, *Fantasia of the Unconscious*, p. 210; quoted in Witter Bynner, *Journey with Genius* (New York, 1951), p. 95.

39. D. H. Lawrence, "The Crown," *Reflections on the Death of a Porcupine* (Philadelphia, 1925), pp. 66–67.

40. The sexual excitement of murder, which Jack describes in *Kangaroo*, recurs in *The Plumed Serpent*: "The striking thud of a heavy knife, stabbing into a living body, this is the best. No lust of women can equal that lust" (p. 148).

41. See Ronald Atkin, *Revolution! Mexico, 1910–1920* (London, 1969), pp. 299–300.

42. See James Wilkie and Albert Michaels, *Revolution in Mexico, 1910–1940* (New York, 1968), p. 195.

43. Lawrence, "Au Revoir, U.S.A.," *Phoenix*, p. 105.

44. *Ibid.*, pp. 940, 945.

45. Lawrence, "Note to *The Crown*," *Phoenix II*, p. 364.
46. Lawrence, *The First Lady Chatterley*, p. 243.
47. D. H. Lawrence, *John Thomas and Lady Jane* (London, 1973), p. 369.
48. Lawrence, *Movements in European History*, p. 317; D. H. Lawrence, *St. Mawr* and *The Man Who Died* (New York, 1960), p. 70.
49. Lawrence, *Letters*, ed. Huxley, p. 713. Thomas Mann's "Mario and the Magician" (1929) is an allegory on this theme.
50. Lawrence, *Letters*, ed. Moore, p. 1045. *Miles* is Latin for soldier; *ich dien* (I serve) was the motto of the Prince of Wales, whom Lawrence describes in "Elephant."
51. John Strachey, *Literature and Dialectical Materialism* (London, 1934), p. 18.
52. Delavenay, *D. H. Lawrence: The Man and His Work*, pp. 255–256.
53. Ernest Seillière, *David-Herbert Lawrence et les récentes idéologies allemandes* (Paris, 1936), p. 256.
54. William York Tindall, "Lawrence Among the Fascists," *D. H. Lawrence and Susan His Cow* (New York, 1939), pp. 174–175, 177. See William Empson's review in *Horizon*, 2 (December 1940), 344. John Lehmann, *New Writing in Europe* (London, 1940), p. 22, also equates Lawrence's ideas with modern Fascist theories.
55. Stebelton Nulle, "D. H. Lawrence and the Fascist Movement," *New Mexico Quarterly*, 10 (1940), 4, 8, 12.
56. Cecil Gray, *Musical Chairs* (London, 1948), pp. 130–131.
57. Bertrand Russell, *Autobiography* (New York, 1968), 2: 14; Bertrand Russell, "D. H. Lawrence," *Portraits From Memory* (New York, 1953), pp. 112, 114.
58. John Harrison, "D. H. Lawrence," *The Reactionaries* (New York, 1967), p. 188.
59. E. R. Dodds, *Missing Persons* (Oxford, 1977), pp. 59–60.
60. Wyndham Lewis, *The Art of Being Ruled* (London, 1926), p. 89.

CHAPTER 8: THE PAINTINGS

1. Lawrence, *Letters*, p. 945; D. H. Lawrence, *Letters from D. H. Lawrence to Martin Secker, 1911–1930* (Bridgefoot Iver, Bucks.: privately printed, 1970), p. 79; Lawrence, *Letters*, p. 982.
2. Lawrence, "Making Pictures," *Phoenix II*, p. 606. Lawrence refers to Angelico's *Flight into Egypt* (1451, Museo di San Marco, Florence); Gherardo Starnina's *The Thebiad* (c. 1400, Uffizi, Florence)—originally attributed to Pietro Lorenzetti; Carpaccio's *Dream of St. Ursula* (c. 1495, Accademia, Venice); Piero di Cosimo's *Death of Procris* (c. 1506, National Gallery, London); probably Bernardo Strozzi's *The Parable of the Wedding* (c. 1636,

Uffizi, Florence); and Giotto's frescoes (c. 1305, Arena Chapel, Padua).

3. See Jeffrey Meyers, "Maurice Greiffenhagen and *The White Peacock,*" and "Fra Angelico and *The Rainbow,*" *Painting and the Novel* (Manchester, 1975), pp. 46–64.

4. Merrild, *A Poet and Two Painters,* p. 213; Lawrence, *Phoenix II,* p. 320.

5. Dorothy Brett, *Lawrence and Brett* (Philadelphia, 1933), p. 193.

6. Lawrence, *Letters,* p. 949; Lawrence, "Making Pictures," *Phoenix II,* pp. 603–604.

7. Charles Baudelaire, *The Life and Work of Eugène Delacroix* (1863), in *The Mirror of Art,* trans. and ed. Jonathan Mayne (New York, 1956), p. 309; Mervyn Levy, ed., *The Paintings of D. H. Lawrence* (London, 1964), p. 10.

8. Marcel Proust, "John Ruskin," *A Selection of His Miscellaneous Writings,* trans. and ed. Gerard Hopkins (London, 1948), p. 64.

9. See Raymond Bloch, *Etruscan Art* (Greenwich, Conn., 1959), plates 32 and 48.

10. *D. H. Lawrence and Italy,* pp. 35, 68.

11. See Bloch, *Etruscan Art,* plates 34 and 55.

12. *D. H. Lawrence and Italy,* pp. 46–47.

13. M.-F. Briguet, *Etruscan Art* (London, 1962), p. [10].

14. John Russell, "D. H. Lawrence and Painting," *D. H. Lawrence: Novelist, Poet, Prophet,* p. 234.

15. Lawrence, *Letters,* p. 1077; Lawrence, "Introduction to These Paintings," *Phoenix,* p. 561.

16. Lawrence, *Letters,* p. 964; Herbert Read, "Lawrence as a Painter," *The Paintings of D. H. Lawrence,* p. 63.

17. Lawrence, *Letters,* pp. 967, 969.

18. *Ibid.,* p. 945.

19. Richard Aldington, "Introduction" to *Apocalypse,* p. xxi; Lawrence, *Phoenix,* p. 177.

20. Boccaccio, *The Decameron,* trans. John Payne (New York, n.d.), pp. 206, 211–212; Peter Irvine and Anne Kiley, "D. H. Lawrence and Frieda Lawrence: Letters to Dorothy Brett," *D. H. Lawrence Review,* 9 (1976), 71–72.

21. Quoted in Nehls, *Composite Biography,* 3: 334.

22. Lawrence, *Letters,* ed. Huxley, p. 756.

23. Lawrence, *Mornings in Mexico,* pp. 58, 60.

24. Lawrence, *Women in Love,* p. 263.

25. Lawrence, *Letters,* pp. 965, 1013; Nehls, *Composite Biography,* 3: 332.

26. Lawrence, *Letters,* p. 981; Lawrence, *Apocalypse,* pp. 46–47.

27. Lawrence, *Letters,* p. 1164.

28. *Ibid.,* p. 1176.

29. Lawrence, *Complete Poems,* 2: 579–580.

CHAPTER 9: THE RESURRECTION THEME

1. Quoted in Frieda Lawrence, *Not I, But the Wind,* p. 151.
2. Lawrence, *Apocalypse,* p. 3; Lawrence, *Letters,* p. 765; Luhan, *Lorenzo in Taos,* p. 326.
3. Quoted in Brett, *Lawrence and Brett,* p. 240; Lawrence, "Introduction to These Paintings," *Phoenix,* p. 569; Lawrence, *Apocalpyse,* p. 199.
4. Frieda Lawrence, *Not I, But the Wind,* pp. 195, 292.
5. Nehls, *Composite Biography,* 1: 197, 3: 424.
6. Lawrence, *Letters,* pp. 1231–1232.
7. *Ibid.,* pp. 1241, 1243, 1245.
8. Aldous Huxley, *Letters,* ed. Grover Smith (New York, 1969), p. 364. Huxley portrays this healing aspect of the Frieda-Lawrence relationship in the marriage of Katy and Henry Maartens in *The Genius and the Goddess* (1955).
9. Frieda Lawrence, *Not I, But the Wind,* pp. 288–289.
10. See Jeffrey Meyers, "'The Voice of Water': Lawrence's *The Virgin and the Gipsy,*" *English Miscellany,* 21 (1970), 199–207.
11. Quoted in Earl Brewster, *D. H. Lawrence: Reminiscences and Correspondence,* p. 288; Lawrence, "The Flying Fish," *Phoenix,* p. 785.
12. Lawrence, *Letters,* pp. 644, 973; Lawrence, *Apocalypse,* pp. 47, 200.
13. D. H. Lawrence, *Lady Chatterley's Lover* (New York, 1959), pp. 65, 73.
14. Luhan, *Lorenzo in Taos,* p. 117.
15. D. H. Lawrence, "Sun," *Complete Short Stories* (New York, 1964), 2: 529.
16. D. H. Lawrence, *Sun* (Paris, 1928), p. 38.
17. Quoted in Frieda Lawrence, *Memoirs and Correspondence,* p. 248.
18. Moore, *The Priest of Love,* p. 532; Lawrence, *Lady Chatterley's Lover,* p. 80. A photograph of Lawrence writing under an olive tree at the Villa Mirenda appears on the dust jacket of *D. H. Lawrence: Novelist, Poet, Prophet.* Lawrence, "Man Is a Hunter," *Phoenix,* p. 33.
19. Lawrence, *Letters,* ed. Huxley, p. 717; Lawrence, "A Propos of *Lady Chatterley's Lover,*" *Phoenix II,* p. 515.
20. *Letters,* ed. Huxley, p. 792.
21. Frieda Lawrence, "Introduction" to *The First Lady Chatterley,* p. 130.
22. See Robert Lucas, *Frieda Lawrence* (New York, 1973), pp. 238, 242.
23. Frieda Lawrence, *Memoirs and Correspondence,* p. 389.

24. Mark Schorer, "Introduction" to *Lady Chatterley's Lover* (New York, 1966), p. 29.

25. The photograph and Lawrence's comment are printed in Harry Moore, *D. H. Lawrence and His World* (New York, 1966), p. 19. Compare this to *Lady Chatterley,* pp. 185–186.

26. Schorer, "Introduction," p. 26; Merrild, *A Poet and Two Painters,* pp. 74, 76.

27. Lawrence, "A Propos of *Lady Chatterley's Lover,*" *Phoenix II,* p. 510.

28. Quoted in Chambers, *D. H. Lawrence,* p. 80; Lawrence, "Red Trousers," *Phoenix II,* p. 564.

29. Lawrence, *Letters,* ed. Moore, p. 967.

30. Lawrence, *Women in Love,* p. 403; André Malraux, "D. H. Lawrence and Eroticism: Concerning *Lady Chatterley's Lover*" (1932), *Yale French Studies,* 11 (1953), 57.

31. T. E. Lawrence, *Letters,* ed. David Garnett (New York, 1964), p. 687. For the relation of this statement to T. E. Lawrence's own work, see Jeffrey Meyers, "Sexual Pathology," *The Wounded Spirit: A Study of 'Seven Pillars of Wisdom'* (London, 1973), pp. 114–129.

32. W. B. Yeats, *Letters,* ed. Allan Wade (London, 1954), p. 810.

33. See T. E. Lawrence, *Letters,* p. 420: "Had the world been mine I'd have left out animal life upon it."

34. Edmund Wilson, "Signs of Life: *Lady Chatterley's Lover*" (1929), *The Shores of Light* (New York, 1961), p. 405.

35. Quoted in Moore, *Priest of Love,* p. 417.

36. *D. H. Lawrence and Italy,* p. 66.

37. In "Pornography and Obscenity," *Phoenix,* p. 186, Lawrence states that the grey censors "would suppress Benvenuto tomorrow, if they dared. But they would make laughing-stocks of themselves, because *tradition* backs up Benvenuto."

38. Lawrence, "A Propos of *Lady Chatterley's Lover,*" *Phoenix II,* p. 499.

39. Friedrich Nietzsche, *The Portable Nietzsche,* trans. and ed. Walter Kaufmann (New York, 1966), pp. 585–586; Gabriele D'Annunzio, *The Maidens of the Rocks,* trans. Anna and Giuseppe Antona (New York, 1926), pp. 20–21.

40. Lawrence, *Letters,* ed. Moore, p. 75; Lawrence, *The Rainbow,* pp. 272, 283.

41. Lawrence, *The Symbolic Meaning,* p. 255; Lawrence, *Letters,* ed. Moore, p. 1115; Lawrence, *Phoenix II,* p. 575.

42. Lawrence, *Letters,* ed. Moore, p. 975.

43. Lawrence, *St. Mawr* and *The Man Who Died,* p. 201.

44. Lawrence, *Sea and Sardinia,* p. 123.

45. Lawrence, *Letters,* ed. Moore, p. 255.

46. Lawrence, *Aaron's Rod,* p. 72.

47. *D. H. Lawrence and Italy,* p. 10.

Index

Aiken, Conrad, 75
Aldington, Richard, 20, 22, 43, 46, 143; *Life for Life's Sake,* 47; *Pinorman,* 47; *Portrait of a Genius, But,* 47
Alldritt, Keith, 5
Angelico, Fra, *Flight into Egypt,* 138; *The Last Judgement,* 138
Arnold, Armin, 67
Auden, W. H., 28, 50

Balzac, Honoré de, *Père Goriot,* 54
Baudelaire, Charles, 139
Bergin, Thomas, 50–51
Boccaccio, *The Decameron,* 143
Borg, Michael, 36, 37, 43, 45, 46
Brett, Dorothy, 19, 41, 139, 150
Brewster, Achsah, 18, 64
Brewster, Earl, 18, 25, 139, 141, 145
Brooke, Rupert, 13
Brueghel, Pieter, *The Harvesters,* 143

Burgess, Anthony, 20, 22
Burns, Robert, "To a Mouse," 85–86
Butler, Samuel, 12; *Alps and Sanctuaries,* 172n2
Bynner, Witter, 131

Cannan, Mary, 8, 36
Carpaccio, Vittore, 138
Carrington, Dora, 139
Carswell, Catherine, 19
Cecchetti, Giovanni, 66–68
Cerni, Orazio, 102
Chambers, Jessie, 5, 7, 73–74, 158, 160; *D. H. Lawrence: A Personal Record,* 4, 20, 84
Coleridge, Samuel Taylor, 90
Conrad, Joseph, *Heart of Darkness,* 23; *Victory,* 31
Cooper, James Fenimore, 69, 100
Corsani, Mary, *D. H. Lawrence e l'Italia,* 67–68, 171

Cosimo, Piero di, *Death of Procris,* 138
Cunard, Nancy, 38–39; *Grand Man,* 47–48

D'Annunzio, Gabriele, 108, 109; *Le Vergini delle rocce,* 165
Davidson, Jo, 139
Dax, Alice, 156
Delavenay, Emile, 132, 135
Deledda, Grazia, 51, 59
Dickinson, G. L., 107
Dodds, E. R., 135
Douglas, Norman, 12, 24, 30–33, 37–38, 41, 46–48, 112; *D. H. Lawrence and Maurice Magnus,* 42–44; *Experiments,* 45; *Fountains in the Sand,* 44; *Late Harvest,* 47–48; *South Wind,* 44
Durrell, Lawrence, 28

Freud, Sigmund, 5
Frost, Robert, "To a Moth," 89
Fuller, Roy, "The Giraffes," 89
Fussell, Paul, 22, 24, 26

Gambrosier, Ettore, 8
Garnett, David, 177n15
Gauguin, Paul, 13–14
Gee, Collingwood, 46
Gertler, Mark, 139
Giotto, 138
Goldring, Douglas, 41
Gotzsche, Kai, 139
Gray, Cecil, 116; *Musical Chairs,* 133–34, 135
Grazzini, A. F., *The Story of Dr. Manente,* 51
Greene, Graham, 28, 40, 44
Gregory, Horace, 93
Greiffenhagen, Maurice, *The Idyll,* 138

Hardy, Thomas, 70
Harrison, John, 134–35
Hitler, Adolf, 132, 133, 134, 135
Hocking, William Henry, 41, 121
Holloway, Mark, 44, 46
Hough, Graham, 120–21; *The Dark Sun,* 178n4
Huxley, Aldous, 28, 82, 137, 151, 152;

The Genius and the Goddess, 183n8
Huxley, Maria, 18, 139, 146

Isherwood, Christopher, 19, 28
Italy: Capri, 8–9, 29, 33; Civitavecchia, 24; Etna, 9, 154; Fiascherino, 4, 8, 166; Florence, 11, 19, 29, 30, 88, 90, 110, 112–13, 117; Forte dei Marmi, 11; Lake Garda, 3, 6, 8, 13, 20, 94; Lerici, 19; Malta, 29, 36; Montecassino, 29, 33–34, 41, 94–95, 102, 138; Picinisco (Abruzzi), 8, 33, 95, 102–3; San Gaudenzio, 75; San Terenzo, 8
Sardinia, 13, 20, 23, 24–25, 59; Cagliari, 24; Nuoro, 24; Orosei, 24; Siniscola, 24; Sorgono, 24; Trapani, 24
Scandicci (Tuscany), 10, 18, 156
Sicily, 9, 13, 20, 23–25, 50–53, 57–59, 69–71, 89, 93, 154; Messina, 24; Palermo, 24; Syracuse, 29, 36; Taormina, 9, 18, 29, 34, 94, 142, 153
Spotorno, 10, 153; Venice, 162–64

James, Clive, 20
Jarrell, Randall, "Bats," 85, 88
Juta, Jan, 139

Keats, John, "Ode on a Grecian Urn," 25; "Ode to a Nightingale," 85; "When I Have Fears," 78
Keynes, J. M., 107
Kipling, Rudyard, 13

Lampedusa, Giuseppe Tomasi di, *The Leopard,* 58, 168
Larkin, Philip, 2
Lawrence, D. H.
    Ideas: attitude to Fascism, 27, 105, 108, 109–11, 116, 117–18, 122, 127–28, 129–36; Australian setting, 111–12, 117–22; authoritarian beliefs, 58, 70–71, 105–6, 107–8, 111–18, 121–22, 123, 125–29, 130, 132–33, 136; biblical allusions, 78, 81, 82, 87, 96, 101, 159, 167; criticism of Christianity, 13, 21, 32, 34, 40, 60, 70, 137, 141, 142, 145–46, 149–

50, 159, 164–66; criticism of civilization, 13–14, 16, 20, 22–23, 27; Etruscan art, 4, 13, 25–27, 99, 140–41, 144, 153, 168; health and illness, 3, 10, 14–15, 18–19, 149–51, 153, 167, 168; homosexual theme, 30–34, 38, 40–44, 48, 79, 96, 112–13, 116, 118–22, 125; male-female conflict, 74–85, 90–93, 96–102, 114–16, 123, 126–27; Mexican setting, 2, 18, 19, 111–12, 123–29, 149; painting, 138–44, 147–48; peasant life, 3–6, 10, 22, 26, 32, 51–53, 58, 59–64, 69–70, 102, 140, 155, 156; political ideas, 105–36; primitivism, 4–6, 13, 16, 20, 25–27, 95, 102–3, 124–25, 137, 144, 150, 153–54, 166; resurrection theme, 1, 26, 96, 137, 142, 144–46, 149–53, 159–60, 165–69; search for ideal community, 12, 13, 14, 18, 19–20, 40, 107, 135; translations, 1, 51, 55, 64–69, 70–71, 137, 174–75n1, 175n20; travel writing, 1, 12–25; vitalism, 5, 7, 26–27, 32, 63, 69

Books: *Aaron's Rod,* 4, 9, 17, 30–31, 41, 43, 44, 47, 48, 64, 71, 96, 110, 111, 112–16, 123, 126, 133, 135–36, 152, 160, 163, 167; *Apocalypse,* 5, 99, 142, 150, 152, 153; *Birds, Beasts and Flowers,* 9, 73, 84–93, 96; *Etruscan Places,* 25–28, 88, 95, 137, 140–41, 142, 152, 168; *Fantasia of the Unconscious,* 77, 111; *The First Lady Chatterley,* 130; *John Thomas and Lady Jane,* 130, 163; *Kangaroo,* 17, 30, 64, 71, 95, 96, 105, 110, 111, 116–23, 133, 135–36; *Lady Chatterley's Lover,* 7, 10, 22, 53, 63, 70, 71, 83, 91, 93, 96, 130, 131, 136, 137, 141, 146, 148, 152, 153–54, 156–64, 166; *Look! We Have Come Through!,* 4, 8, 72–84, 90–91, 95, 152; *The Lost Girl,* 1, 2, 3, 7, 8, 31–32, 40, 71, 93, 94–104, 112, 152, 164, 178nn4 and 5; *Mornings in Mexico,* 2, 121, 144; *Movements in European History,* 110, 111, 130–31; *Nettles,* 147; *Pansies,* 157; *Phoenix,* 150; *The Plumed Serpent,* 2, 7, 41, 58, 60, 63, 71, 93, 96, 111, 124–29, 131, 133, 135–36, 149, 160, 167, 180n40; *The Rainbow,* 5, 8, 21, 38, 58, 70, 71, 76, 95, 96, 105, 108, 138, 146, 152, 164, 165; *Sea and Sardinia,* 2, 9, 16, 20, 23, 24–25, 26, 27, 53, 71, 95, 102, 103, 142; *Sons and Lovers,* 5, 8, 22, 38, 53, 71, 138, 152, 156, 160; *Studies in Classic American Literature,* 13; *Twilight in Italy,* 8, 20–22, 26, 71, 79, 95, 102, 109, 142; *The White Peacock,* 41, 53, 71, 95, 96, 137, 167; *Women in Love,* 21, 22, 41, 54, 76, 81, 82, 83, 91–92, 93, 95, 96, 102, 103, 112, 134, 138, 144–45, 161

Essays: "A Propos of *Lady Chatterley's Lover,*" 159; "The Flying Fish," 152–53; Goats and Compasses," 41, 121; "Introduction to Maurice Magnus' *Memoirs of the Foreign Legion,*" 1, 9, 29–49, 95, 97, 138; "Note on Giovanni Verga," 53; "Nottingham and the Mining Countryside," 5; "Poetry of the Present," 72–73, 75; "Pornography and Obscenity," 143, 184n37; "Preface to *Cavalleria Rusticana,*" 70–71; "The Reality of Peace," 76; "The Risen Lord," 152, 165–66; "The Spirit of Place," 93; "Study of Thomas Hardy," 138

Paintings: *Boccaccio Story,* 137, 143, 146; *Close Up: Kiss,* 142; *Contadini,* 143–44; *Dance Sketch,* 144; *Family on a Verandah,* 142; *Fauns and Nymphs,* 144; *Fight with an Amazon,* 142, 146; *Fire Dance,* 144; *Flight Back into Paradise,* 145; *A Holy Family,* 142; *Italian Landscape,* 142–43; *Italian Scene with a Boat,* 142; *The Kiowa Ranch,* 139; *Leda,* 142; *The Lizard,* 137, 142; *The Mango Tree,* 142; *The Rape of the Sabine Women,* 142; *Red Willow Trees,* 140; *Renascence of Men,* 140, 144–45; *Resurrection,* 137, 145–46, 166; *Throwing Back the Apple,* 145; *Under the Hay-Stack,* 142; *Yawning,* 144

Plays: *The Daughter-in-Law*, 8; *The Fight for Barbara*, 8

Poems: "Bavarian Gentians," 152, 159; "Blessed Are the Powerful," 111; "Cypresses," 140; "First Morning," 158; "Hibiscus and Salvia Flowers," 111; "The Ship of Death," 152, 153, 168–69; "Snake," 69–70, 155

Stories: "The Fox," 71; "The Horse-Dealer's Daughter," 71; *The Man Who Died*, 96, 137, 152, 153, 164–68; "The Man Who Loved Islands," 47; "Odour of Chrysanthemums," 71; "The Princess," 71, 96; *St. Mawr*, 131, 152; "Sun," 7, 58, 137, 152, 153–56, 166; *The Virgin and the Gipsy*, 152; "The Woman Who Rode Away," 71, 96, 152, 153

Lawrence, Frieda, 2, 5, 6, 7, 8, 10, 18, 19, 24, 37, 38, 41, 48, 62, 72, 73–83, 104, 134, 139, 149, 151–52, 154, 157–58, 177n15; *Not I, But the Wind*, 35, 74

Lawrence, T. E., 161–62, 184n31

Lehmann, John, 135, 181n54

Levy, Mervyn, 139

Lewis, Wyndham, 136

Linati, Carlo, 66, 67

Lorenzetti, Pietro, *The Thebiad*, 138, 181n2

Lowell, Amy, 33, 73, 75

Luhan, Mabel Dodge, 9, 15, 18, 137, 150, 154

Mackenzie, Compton, 8, 47, 178n30

Magnus, Maurice, 29–49, 94, 97–98; *Memoirs of the Foreign Legion*, 29, 33, 38–39, 42–46

Malraux, André, 161

Mann, Thomas, 6, 40; "Tonio Kröger," 11

Mansfield, Katherine, 15, 19, 103–4

Manzoni, Alessandro, *I Promessi Sposi*, 61

Marshall, Tom, 75

Mascagni, Pietro, *Cavalleria Rusticana*, 69

Melville, Herman, 69; *Moby Dick*, 92; *Omoo*, 13; *Typee*, 13

Meredith, George, *Modern Love*, 75, 82

Merrild, Knud, 19, 124, 138, 159

Miller, Henry, 28

Monash, Sir John, 117, 180n24

Moore, Harry, 20, 31, 144, 156

Morland, Dr. Andrew, 151

Morrell, Ottoline, 19, 41

Morris, William, 160

Moynahan, Julian, *The Deed of Life*, 178n4

Muir, Edwin, 66, 67

Murry, John Middleton, 19, 41, 103, 125; *Son of Woman*, 2

Mussolini, Benito, 109, 130, 133, 135

Nehls, Edward, 1

Nietzsche, Friedrich, 27; *The Antichrist*, 165

Nulle, Stebelton, 133, 135

Oates, Joyce Carol, 85

O'Brien, Frederick, *White Shadows on the South Seas*, 14

Orioli, Pino, 11, 46, 47, 147

Osbourne, Fanny, 15

Pini, Pietro, 143–44

Plato, *Phaedo*, 168; *The Symposium*, 92

Proust, Marcel, 140

Ravagli, Angelo, 10, 62, 157–58

Read, Herbert, 141

Richards, Grant, 46

Roethke, Theodore, "Snake," 85–90

Rolfe, Frederick (Baron Corvo), *Hadrian the Seventh*, 40

Ruskin, John, 12, 160

Russell, Bertrand, 82, 105, 107, 111; *Autobiography*, 134; *Portraits From Memory*, 134

Russell, John, 141

Rutter, Frank, 144

Salomone, Walter, 36

Schorer, Mark, 17, 18, 158

Secker, Martin, 10, 137

Seillière, Ernest, 132, 135

Seltzer, Thomas, 33, 45, 51

Starnina, Gherardo, *The Thebiad,* 181n2

Stevenson, Robert Louis, 2, 13–17; *An Inland Voyage,* 16; *The Silverado Squatters,* 15; *Travels with a Donkey,* 16

Strachey, John, *Literature and Dialectical Materialism,* 132, 134, 135

Strozzi, Bernardo, *The Parable of the Wedding,* 138, 160

Swinburne, Algernon Charles, "Hymn to Proserpine," 159

Tennyson, Alfred Lord, "Maud," 78

Tindall, William York, *D. H. Lawrence and Susan His Cow,* 132–33, 135

Tomlinson, H. M., 13; *Gifts of Fortune,* 19

Tracy, Billy, 172

Trotter, Philip, 145

Twain, Mark, 13

Verga, Giovanni, 4, 48–71, 95; *Cavalleria Rusticana,* 50, 62–64, 66, 68, 69, 70–71, 137; *I Malavoglia,* 50, 51–52; *Mastro-don Gesualdo,* 50–51, 52–57, 60, 64, 66, 68, 71, 175; *Novelle Tusticane,* 50, 59–62, 67

Warren, Dorothy, 146

Weekley, Ernest, 62, 77, 79, 104

Whitman, Walt, 15, 41, 42, 73, 120, 165; "Dalliance of the Eagles," 85

Wilkin, Andrew, 67, 69, 176n28

Wilson, Edmund, 162

Worthen, John, 94, 122

Yeats, W. B., 162

Young, Brett, 8